Structuring Diversity

STRUCTURING DIVERSITY

Ethnographic Perspectives on the New Immigration

Edited by
Louise Lamphere

THE UNIVERSITY OF CHICAGO PRESS / CHICAGO AND LONDON

The University of Chicago Press, Chicago 60637
The University of Chicago Press, Ltd., London

Printed in the United States of America
01 00 99 98 97 96 95 94 5 4 3

ISBN (cloth): 0-226-46818-6
ISBN (paper): 0-226-46819-4

Library of Congress Cataloging-in-Publication Data

Structuring diversity : ethnographic perspectives on the new immigration / edited by Louise Lamphere.
p. cm.
Includes bibliographical references and index.
1. Immigrants—United States. 2. Minorities—United States. 3. United States—Ethnic relations. 4. United States—Emigration and immigration. I. Lamphere, Louise.
E184.A1S94 1992
305.8'00973—dc20 91-41183
CIP

∞The paper used in this publication meets the minimum requirements of the American National Standard for Information Sciences—Permanence of Paper for Printed Library Materials, ANSI Z39.48-1984.

CONTENTS

PREFACE

From the perspective of the early 1990s, it is clear that the face of urban America is changing. United States cities, particularly in the East and Midwest, have always been centers for receiving immigrants both from rural hinterlands and from abroad; they have been the places where primarily white European immigrants have forged ethnic communities and become part of the American mainstream. Due to the post–World War II urban migration of blacks, Native Americans, and native-born Hispanics, most minorities are now living in urban areas. In addition, large numbers of new immigrants have been drawn to U.S. urban centers since 1965, when immigration laws changed to include more immigrants from Asia and Latin America.

These newcomers are the newest and most important force in the changing face of American cities. They are nationally diverse, coming, for example, from Mexico, Haiti, Poland, Korea, Vietnam, Taiwan, Guatemala, and Cuba. Unlike previous immigrant streams, most of whom came from peasant and working-class origins, post-1965 immigrants represent a wide range of class backgrounds, from wealthy businessmen to middle-class shopkeepers and professionals, to rural peasants and service workers. By their very presence, newcomers are transforming urban workplaces, neighborhoods, schools, and local governments. They have helped create the more linguistically, culturally, and racially diverse urban American of the 1990s.

This collection of articles explores the interaction of America's newcomers with established residents (black, white, Hispanic, and Asian-American) in six U.S. cities: Miami, Chicago, Houston, Philadelphia, Monterey Park (California), and Garden City (Kansas). Our results are based on qualitative, ethnographic research conducted by multiethnic teams as part of a project on "Changing Relations: Newcomers and Established Residents in U.S. Communities." The project, funded by the Ford Foundation through the Research Foundation of the State University of New York, focused not on dramatic incidents of conflict between new immigrants and established residents but on everyday interactions that take place in the workplace, in apartment complexes and neighborhoods, in schools and community organizations.

We discovered, to use Robert Bach's phrase from the project's Final Report, that newcomers and established residents live in "divided social worlds" characterized by separation and social distance. In the articles in this collection we explore the social structural bases of this separation by examining work sites in Garden City and Miami, housing arrangements in Albany Park, Chicago, and Houston, schools in three neighborhoods in North Philadelphia, and local government in Monterey Park. We argue what is perhaps a controversial thesis: separation and division are not merely a matter of choice, language barriers, or cultural differences too difficult to bridge. They are also patterns supported and even created by the structure of the institutions in which newcomers interact with established residents. These institutions—corporations, school systems, city governments, and housing corporations—mediate and shape interrelations, often making it difficult for bridges to be built between new immigrants and others. Where interaction is fluid and where boundaries are transcended, the institutions themselves are being structured or even transformed to make participation and integration more possible. Our analysis teases out the importance of class and power as they operate in these local "microlevel" settings, often pushing immigrants aside or giving them little voice in their everyday lives. It focuses our attention on the possibility and the necessity of changing these institutions if newcomers are to become more fully integrated into American life.

This collection has been a collaborative effort from its very beginnings, and therefore we are grateful for the support and input of many individuals. We would like to thank Shepard Forman, of the Human Rights and Governance Division of the Ford Foundation, as well as Diana Morris, who served as our first program officer. William Diaz served as the program officer between the official beginning of the project in 1988 and its conclusion in February 1990. We are grateful for his advice and leadership at all stages of the project, but particularly during our lengthy quarterly meetings. Mary McClymont and Andrea Taylor also participated in a number of our project meetings and offered important commentary and insight.

We would also like to thank Karen Ito, chair of the board of the Changing Relations project, and Robert Bach, codirector of the project, for their input into the research from its inception to the delivery of the final reports. Board members Niara Sudarkasa and Rudolfo de la Garza visited several research sites and provided helpful commentary as well as critical discussion of the teams' interim and final reports. Roger Sanjek, who served as codirector during 1988, also was an important source of guidance and support for many of the teams.

The authors of each of these articles were part of larger research teams who carried out additional components of the research in each of the communities.

The efforts of other team members are gratefully acknowledged, and their contributions are cited at the beginning of each individual article. I would also like to thank my research assistants Mary Jane McReynolds, Jocelyn DeHaas, and Art Martin for all the library research, phone calls, photocopying, and mailing that they did over the past two and one-half years on behalf of the project.

We have also enjoyed an excellent working relationship with the staff of the University of Chicago Press. We would like to thank our editor, Douglas Mitchell, our designer, Martin Hertzel, and our copyeditor, Ruth Stewart, for the time and effort they have given us in turning our manuscript into a book. We are also indebted to Laura Kriegstrom Poracsky, graphic designer for the Institute for Public Policy and Business Research at the University of Kansas, who produced a number of the illustrations used in this book.

Editing a collection is often said to be a thankless job and one filled with difficulties and delays. In this case, bringing *Structuring Diversity* into print has been a remarkably easy task, thanks, in particular, to the cooperation and goodwill of all the contributors who completed their manuscripts on time, answered my phone calls, and met deadlines efficiently. I was particularly impressed with the amount of collegiality and collaboration that we managed to retain, not only during the actual research, but during the two years that it took to bring this book to completion. We are, of course, all indebted to the newcomers and established residents who welcomed team members into their lives, willingly gave interviews, and articulated their sense of what America is becoming.

LOUISE LAMPHERE

INTRODUCTION: THE SHAPING OF DIVERSITY

Louise Lamphere

Bernadette, a recent Haitian immigrant who worked for a firm that made high-fashion men's sport jackets, found her job a daily struggle, although she had worked in other apparel plants in Miami. As she tried hard to make the piece rate, she said, "I will not have the time to talk to people because I am worrying about the job, so that I can make more money." As one of the few Haitians recently employed in a plant dominated by a female Cuban work force, she worked side by side with Cuban immigrants, yet had little time to interact with them. Cubans dominated the informal culture of the plant to the extent that two recently hired Haitian women thought the newly installed food warmers must be only for Cuban use. In this context it is not surprising that Bernadette felt excluded from a lunchtime party. "I saw groups of Cubans and Haitians together. I see them in the backyard. But no one told me whether I had to give money or to help in any way. They did not tell me anything."

On the other side of Miami, Joe, an American-born white carpenter, was employed on the huge Miami Convention Center construction site. He had quite cordial relations with a Cuban coworker; as he quipped, "I've known that son of a bitch for years; we're brothers in wood." Both were friendly with a Haitian carpenter, whom they admired for going to school, learning English, and saving money. In contrast to the high level of interaction between this established resident and a relative newcomer, trade segregation and the isolation of work on such a large project distanced Joe and his Cuban coworker from most of the African Americans and Haitians who were laborers rather than skilled tradesmen. Carpenters and laborers had separate sites in which to congregate at lunch or during break times.

Over two thousand miles away in Albany Park, Chicago, the "Courtyard Kids" at "Big Red," a dilapidated brick apartment complex, were a mix of Puerto Ricans, Mexicans, Hmong, Cambodians, Assyrians, Appalachians, and African Americans—predominantly new immigrants but also some whose parents and grandparents were American citizens. They terrorized the Appalachian white janitor (whom they called "Mr. Jethro") when he roped off their play area in order to transform it into a lawn. Eventually he became conciliatory and even hooked up a water sprinkler in which they could play. A few months later the Courtyard Kids were dispersed, since the American owner of the apartment complex declared bankruptcy and the new owner evicted tenants in order to rehabilitate the building.

At Peterson grade school in Philadelphia, Maria, a Puerto Rican student, read a letter from her friend Alícia, who had recently returned to Portugal, her native country. As Maria read, she was sitting next to her two best friends, who were white, born in the United States, and from European ethnic backgrounds. Several miles away at Dixon, another public grade school, Puerto Rican students sat in their own clusters in the cafeteria, speaking Spanish and spatially distant from both Euro-American ethnics and the few African-American students who gathered at their own separate tables.

These examples illustrate a wide a range of relations between new immigrants and established residents and suggest that interrelations are not just a matter of race, ethnicity, or immigrant status but can be influenced by the organization of a workplace, apartment complex, or school.

In the 1990s, new immigrants are an increasingly important part of our population, particularly in urban areas. While in 1980 there were 14.1 million foreign-born in the U.S. population, or 6.2 percent of the total, by 1990 cities like Miami, Chicago, and Los Angeles were dominated by populations that had immigrated to the United States since 1965. New immigrants experience American life in the context of our major institutional settings: workplaces, schools, rental housing complexes, retail businesses, and community organizations. These settings offer a wide variety of examples of the interaction between established residents and new immigrants and between individual newcomers from divergent cultural and national backgrounds. Everyday experience ranges from the kind of distance and separation Bernadette and Dixon students experienced, to the intermittent tension and conflict engendered between the Courtyard Kids and Mr. Jethro, to the inclusive nature of both newcomer–newcomer bonds and newcomer–established resident ties illustrated by the friendships of the students at Peterson, the long-term tie between Joe and his Cuban coworker, and the composition of the Courtyard Kids group itself.

Newspaper and television coverage has often highlighted conflict and violence between newcomer groups and between new immigrants and established residents, creating the widespread notion that relations between these various groups are always volatile and full of tension. Three examples over a two-year period illustrate the kinds of incidents that have come to public attention. In January 1989, the "Super Bowl riots" erupted in Miami when a Cuban policeman was involved in the death of a black resident of Overtown, a predominantly black section of the city. The following summer, in Philadelphia, the white son of a police officer was beaten and shot to death as Puerto Rican youths sought to avenge an attack by white youths in the Port Richmond area of the city. This incident and the subsequent arrest of seven youths led to extensive press coverage, while the death of a Puerto Rican teenager from a beating with a lead pipe by a white youth was much less publicized (*Philadelphia Inquirer,* 22 May 1989, p. 1; 7 July, 1989, Metro section, p. 1). In May 1990, newcomers from the Caribbean continued a four-month boycott of two Korean-owned grocery stores, alleging that a Haitian woman had been attacked by a store employee (*New York Times,* 11 May 1990). Finally, in August 1991, tensions rose in southwest Philadelphia after a Chinese-Vietnamese youth had been arrested for the slaying of an eighteen-year-old white basketball star. The house of the sister of the accused was guarded by the police, and Southeast Asian immigrants feared reprisals (*New York Times,* 3 September 1991, A12).

As dramatic and as disturbing as these incidents are, there is evidence that they are not typical of newcomer–established resident relations and that violence may not always erupt along racial or ethnic lines. Korean merchants in Olney in northern Philadelphia and in Albany Park, Chicago, have learned to hire local residents, especially in stores that cater to non-Asian customers (Goode n.d.). Although there have been protests over the use of Korean-only signs, Koreans have been able to accommodate to community demands, and they have avoided the kind of long-term confrontation found in Flatbush (Goode 1990:125–53). In Albany Park, where neighborhoods are made up of newcomers of all ethnicities, teenage boys join multiethnic gangs, and teenage violence and gang-related killings have not been racially or ethnically motivated (Conquergood et al. 1990).

These counterexamples suggest that relations between new immigrants and established residents in the United States are more complex than media images suggest. In this book we argue that a focus on relationships is of key importance for understanding the changing nature of U.S. cities in the 1980s and 1990s; but to understand these relations we need to get beyond the more sensational instances of violence and to concentrate on the more mundane, everyday experiences of new immigrants and established residents. This means two things: extensive use of qualitative ethnographic data that capture the content and context of interrelations, and a study of interrelations within what we call "mediating institutions"—workplaces within industrial firms, school systems, rental housing complexes owned by individuals or corporations, community organizations, and local governments.[1]

1. During the course of the project we used the term "arena" to specify those contexts in which newcomers and established residents interact. We chose "arena" as a rough-and-ready label for contexts—workplaces, political settings, community organizations, public space, and churches, to name a few. In this collection we have shifted our focus to mediating institutions—not the spatial contexts in which people interact, but the institutional settings (which are often not localized), as well as particular "sites" within an institution. The distinction is between a "workplace" as an "arena," a corporation as a mediating institution, and a particular plant as a site. Similarly, "the schools" as an educational arena become a school system as an institution and a particular elementary school as a "site of interaction."

We use "institutions" to denote formal organizations that are hierarchically organized and "institutionalized," that is, they have a structure that continues on beyond the lives of the individuals who are involved in them at any particular time. We have focused on the *mediating* functions of institutions with regard to new immigrants in two senses. First, they mediate or serve to channel larger political and economic forces into settings that have impact on the lives of individuals—both new immigrants and established residents. Thus, a meatpacking firm, in response to a need to retain profits and compete, might build a new plant and put into practice a set of policies that lead to the hiring of new immigrants but also encourage high turnover. These policies shape newcomer–established resident relationships. Or, in response to a shrinking tax base, a school system might institute hiring and wage policies that create high teacher turnover, which, at any particular school, might have an important impact on programs for immigrants and other students. In both these examples, an individual workplace or school (through policies sometimes made at the level of a corporate headquarters or school system) is where macro-level forces are brought to bear on micro-level relationships.

Second, these institutions mediate the interaction between newcomers and established residents. Particular sites within mediating institutions are where people from diverse backgrounds are thrown together to live, work, learn, and participate in local government or community activities. Although interaction between new immigrants and established residents may often take place in more fluid, informal settings—in neighborhoods, on the street, in parks, on subways, or at publicly sponsored festivals—most such interaction takes place in formal settings where relationships are defined and circumscribed through well-defined roles such as management-worker, owner-tenant, teacher-student, and elected official–voter. Since mediating institutions are hierarchically organized, owners, managers, and superintendents are at the top and workers, students, and tenants are at the bottom. Usually established residents hold the positions of power within these organizations, and newcomers are predominantly at the bottom. There may, of course, be a significant number of established residents who work, study, and live alongside new immigrants and who are also workers, students, or tenants, depending on the history of a particular factory, school, or apartment complex. Given this distribution, newcomers and established residents often interact in situations in which the established residents have de facto power over immigrants by dint of the structure of the mediating institution itself. A focus on mediating institutions places issues of class and power at the center of the analysis.

Mediating institutions shape, structure, and constrain interrelations. Thus, we would argue, Bernadette's distance from her Cuban coworkers and Joe's lack of interaction with black and Haitian workers has more to do with the structure of their respective work sites than with cultural and racial barriers per se. Many of the case materials used throughout this book suggest that exclusion, distance, and isolation may be more common experiences for new immigrants than either conflict with established residents or instances of frequent interaction and integration.

An emphasis on mediating institutions and interrelations, rather than on issues of conflict, also helps us to uncover a larger set of issues: whether and how new immigrants are being integrated into the major structures of urban life. That both the Courtyard Kids and Mr. Jethro were pushed out of Big Red is an example of how larger political and economic forces are played out in the context of class and power relations in mediating institutions. Studying interrelations in these contexts thus raises a number of important questions. Are new immigrants being incorporated into local economies, gaining access to higher-paying jobs, and acquiring skills, or are they facing discrimination and finding themselves trapped in low-wage, unstable employment? Are they living in neighborhoods alongside established residents, or is their access to housing characterized by segregation and exclusion? Are schools fostering interaction between new immigrants and children of other backgrounds and providing immigrants with access to the educational skills necessary to improve their economic and political position? And are newcomers sharing political power with more established groups, or are they remaining marginal to the urban political scene? These questions point to the larger issue of whether the political and economic structure of America is being transformed. If the urban landscape is "changing color" as new immigrants settle in U.S. cities, are the institutions within cities also changing, or are they merely reproducing older patterns of class, power, and segregation?

We are better able to answer these questions because of a Ford Foundation project titled "Changing Relations: Newcomers and Established Residents in Six U.S. Communities." The project, which began in January 1988 and was completed in February 1990, focused on the ways new immigrants and established residents have adjusted to one another in five urban areas (Miami, Los Angeles, Chicago, Philadelphia, and Houston) and one small city (Garden City, Kansas). Its purpose was to "uncover a more representative portrait of the full range of relationships between immigrants and established residents, including interactions that may produce conflict, accord, and other modes of accommodation" (Ford Foundation 1987:1). In each community, a team of researchers (including faculty, graduate students, and some community-based researchers) focused on the ethnography of interrelations. Through participant observation and intensive interviewing, team members examined interrelations in everyday life in formal mediating institutions (such as school systems and corporate workplaces) and also in informal settings such as neighborhoods, festivals, and public places. Researchers gathered information about the local economy, demographic change, and power relations to understand the broader context in which face-to-face relations were taking place.

These "micro-level" qualitative observations, used in combination with "macro-level" data on local political economy, are characteristic of recent approaches to urban ethnography. Such a combination is necessary, we argue, if we are to understand the complexities of the new immigration and the variety of relationships that are being forged—ranging from access and integration, on the one hand, to patterns of distance or conflict, on the other.

The Changing Relations project was distinctive in several other ways. Commitment to team rather than individual research, and to the use of researchers from different disciplinary backgrounds (anthropology, geography, sociology, political science, communication, and urban studies), meant that in each community we were able to examine topics in more depth from multiple perspectives. Central to this ability to get at complexity was the fact that teams were composed of researchers from a variety of cultural and ethnic backgrounds, many of them having familiarity with the languages of the newcomer groups being studied. Finally, the selection of six communities within one coordinated project, with the six research teams all focused on collecting data on the same five questions, gave this enterprise a degree of integration that much urban research lacks. Each of these characteristics by itself (ethnography, team research, multidisciplinary research with multicultural investigators, and a coordinated, multicommunity effort) is not unique. However, the combination within one project means that the Changing Relations project has much to contribute to our understanding of the new immigration and its impact on America.

This collection of essays highlights some of the findings that have emerged from the Changing Relations project. It also demonstrates the strength of combining ethnography with macro-level data on urban economies. Throughout the collection we will argue that macro-level political and economic forces shape relationships between newcomers and established residents in each community we have studied. Each contribution will explore these forces within a particular mediating institution—workplaces within industrial and construction firms, rental housing complexes owned by private entrepreneurs and corporations, schools in both public and parochial systems, and public settings managed by local government. Each will analyze how newcomers and established residents interact in these particular mediating institutions and how this interaction has been shaped and often transformed by both the structure of the institution and the larger political economy. These six case studies thus bring us face to face with issues of class and power as they are played out in various settings.

Changing Relations in the Context of Economic and Political Transformation

The increase of new immigrants to the United States is taking place in a historical context that has included restructuring of the U.S. economy and the advent of a more conservative political climate. Both of these factors have shaped the urban environments in which immigrants have settled, and both have had an important impact on localized sites within mediating institutions—for example, particular work sites or apartment complexes.

The immediate cause of the increased flow of new immigrants to the United States was amendments to the 1952 Immigration and Nationality Act, passed in 1965, during the economic expansion that accompanied the buildup of the Vietnam War. The 1965 amendments abolished the country-by-country quotas that since 1924 had made it difficult for anyone except Northern Europeans to immigrate to the United States. Instead, the amendments established a limit for new immigrants from both the Western and Eastern hemispheres.

One goal of these amendments was to reunite families of citizens and legal permanent residents and to admit needed workers. Under the 1965 law, the spouse, parents, and unmarried minor children of U.S. citizens can become permanent immigrants. Between 1965 and 1990, an additional 270,000 were admitted each year under a preference system. There are six preference categories referring to particular family relationships and occupational groups, each with a specific numerical limit.[2] The numerical ceiling in most of the preference categories were raised (particularly those admitting workers and professionals) through congressional legislation in 1990, so that the total number of annual visas would be increased to 406,000 between 1991 and 1994 and to 421,000 thereafter.

A second important group of new immigrants is refugees. Until 1980, refugees were admitted on an ad hoc basis: the attorney general could admit groups on a parole status. Then Congress passed individual laws giving refugees legal status and associated benefits. Cubans, Vietnamese, and other Southeast Asians were admitted to the United States under these conditions. The 1980 Refugee Act provided a regular legal mechanism though which the president could admit refugees. Legal entries into the United States, including refugees, were about 500,000 a year during the 1980s.

Finally, a significant number of newcomers have entered the United States illegally, most over the U.S.-Mexican border. Estimates of illegal immigrants in 1980 ranged from 2.5 million to 3.5 million (Bean, Vernez, and Keely 1989:82), 50–60 percent of them coming from Mexico.

The 1965 Immigration Act amendments, the increase in the number of refugees, and economic and political changes that have led to large numbers of undocumented immigrants have all encouraged Latin and Asian immigration and thus a very different population of immigrants from those who came to the United States before 1924. Overall there has been a substantial increase in the proportion

2. The first category consists of unmarried adult sons and daughters of citizens, and the second category includes spouses and unmarried children of permanent resident aliens. The fourth preference category is married children of U.S. citizens, while the fifth includes sisters and brothers of U.S. citizens. The third and sixth preference categories consist of professionals or workers in occupations in short supply (Kubat 1979:56–57; Bean, Vernez, and Keely 1989:18).

of Asians within the documented immigrant population, while the absolute number of Mexicans and Central Americans has increased, with only slight increases in the proportion (see figure 1). More immigrants from these areas are undocumented. Newcomers who have come into the United States since 1965 have included large numbers of Vietnamese, Chinese from Hong Kong and Taiwan, Koreans, Filipinos, Cambodians, Laotians, and Hmong. There has also been a substantial flow of Mexicans, Cubans, Colombians, and Dominicans, as well as some blacks from Caribbean countries (Haitians and Jamaicans; see figure 2).

As Alejandro Portes and Ruben Rumbaut demonstrate, immigrants are dispersed throughout all fifty states but are concentrated in six (California, New York, Florida, Texas, New Jersey, and Illinois). Moreover, 42 percent of legal immigration during 1987 was to six major cities—Los Angeles, New York, Miami, Chicago, Washington, D.C., and San Francisco (Portes and Rumbaut 1990:34–37). Finally, whether a particular population of new immigrants is relatively dispersed or concentrated varies among these cities. Three of the teams within the Changing Relations project studied interrelations in cities where immigrants have concentrated (Chicago, Los Angeles, and Miami). Three other teams focused on relationships in cities where new immigrants are a significant but less dominant part of the population: Houston, Philadelphia, and Garden City, Kansas.[3] This range of immigrant destinations also provided a broad sampling of the different newcomer populations that have arrived in the United States since 1965: Cubans and Haitians in Miami; Chinese in Los Angeles; Lao, Hmong, Mexican, Assyrian, and Korean immigrants in Chicago; Mexican and Central American immigrants in Houston; Puerto Rican, Polish, and Korean newcomers (among others) in Philadelphia; and Vietnamese and Mexican immigrants in Garden City.

The newcomers studied in the Changing Relations project represent a variety of class backgrounds. While previous immigrant streams have been largely composed of persons from peasant or working-class backgrounds, since 1965 newcomers have come from middle-class or even upper-class professional and entrepreneurial backgrounds, as well as from rural and working classes (see Portes and Rumbaut 1990, chapter 3, for a discussion of the class diversity among immigrants and the variety of class adaptations that they have made once in the United States). Our research reflects this diversity, and class difference is one of the most salient aspects of our analysis. Koreans in both Philadelphia and Chicago were middle-class shopkeepers and entrepreneurs, while Mexican and Central American immigrants in Houston and Garden City were often from

3. Roger Sanjek and a team of researchers have been studying changing relations between new immigrants (Dominicans, Colombians, Chinese, and Koreans) and established residents (African Americans and white ethnic Americans) in Queens, New York. This project had been a seventh site within the Changing Relations project until January 1989, when Sanjek resigned as cochair of the Changing Relations board. For data on interrelations from the New York City area that are comparable to those collected on the Changing Relations project, see Sanjek's publications (1988, 1989).

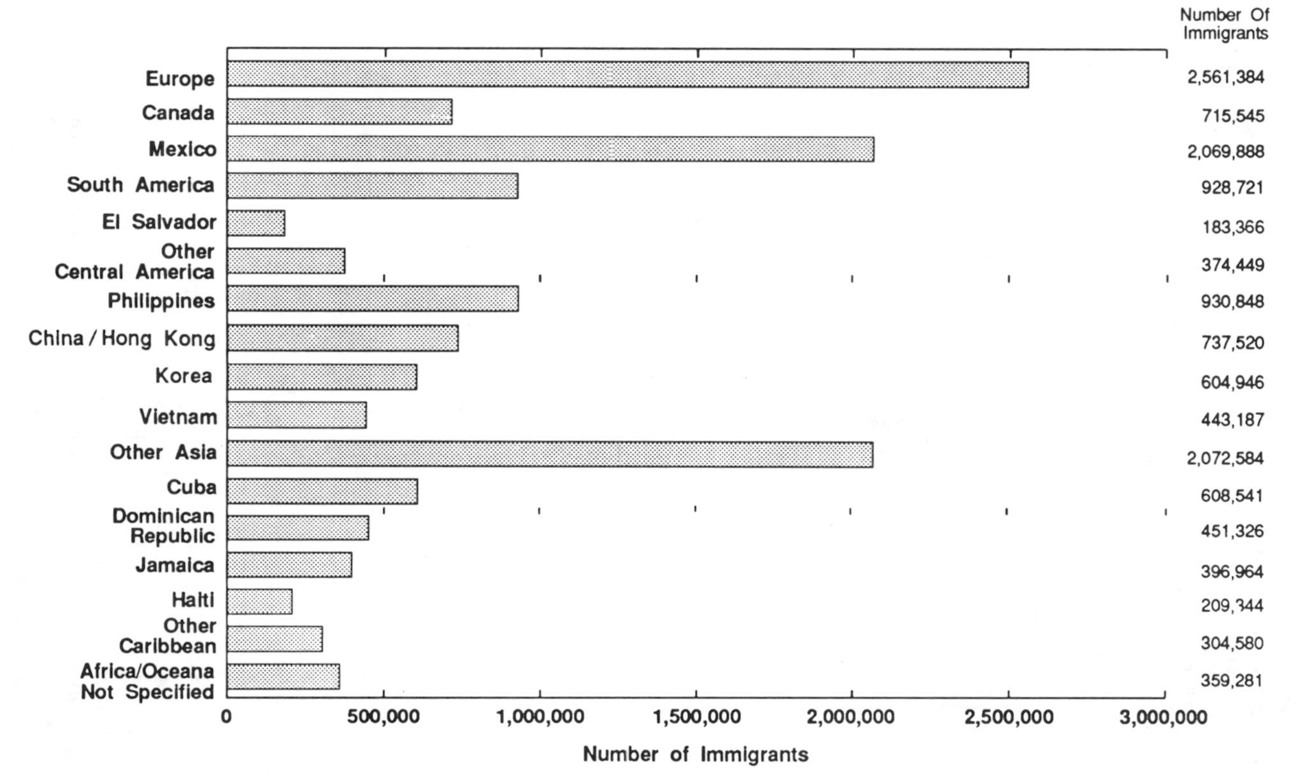

Figure 1. Legal immigration to the United States by area, 1961–89
Source: U.S. Immigration and Naturalization Service

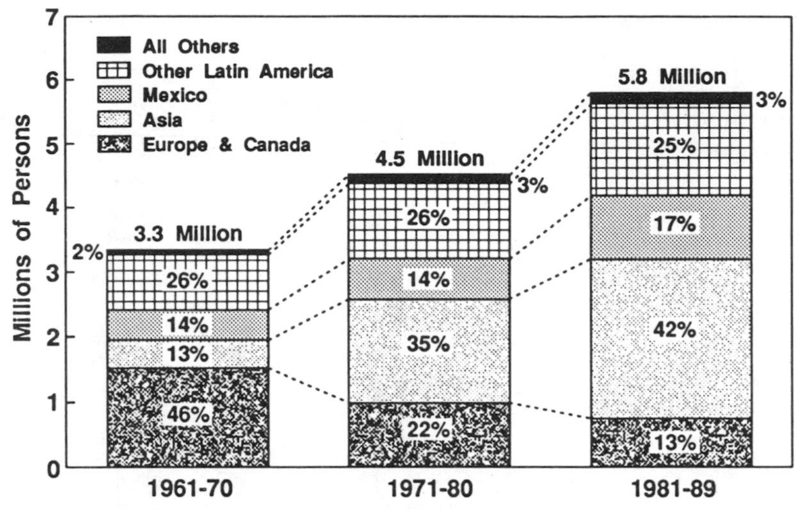

Figure 2. Legal immigration to the United States by country or region, 1961/70 to 1981/89
Source: U.S. Immigration and Naturalization Service

rural backgrounds and held working-class or service jobs once in the United States. Chinese immigrants to Monterey Park included professionals and wealthy bankers and developers, while Vietnamese immigrants to Garden City included a few professional families but also a large segment from a rural fishing village. The Cuban population in Miami contains perhaps the widest range of class positions, with important contrasts in terms of wealth and occupation. To sample this diversity, the Miami team studied influential Cuban members of the city's elite as well as the apparel and construction workers who are the subject of a contribution to this volume.

New immigrants began coming to the United States during a period of economic expansion, but there were severe recessions in 1974–75 and 1982–83. During the 1980s, the U.S. economy was being transformed by increased competition with European and Asian countries. Barry Bluestone and Bennett Harrison, in *The Deindustrialization of America,* estimate that

> between 450,000 and 650,000 jobs in the private sector, in both manufacturing and non-manufacturing, were wiped out somewhere in the United States by the movement of both large and small runaway shops. But it turns out that such physical relations are only the tip of a huge iceberg. When the employment lost as a direct result of plant, store, and office *shutdowns* during the 1970s is added to the job loss associated with runaway shops, it appears that more than 32 million jobs were destroyed. Together, runa-

> ways, shutdowns, and permanent physical cutbacks of complete closure may have cost the country as many as 38 million jobs. (Bluestone and Harrison 1982:26)

Some industries moved to suburban areas, others to the Sun Belt states, and still others abroad. Bluestone and Harrison point out, however, the deindustrialization has been uneven. Southern towns were victims of plant closings (particularly in the textile industry), and even Los Angeles experienced numerous shutdowns. In 1980 alone, 150 major plants closed, displacing 37,000 workers (Bluestone and Harrison 1982:40). Much of this restructuring involved the decline of heavy industries like auto, steel, and rubber, along with the relocation of lighter manufacturing firms (apparel and textiles) and the expansion of some new high-tech industries (often defense-related), primarily in the South and West (Sawers and Tabb 1984; Markusen, Hall, and Glasmeier 1986).

Restructuring has also taken place on a worldwide level, as European and Asian corporations have overshadowed American firms and begun to invest in U.S. holdings. Production in electronics, apparel, and other industries has moved to Third World countries, but "runaway shops" are only part of the story. There have also been an infusion of foreign capital and a reorientation of some American cities toward potential markets abroad. The growth of Miami and Los Angeles in relationship to Latin American markets and the investment of Asian capital in Los Angeles and San Francisco are the most obvious examples over the decade of the 1980s.

Most cities, however, have suffered rather than grown as a result of restructuring. As the 1980s progressed, some Western cities were hard hit by the recession of 1982–83—particularly Houston, Denver, and Tulsa, which suffered from the decline in the oil industry. Overall there has been a decrease in high-paying manufacturing jobs and an increase in lower-paying service and clerical jobs. But this scenario has been unevenly played out in different regions of the country. This points to the importance of understanding a local political economy and examining the ways it has been shaped over the past twenty-five years.

Such an approach is particularly important in studying the relationships between newcomers and established residents. Immigrants themselves have been pulled into, pushed out of, or encouraged to stay in very different economic settings throughout the United States. A growing local economy in the early 1970s might have declined in the mid-1980s. Another urban area might have grown enormously in the 1980s, but in the peripheral suburbs rather than in the central city. These patterns of growth and decline not only create and take away jobs but also establish the tax base and the amount of public services, including school resources, available to a city's population. In other words, economic and political conditions set the stage for relations of cooperation, conflict, adjustment, or isolation.

The six communities selected for the Changing Relations project not only include cities that have been the destination of many immigrants but also represent a wide range of economic transformations over the past twenty-five years. Philadelphia and Chicago are examples of industrial cities in the East and Midwest that have experienced a substantial loss of jobs as firms have moved to the suburbs and industries have declined. Houston was a classic example of Sunbelt growth and expansion during the 1970s, with its dependence on oil and the space industry; however, with the decline in oil prices in the early 1980s, the city suffered high unemployment and population decline (Shelton et al. 1989).

In contrast, Miami, another Sunbelt city with a history of economic booms and busts, experienced growth and development during the 1980s as its economy became more oriented toward Latin America. Not only has it become a banking and trade center, but it has been the recipient of some industrial relocation as well (Stepick et al. 1990:34–36). Los Angeles also continued to grow and expand during the 1980s, attracting high-tech industry and becoming a center for trade with both Latin America and Asia (Horton 1990:51–53). It is worth noting, however, that the Changing Relations field research predated the recession of 1990–91, which may have had an adverse economic impact on both of these urban areas.

Finally, Garden City, Kansas, is an example of industrial restructuring within small-town America. Over the course of a century Garden City has experienced several "waves" of capital investment—first cattle, then sugar beets, and more recently cattle feeding. In the early 1980s, two large beef-packing plants located in Garden City—part of the industry's move out of older unionized centers, such as Chicago, to rural, nonunion, low-wage locations in southwest Kansas and Texas (Broadway 1990:77). Each of these local economies has had a role in attracting and holding new immigrant populations.

Contributions to this volume use the concept of restructuring in a number of different ways, all of which stem from the restructuring of the U.S. economy in the 1970s and 1980s, which set in motion a number of processes in which immigrants have played a key role. Donald Stull, Michael Broadway, and Ken Erickson, in their analysis of relations between newcomers and established residents in Garden City, begin with the restructuring of the meat-packing industry, a classic example of the relocation of industry in the Bluestone and Harrison mold. Guillermo Grenier, Alex Stepick, and their fellow researchers also focus on industrial restructuring. They examine the apparel and construction industries, not so much on a national level, but in the Miami/Dade County area. Here restructuring is about the changing ethnic composition of the work force, home work in the apparel industry, and nonunion work sites in construction—all results of employers' attempts to keep wages down through the recruitment of an immigrant labor force. While meat packers came to Garden City first and recruited immigrants later, the major changes in Miami's apparel and construction industries went hand in hand with the influx of Cuban and later Haitian immigrants. There is a dialectical relationship between the structure of these industries and the influx of immigrants—each feeds on the other and produces a gradual set of transformations.

Nestor Rodriguez and Jacqueline Hagan examine restructuring not in industry but within the rental housing market; thus their focus is on immigrants as consumers rather than as workers. The decline of the Houston economy (due to the restructuring of the oil industry) reverberates at two "lower" levels—the restructuring of the rental housing market on the west side of Houston and the recomposition of a particular tenant population in Arborland. Then, when the economy recovered, a second phase of restructuring took place at both levels, again recomposing tenant populations and changing newcomer–established resident relationships.

In a third use of the concept, John Horton begins his analysis of Monterey Park with a discussion of economic and demographic restructuring and takes it into the arena of political restructuring (and local government as a mediating institution). The changing economy of Monterey Park is an outgrowth of Los Angeles' expanding relationship with Asia, both through the immigration of Chinese newcomers with capital and the development of Asian trade relations. The influx of newcomers and the altered economy brought first a backlash among Anglo-American residents and later a defeat of nativism and the emergence of coalition politics based on ties between some Latino, Anglo, and Jewish established residents and Chinese newcomers.

While restructuring has been a major trend at several different levels, it is important to remember that these economic changes have taken place at the same time that the United States has experienced a wave of political conservatism. Conservative policies have had a major impact on government funding, which in turn has added to the difficulties experienced in urban areas with high levels of unemployment. The Reagan administration made major cuts in federal aid to cities by reducing federal grants to local governments. At the same time, more programs had to be administered and funded at the local level. Block grants also diminished the possibility of community control over programs. In addition, entitlement programs were cut in the early 1980s, and many neighborhoods have been demolished or undergone "gentrification" (Mullings 1987: 10–11).

Some aspects of this conservative political climate are in fact reactions to the increased number of new immigrants. For example, in 1986, the Immigration Reform and Control Act (IRCA) was passed to control and contain illegal immigration, primarily through employer sanctions against those hiring undocumented workers (Bean, Vernez, and Keely 1989:25). IRCA also contained a legalization program to regularize the status of undocumented aliens who had resided in the United States since 1982 and a large group of agricultural workers. The passage of the act indicates the depth of the ambivalence Americans feel toward immigrants and the sense that the numbers of illegal immigrants were increasing. It amounts to "closing the back door" to the United

States (Bean, Vernez, and Keely 1989:6). This ambivalence has continued. A recent Roper poll indicates that 48 percent of Americans believe U.S. law allows too many immigrants into the country, while over 70 percent oppose legislation that would double the number of immigrants allowed to enter the country legally every year. Despite IRCA, 79 percent of respondents believe that the federal government is doing no better than a fair job in controlling illegal immigration (*Albuquerque Journal,* 5 June 1990, pp. 1, 3).

Another indication of anti-immigration and perhaps anti-immigrant attitudes has been the passage of "English only" legislation in states with large Spanish-speaking populations (including California, Florida, Arizona, and Colorado).[4] For example, in 1988, 84 percent of Florida voters cast their ballots in favor of an amendment to the state's constitution declaring English the official language. Although surveys before the election indicated that voters still favored bilingual education, most had intense feelings about the role of language and national identity (agreeing with the statement, "If you live in America you should have to learn English"). Also, many voters expressed fears about new immigrants (agreeing that "we are losing control of our state to foreigners"). According to one estimate, 86 percent of Hispanics voted against the amendment, while 80 percent of white Americans and 80 percent of black Americans voted in favor (Castro 1989). Efforts to restrict immigration and to make English the official language come at a time when cities have become hosts to increasing numbers of new immigrants, yet federal funds for services and programs have been cut, so that competition for scarce resources among newcomers and established residents has been exacerbated.

These economic and political forces have had a differing impact on newcomer–established resident relations in each of the cities studied by the Changing Relations project. Economic restructuring has been complex and uneven, so that it would be simplistic to assume that interrelations would be understandable in terms of a simplistic Frost Belt–Sun Belt dichotomy. Instead, we argue for an examination of the particular configuration of economic and political forces that have developed in each city over the past few decades, as they shape relations between new immigrants and established populations.

Developing the New Ethnography to Study Interrelations

To understand the place of new immigrants in U.S. cities, we need an approach that combines consideration of these structural and political changes with the insights ethnography can provide into the patterning and nature of relations. We

4. Anti-immigrant sentiment, of course, is nothing new in American history. Beginning with the Irish immigration of the 1840s and culminating with the imposition of immigration restrictions in 1924, the United States has experienced a number of distinct waves of anti-immigrant sentiment, which have often resulted in illegal and legal forms of discrimination and restriction.

characterize this approach as one that integrates macro-level quantitative data with micro-level qualitative participant observation and intensive interviews—a mix that has come to characterize the best in most recent urban research.

The ethnographic tradition in urban research began with early studies by sociologists of the Chicago School during the 1920s. Some of these ethnographies provided a descriptive "slice of life" from the marginal world of hobos and taxi-dance girls (e.g., Anderson 1923; Cressey 1932) or combined social history with personal documents and cultural analysis to describe the urban ecology of neighborhoods (Wirth 1928; Zorbaugh 1929). These micro-level studies were not well integrated with the more "macro-level" analysis of the city provided by Robert Park, Louis Wirth, and Edward Burgess, the major theorists of the Chicago School (Park 1916; Wirth 1938; Burgess 1967). There was also a tendency to view "the city" as a distinct and isolated unit to be contrasted with rural life, as in the work of Robert Redfield, the major anthropologist connected with the Chicago School (Redfield 1941, 1947, 1955).

When anthropologists began to conduct research in U.S. urban areas during the late 1960s and early 1970s, there was a resurgence of rich ethnographic descriptions, in this instance focused either on street-corner groups (Liebow 1967; Keiser 1969; Spradley 1970) or families and kin networks (Stack 1974). Despite the impulse to select a problem or present data in light of larger social and political issues, these ethnographies were self-contained. They did not utilize macro-level data on unemployment, family income, arrest rates, or school dropout rates to frame a study of a local population. Furthermore, the class structure and political economy of a particular city were not analyzed in order to explore the possible roles that macro-level forces could play in shaping a particular set of behaviors.

During this period there was a debate over whether cities should be treated as "cultural wholes" (Fox 1977; Gulick 1968) and as unique institutions (an extension of the Chicago School approach; see Peattie and Robbins 1984), or whether they should be studied as localities within a larger investigation of industrial and complex societies (Leeds 1973). There was a clear sense that urban anthropology should be more than "anthropology *in* the city," small, piecemeal studies by anthropologists that just happened to be in urban settings. Nevertheless, both positions often led to more emphasis on the macro-level, with less attention to how micro-processes could be linked to a larger framework.

Only in recent years has urban ethnography been rejoined with a more macro-level approach, this time not with a focus on "the urban" or the character of "the city" but with attention to local political economies within the larger nation-state (see Gulick 1984; Lynch 1984; Goode 1989). In a recent review of "urban anthropology," Roger Sanjek argues that the "urban anthropology of the 1950s to 1970s is dead." The balkanization of social and cultural anthropology into subfields such as urban anthropology is being overcome as more studies done in cities are reintegrated into a social-cultural anthropology that focuses on a connection between what we are calling micro- and macro-level data. We would agree with Sanjek's statement,

> One of the strongest theoretical messages of urban anthropology was argued eloquently from the mid-1960s on by Leeds—"No Towne is an Island of Itself." Cities are nodes within societies, or social formations. Urban social relations are conducted within and contextualized by state and state-regulated institutions concerned with education, communication, transportation, production, commerce, welfare, worship, civic order, housing, and land use. Leeds has been heard, or his message is at least now more nearly taken for granted. Accordingly, the study of such relations and institutions in ex-urban or trans-urban settings is difficult and unnecessary to separate from "urban anthropology." (Sanjek 1990:7)

Following Sanjek's view, this collection follows in the footsteps of one recent collection that exemplifies the new urban ethnography, *Cities of the United States: Studies in Urban Anthropology,* edited by Leith Mullings (1987). The Mullings collection combines micro-level ethnographic observations with macro-level data and demonstrates the ways in which macro-level forces actually shape behavior.

In this collection, we do not thoroughly examine the enormous literature on immigration, race, and ethnic relations, nor do we discuss some of the important debates surrounding the new immigration—for example, whether new immigrants are displacing American workers. These issues are taken up in the final report of the Changing Relations project, issued through the Ford Foundation (Bach et al. 1991). Nevertheless, our approach in this collection provides a different slant on immigration and interethnic relations from that of most studies on immigrants to the United States.

Classical approaches to immigration in the United States have been preoccupied with issues of assimilation (Gordon 1964; Glazer and Moynihan 1970) or mobility (Handlin 1974; Thernstrom 1973). Although some of these studies have been comparative, there is a tendency in the literature to focus on the experience of one ethnic group. Thus there are a large number of studies on European ethnics such as Irish, Italian, Portuguese, and Polish immigrants (Handlin 1974; Gans 1962; di Leonardo 1984; LaRuffa 1988; Anderson 1974; Lopata 1976) and on ethnic minorities: African Americans (Stack 1974; Liebow 1967; Hannerz 1969), Mexican Americans (Zavella 1987; Keefe and Padilla 1987; Moore and Pachon 1985), Japanese Americans (Peterson 1971; Glenn 1986; Yanagisako 1985), and Chinese Americans (Wong 1982). The best of the comparative studies have focused on several ethnic groups within one urban context (Thernstrom 1973; Bodnar, Simon, and Weber 1982; Hershberg et al. 1979; Portes and Stepick 1985).

The literature focuses on both the creation of ethnic identities and groups out of populations that had no previously cohesive identity or organization, yet shared a place of origin (Schiller 1977; Aronowitz 1973), and structural barriers and constraints such as residential segregation, legal status, employment opportunities, and the structure of a local economy (Yancey et al. 1976; Portes and Rumbaut 1990). Our approach takes the analysis one step further and examines interactions at a more micro-level within what we are calling mediating institutions. Ever since Barth (1969) showed us how important it is to look at the boundaries between ethnic groups, it has been important to focus on interrelations, as well as the issues of identity, cultural values, and group cohesiveness that the literature on ethnicity has traditionally emphasized. Our assumption is that change and transformation, on the one hand, and processes of isolation or containment as well as conflict, on the other, take place across boundaries or at their interface. Thus our emphasis on the categories of "newcomer" and "established resident" and our focus on interaction within mediating institutions allow us to understand what is happening across these boundaries. By examining mediating institutions within changing local economies, and by combining macro-level data with ethnographic insight, we are able to get at power and class as they shape the strategies and choices of new immigrants.

We do not assume that assimilation and change take place in some abstract way, through unspecified exposure to or contact with American culture and society. Rather, they take place in the context of specific institutions where newcomers and established residents interact and have differential access to power. Such a framework also leaves open the possibility that interaction has an impact on established residents and that change is not only something that new immigrant populations experience. In some instances, the structures of mediating institutions themselves can be changed, and newcomers can have an impact on the cultural values or identities expressed through those institutions.

Critical Tales about Interrelations

In this collection we have developed the notion of the "critical tale," a term used by John Van Maanen to characterize ethnographic description that is "strategically situated to shed light on larger social, political, symbolic or economic issues" (Van Maanen 1988:127). Van Maanen does not discuss his notion of the critical tale in great detail, but we have taken it to mean a form of ethnographic writing that not only reveals the meanings and actions of those being studied but also connects these to an analysis of structure and power. Each essay in this book begins with an ethnographic vignette that sets the stage for examining relations between newcomers and established residents in a particular arena. Then, through a combination of analysis and ethnographic description, each chapter explores how relations are shaped by larger economic and political forces as they are played out in a particular setting. We have chosen to develop the notion of the "critical tale" rather than other types of recent ethnographic writing (for example, the confessional and impressionist tales identified by Van Maanen [1988] and the more dialogic efforts of Dwyer [1982] and March [1990]), since it allows us to pull together macro- and micro-level data in interesting ways. The construction of class, race, ethnicity, and gender can be laid bare through such critical description, yet it can also give primacy to the meanings and activities of both newcomers and established residents.

Methodological Issues

As each of the six teams that were part of the Changing Relations project continued their research between 1988 and 1990, definitions of our key categories (newcomers and established residents) evolved, as did access to various sites within mediating institutions and the roles of individual researchers.

We defined newcomers as members of populations that have come to the United States since the 1965 amendments to the Immigration and Nationality Act. Though some Cubans came to the United States as early as 1960, we viewed the Cubans as "newcomers," since large numbers of them, particularly the Mariel refugees, continued to arrive in Miami between 1980 and 1990 and since their advent coincided with a restructuring of the local economy. Puerto Ricans in Philadelphia are also considered newcomers. Although they are American citizens, because of language and cultural differences they are often perceived as immigrants, and in Philadelphia their numbers have increased substantially since 1965. We defined "established residents" as members of minority or majority populations that have resided in the United States for one or more generations. Thus, Mexican Americans and other Hispanic Americans in Monterey Park and Garden City were established residents, while Mexican immigrants to Garden City and Guatemalans in Houston were defined as newcomers.

These were "rough-and-ready" categories, and as fieldwork progressed, researchers discovered that there was often considerable diversity within a newcomer population, depending on the time of arrival. For example, early Cuban arrivals were distinguished from Mariel refugees in Miami, and early Vietnamese immigrants (those who came to the United States before 1978) formed a very different subpopulation from immigrants from fishing villages who arrived several years later. In some cases established residents were newcomers to a neighborhood or city (for example, blacks who had moved from more traditionally black neighborhoods in Chicago to Albany Park on the North Side, or middle-class whites who arrived in Garden City); nevertheless, their American background and their socialization to American institutions (corporate work places, school systems, churches, government structures, etc.) justified their categorization as established residents.

The focus on interrelations and the use of the categories "newcomer" and "established resident" were designed to keep us from thinking of populations in terms of "ethnicity" and ethnic-group formation—to center on interaction between individuals and between groups rather than the formation of monolithic bounded groups. Such an approach recognizes that ethnic, racial, and class identities are socially constructed in the course of interaction and may be more or less inclusive and multilevel. We have not focused primarily on ethnic labels, realizing that in certain contexts individuals may identify themselves or be identified differently—to use two examples—as members of a village, Vietnamese, Asians, or Asian Americans, or as Mayans, Guatemalans, or Central Americans, depending on the knowledge of the speaker or the context.

The contrast between newcomers and established residents allowed researchers to focus not on ethnicity and issues of identity and assimilation but on interrelations as they are enacted in particular situations and on strategies that produced a wide range of outcomes, from conflict to competition to accommodation.

In each community, teams focused on particular "sites" of interaction within a larger mediating institution: one or more schools within a school system, an apartment complex within a large real estate corporation, a individual church within a denomination, or a factory or construction site owned by a larger corporate entity. Some researchers gathered most of their data at the individual site they were studying. Others found it difficult to pursue the study of interrelations in a particular locale. As John Horton says of the Monterey Park team's focus on City Hall, "We did, of course, attend city council meetings but meetings were not only episodic, but they represented, if not the endpoint, then only one stage in the unfolding of events and issues in this realm" (Horton 1990:14). In order to involve themselves in the more informal and "behind-the-scenes" politics, the Monterey Park team identified a number of issues that crossed several different sites and began to follow and become part of key groups and networks of established residents and newcomers. This approach involved examining the formal institutions of city government and small community organizations as well as informal relations outside of but critical to the operation of the more formal institutions. For this team and others, such a research strategy meant finding key consultants or informants as well as conducting more formal interviews with participants in interaction at different sites.

Sometimes the focus on a mediating institution and sites within it shifted as the research progressed and team members gained access to sites that had been unanticipated at the proposal stage of the project. For example, the Chicago team initially proposed to study community organizations, public space, and household networks. Only the community organizations are mediating institutions by our definition; the other two contexts constitute informal relations. Dwight Conquergood began his research by concentrating on interrelations in "public spaces," a much more amorphous topic than that of community organizations. He followed different kinds of interactions between newcomers and established residents in a wide range of sites—from back alleys and streets to restaurants and parks. His analysis of "street sense" (rules for behavior on the streets among those of very different newcomer and established-resident backgrounds) and his relationship with teenage gang members emanate from this more "free-floating" subject area (see Conquergood et al. 1990). Conquergood's experience of living in Albany Park provided data on a site within another mediating institution: a housing complex owned by an individual landlord. His contribution for this collection describes Big Red, where he lived for over a year.

Other teams had to deal with being excluded from a particular site. This was particularly true for researchers in Garden City. At the time they submitted their research proposal, they expected to have access to one of two beef-packing plants; however, this plant was bought by another company, and by the time the project was funded the team had lost their access. Thus their data on work sites were gathered through interviews, informal conversations, interactions at a bar frequented by packing-house workers, and information about the beef-packing industry obtained from plants in other cities and published reports.

Researchers developed a wide range of roles both within teams and within the project as a whole. Some became participant observers, as both Jacqueline Hagan and Dwight Conquergood did in their study of apartment buildings. Steve Morris worked as a carpenter's apprentice for three months on a construction site in Miami. Others were more often observers than participants. For example, Judy Goode, Jo Anne Schneider, and Suzanne Blanc (Philadelphia) spent time observing interrelations in classrooms, on playgrounds, at school meetings, and at public events. Whenever possible, they took on roles as informal classroom and teacher aides. John Horton and Mary Pardo observed city council meetings, public celebrations, and meetings of formal organizations in Monterey Park.

Some researchers combined interviews with participant observation, while others used interviews almost exclusively. For example, Alex Stepick and Guillermo Grenier relied primarily on interviewing in the apparel factory they studied in Miami, until they found a female researcher they could place in the firm as a worker. Don Stull, Michael Broadway, and Ken Erickson interviewed managers and workers connected with Garden City meat-packing plants—a research strategy forged to compensate for their limited access to the plants.

Some researchers combined their research roles with activism. Dwight Conquergood helped residents in Big Red locate city officials to help them deal with a shutoff of water in the apartment building during the summer of 1988. Jacqueline Hagan and two Mexican-American employees at Arborland convinced management to let them conduct a seminar to help non-English-speaking immigrants deal with the problems they encountered with the new security system. Hagan often acted as an intermediary between tenants and management, for newcomers felt more and more disfranchised by the managers' efforts to restructure and upgrade the apartment complex. Others were more formal activists, usually in community organizations in which they were studying newcomer–established resident relations. For example, Jose Calderon was a member of Neighborhood Watch in his locality in Monterey Park, as well as a founder of a chapter of LULAC (League of United Latin American Citizens), which he was also studying. Judy Goode became an active member of several Olney action groups, and Jo Anne Schneider played a role in the Puerto Rican/Port Richmond Task Force that organized after the deaths of two Philadelphia teenagers (one Puerto Rican and one white), mentioned above.

Several members of the project have long careers in applied anthropology, a subdiscipline in which research for a subject population or with policy implications is a long-standing tradition. The activist stance that emerged within each project dovetailed well with these anthropological and applied traditions and with the goals of the Changing Relations project itself. In the project statement (Ford Foundation 1987), the board stressed the importance of disseminating the results of the project, particularly to members of community groups. Policy recommendations were an explicit part of each team's final report, and each team has proposed and carried out a number of dissemination projects, ranging from conferences and the making of a video to the formation of policy groups within the study community.

Six Critical Tales Concerning Relations of Power and Class

We have used the notion of "critical tale" as a vehicle for connecting macro- and micro-level data, and for demonstrating the ways in which macro-level forces shape interaction within a particular institutional setting. Each of these six critical tales illustrates the different ways in which the macro- and micro- links can be made, and each addresses issues of class and power, helping us examine the dynamics of separation and isolation or interaction and integration.

In examining power relations, it is helpful to distinguish between tactical and organizational power on the one hand and structural power on the other. Tactical power, as Eric Wolf points out, is deployed through organizations and constitutes the many and varied ways in which individuals and structural units circumscribe, limit, and define the actions of others (Wolf 1990:586). Structural power has to do with how the political economy is structured and power is deployed to allocate social labor. It shapes the possible field of action so as to make some kinds of behavior possible, while others are less possible (Wolf 1990:587). In our framework, structural power is most visible in macro-level economic and political forces, as industries, corporations, and various levels of government (within the United States and abroad) react to and try to shape movements of capital and labor. Most of our case studies examine tactical and organizational power as it is deployed at a micro-level—at a particular site within a mediating institution. We focus on the policies of managers, owners, school principals, and local government officials as they deploy power and shape the lives of new immigrants and established residents.

"The Price of a Good Steak" connects macro- and micro-levels by simultaneously "looking up and down," exploring in depth the connections between industrial restructuring at a national level and local workplaces within one community. The authors pull together material on the national beef-packing industry that leads them to understand the shaping of relations on the plant floor and in Garden City as a whole. Without a historical understanding of the restructuring of meat packing as well as data on the low profit margins and the attempt to deskill jobs, management's strategies to "get it out the door" and spend little time on training and retention would be incomprehensible. In turn, the pressure on workers to "pull their count," the relative lack of interaction between newcomers and established residents, and the fine line between horseplay and conflict all "make sense" as outcomes of management policy.

Management policy also shapes the possibilities for newcomer–established resident interaction and has consequences for gender relations. An inadvertent consequence of hiring policies and recruitment is that Vietnamese and Hispanics are concentrated in different plants and on different shifts, or within different departments on the same shift. Gender plays a role in job placement as well. Men tend to work in more physically demanding jobs in the Slaughter Department, while women are usually employed cutting up sections of the carcass in the Processing Department. The rigid, hierarchical system that emphasizes technical control through a "disassembly line" shapes relations between newcomers and established residents, as well as between men and women. "Communication must be quick and to the point; workers have little time for idle conversation—or even work-related discussion—when carcasses or boxes are whizzing by at 400 or more an hour" (Stull et al. 1990:97–98). Overall, we see more isolation than interaction within the work site itself.

The workplace is, of course, the quintessential place where relations of class and power are played out. Relations between managers and workers are, after all, class relations—between those who deploy power on behalf of corporate owners and those who are wage workers. Newcomers, though they may be of rural origin, join the working class in the process of migration and entrance into the Garden City economy.

On the plant floor, forms of tactical or organizational power are concretized in the disassembly line, the hierarchy of control, and management's policies concerning hiring, firing, and layoffs. For Garden City's newcomers, the termination of a meat-packing job is not usually a matter of "individual choice" or an attempt at upward mobility, but rather a result of job-related injuries, management's tendency to "write up" or fire workers for minor infractions, and policies that keep turnover high so that benefits or higher wages need not be paid.

The high turnover, in turn, reverberates through the community, creating high population mobility, rapid turnover in the schools, and increases in various indices of social disruption. Newcomers leave Garden City not just to pursue their individual goals in another location, but because the major employers have propelled them out of jobs. The connections among the national characteristics of an industry, local workplaces, and interrelations both at work and in the community are best traced, perhaps, in a small city.

A second article examining interrelations within workplaces builds a *comparative framework* into the body of the paper, in order to sort out the relationship between macro-level forces and micro-level interaction between newcomers and established residents. Here again we are dealing with working-class newcomers in contexts they do not control.

Alex Stepick and Guillermo Grenier compare work sites in two different industries, showing how each industry has been affected by Miami's recent bust-and-boom cycle, which coincided with the influx of Cubans in the early 1960s. They exemplify two forms of organizational power that contrast with those of Garden City's meat-packing plants. The apparel plant has a dominantly female labor force and illustrates the importance of continued growth and restructuring in Miami, through the replacement of a local owner by a "Northern" firm with a more bureaucratized management style. The construction site (the convention center) also reflects Miami's growth through immigration and its increasing role as a tourist and trade center. Its labor force is dominantly male and is structured by the organization of the construction trades as much as by systems of control that emanate from a developer or large construction firm. In both sites, interrelations between new immigrants and established residents were shaped by the work process and the hierarchy of jobs. These factors limited interaction to a large degree, but had differential impact on conflict and cooperation between members of different ethnic groups.

For these workplaces, the Miami research team concluded that the most common and successful strategy for promoting apparent accord was through segregation of social relationships: trade segregation in the construction industry and the intense concentration required for work in an apparel factory, along with compartmentalization of the Haitians in the Pressing Department. "When interaction does occur across normally segregated boundaries, it usually is institutionalized and thus is guided by regular, unwritten rules that allow superficial tolerance and the conduct of daily business. These include such things as not messing with someone else's 'shit' in construction and maintaining a 'normal' pace at work, i.e., fast enough to allow others to proceed, but not so fast as to be a 'rate buster.' Adherence to such rules produces seeming accord," the team stresses (Stepick et al. 1990:145).

The texture of this separation and boundary maintenance may also be gendered, as workers operate within a given labor process and set of employer policies. In the apparel factory, as in many female workplaces, women participate in informal relationships, holding celebrations for birthdays, weddings, and national holidays like Christmas and Thanksgiving. In some work contexts, such parties provide a context for crossing the boundaries between newcomers and established residents (Lamphere 1985, 1987). However, in Miami, Cuban women not only continued to control the seating space in the cafeteria but tended to exclude Haitians from their informal celebrations as well. They maintained boundaries between newcomer populations, though this trend seemed to be breaking down. Men at the construction site maintained boundaries in a different manner—through dyadic interaction, ranging from joking to harassment. The informal system of rules described by Steve Morris of the Miami team helped to ease communication across newcomer–established resident boundaries as well as across ethnic boundaries. Gender differences in relations are constituted in the context of power relationships embodied within the labor process and management policies.

Using a third mode of analysis, the two articles on housing bring together macro-level forces and micro-level relationships by taking a *processual approach*. Both articles guide us through a series of events that resulted in the ejection of newcomer residents from their rental apartments. As in the articles that focus on the workplace, the newcomers studied in both Houston and Albany Park belonged to the working class. Dwight Conquergood describes interrelations in a large housing complex in Chicago's Albany Park, while Nestor Rodriguez and Jacqueline Hagan examine an apartment complex in Houston. Conquergood describes the rich texture of interrelations between neighbors of different ethnic backgrounds in "Big Red," a dilapidated red-brick multiapartment building in Albany Park. The building was owned by a local landlord and is part of a neighborhood called Little Beirut, known for its ethnic diversity, its gangs, and the low income of its residents. In contrast, "Arborland" (pseudonym) is a large, modern apartment complex in the newer southwestern section of Houston. The complex was owned by a California corporation and managed by local Anglos. Tenants had access to a swimming pool and barbecue pits in each courtyard, and the complex has tennis courts, a Jacuzzi, maid service, and an in-house bar and restaurant. Despite these contrasts, newcomers in both complexes were victims of tactics that brought about their ejection.

While workplaces are organized around owner-worker relationships, in apartment complexes power is deployed through the owner-tenant relationship (within what Hagan and Rodriguez call the secondary circuit of real estate capital). These, of course, are class relationships as well. The Houston example is perhaps clearest in illustrating how macro-level economic forces (in this case the decline of the oil industry in the early 1980s) are played out in micro-level contexts. As the larger economic climate shifts, so does the relationship between management (which implements the owner's policies) and tenants.

As a result of the serious downturn in Houston's housing market because of the oil "bust" of the early 1980s, management's initial response to newcomers at Arborland was marked by accommodation. In the late 1980s, however, the

Houston economy began to revive. With an upturn in the housing and rental market, landlords could more easily rent to established-resident Anglos and blacks. At Arborland, policy toward low-income newcomers became one of exclusion. An electronic security system was installed, making access more difficult even for tenants, management posted notices only in English, Spanish-speaking rental agents were no longer hired, and newcomer Latino tenants were placed in the rear buildings. Finally, management raised rents, forcing newcomers to leave and find cheaper housing elsewhere.

Dwight Conquergood's article on Big Red also lays bare important class relations within Albany Park that were articulated in the landlord-tenant relationship. However, in the saga of Big Red's renewal, ownership was shifted from an absentee slumlord to a local community development organization, which turned the building over to a new housing entrepreneur. His eviction of tenants was in the name of preserving the community and rehabilitating Big Red. Conquergood's class analysis reminds us that power is constituted through a power/knowledge nexus (Foucault 1972) and is embedded in language. Conquergood isolates what he calls the "rhetoric of transgression" in the language used to describe Big Red. It was classified as dirty and dangerous; "blight," "cancer," and other terms evoking contagious disease were used. Images of flux and instability ("transience") were associated with the tenants, and notions of progress and development were invoked as part of a "strategic manipulation of time," so that by contrast Big Red and its tenants were seen as dragging the neighborhood backward—the antithesis of renewal and redevelopment.

Despite the displacement of newcomers from Arborland and Big Red, both articles give vivid examples of tenants' resistance to tactical uses of power. Arborland tenants organized to get better information on the new security system, and Big Red tenants orchestrated the restoration of the building's water supply by digging down to the water main. Big Red tenants' daily responses to the difficulties of living in a deteriorating building were particularly resourceful. They created a context in which relations between newcomers of very different cultural backgrounds and between newcomers and established residents could be forged.

A *comparative framework* is also used by Judy Goode, Jo Anne Schneider, and Suzanne Blanc in examining interrelations in elementary schools in North Philadelphia. Here, we see class and power at work in ways that differ from those of the workplace, since the Philadelphia cases focus on the intersection of school systems and the local political economy (which, in turn, shapes the class base of particular neighborhoods). There is no simple relationship among neighborhood, school, and newcomer–established resident relations. Public and parochial schools have very different goals (the public schools focused on individual achievement and the parochial schools on perpetuating religious and moral values).

Schools whose students were able to cross the boundaries between newcomers and established residents were those that were able to control their resources and therefore ensure the stability of teacher and student populations. In addition, interrelations were shaped by the social structure of the school and its ideology (whether it emphasized achievement or family and community values, and how it constructed ethnic "difference"). At Peterson, one of the two public schools studied, newcomer–established resident friendships were common, and no ethnic group dominated the awards at graduation. In this achievement-oriented school, ethnic difference received little emphasis. At St. Ignatius across the street, ethnic boundaries were more visible; this parochial school emphasized strong family ties and supported the notion that each child likes to be with his or her "own kind." In examining schooling as an arena and in understanding the school (and the school system) as a mediating institution, Goode, Schneider, and Blanc show us the complex interconnections between the internal structure of the school (relations among administration, teachers, aides, students, and parents) and the local neighborhood (as it responded to economic decline, immigration, and ethnic diversity).

In addition, each school holds a place in a larger bureaucracy, and schools' ability to control their resources (a stable student body, the retention of teachers, an adequate budget based on tax dollars or parishioners' contributions) varies a great deal. Power here emanates from a wider set of structural relationships that connect a larger political economy with the school systems that depend on it. Even as administrators, teachers, and aides deploy power within a school (controlling students and their interaction), their strategies are constrained by the position of their school in a larger system. Hence the possibilities open to Dixon, a working-class school with marginal resources, were much more limited than Peterson's.

It is interesting that it is the public school (Peterson) in a neighborhood (Olney) where newcomers have middle-class rather than working-class origins that has been most successful in avoiding "the reproduction of preexisting group boundaries." Working-class Puerto Rican newcomer parents at Dixon were at odds with the school, and their children were separated from those of other ethnic backgrounds, while Polish newcomer children were pulled into a homogeneous Polish-American setting that was defensively maintained against encroaching nonwhite newcomers and established residents (Puerto Ricans and blacks).

John Horton's contribution provides an "upbeat" ending for the collection, since it illustrates ways in which effective organizing across newcomer–established resident boundaries can effect political change and redistribute power relationships. One might argue this is a *transformative* "critical tale."

Here newcomer Chinese from Hong Kong, Taiwan, and Southeast Asia have immigrated to Monterey Park, a Los Angeles suburb with considerable capital and economic connections. They own a majority of the businesses, and among them are a large number of the professionals (doctors, dentists, and other medical personnel) in the community. There has been a substantial Anglo backlash: many white residents have left the area, while others have supported restrictions on signs in Chinese, openly argued for "English only," and attempted to send messages of Americanism to the newcomers.

In 1987 the Monterey Park City Council was dominated by Anglo and Latino representatives who were anti-immigrant, but by 1990 there were some signs that the backlash was subsiding and that a coalition of Latino, Asian-American, and white liberals was promoting policies that would build bridges between the various ethnic groups in the community.

As a particular type of "critical tale," Horton's essay dwells on several examples of public occasions where interaction brought about an unintended result—the defeat of a proposal to build a statue of George Washington, and the creation of a Cinco de Mayo celebration for a Chinese audience out of what was to have been a celebration of Monterey Park's Anglo heritage. Like the two articles on housing, Horton's analysis is processual (a series of events that led to a reorganization of community politics), but his scenario is punctuated with "event analyses" that allow us to see how political forces became realigned.

The effect of new immigrants on the local government of Monterey Park as a mediating institution has been to undermine the traditional Anglo hierarchy and open the institution to new contenders for power: grass-roots activists protesting overdevelopment, and Asians and Latinos using their numerical power to demand participation. In this case we are not dealing with a working-class newcomer population, but with upper-middle-class professionals and wealthy business interests. Monterey Park is a class-homogeneous setting, and there is not a class difference between elected and appointed officials and the electorate. The transformation of the mediating institution of local government, though important, did not entail sharing power across class lines.

During the two years of the Changing Relations project, other examples of interaction and accommodation occurred among middle- and upper-class groups, where newcomers of like status were more easily accepted than are those from a working-class background. For example, the white American elite in Miami has begun to include more Cubans in mainstream organizations such as the Greater Miami Chamber of Commerce. A list of eighteen "power brokers" in Miami included eight Cubans. Only five Cubans, however, were included in the forty-nine member "Non-Group," a powerful "old boys' network" that was founded in the early 1970s. In Garden City, middle-class Southeast Asians, some of whom were the first Asians to arrive in the town, tended to be found in white-collar jobs or professional positions. This tiny group with more education and better English skills were better integrated than Vietnamese from village backgrounds. They were often spokespersons for Vietnamese who had less access to schools, medical facilities, or government agencies. Finally, newcomers in Albany Park who sat on the boards of community agencies, such as the Albany Park Community Center and the North River Commission, were often from small business or middle-class backgrounds. They were better integrated into institutions alongside established residents than were the working-class and unemployed residents of Big Red. Overall, among all the newcomer groups studied by the Changing Relations project, well-off Cubans in Miami and upper-middle-class Chinese in Monterey Park were the newcomers who had achieved the greatest economic and political success.

The Role of Gender in Interrelations

The role of gender in each of these case studies is worth noting. Men and women are often differentially located in social situations. They work in different industries (construction versus apparel, for example), and even if they work in the same industry they are likely to work at different jobs in different departments (Slaughter for men and Processing for women in meat-packing plants). In apartment complexes they often frequent different public spaces (the men in the back alley, the women and children in the courtyard of Big Red). Women are more in evidence in schools and social service institutions and may be absent from higher levels of management in private industry.

In local politics (in contrast to the national level), women are playing an increasing role, as evidenced by the number of women on the Monterey Park City Council and by its woman mayor (Judy Chu, who took the position for a year through a rotating mayorship among city council members).

Women are often the actors who make an effort to cross ethnic boundaries and to create coalitions. Horton elsewhere noted that Chu and two other female council members formed a coalition of "pragmatic, female peace-makers" in contrast to the more confrontational males (Horton 1990:134–35). Certainly, in both Big Red and Arborland women were often important in making connections across newcomer–established resident lines. These "connecting activities" were often informal and sporadic—for example, selling food door to door or enlisting aid when a porch collapsed. But such activities are nevertheless crucial in making the connections that are often necessary later for collective action.

Our approach has demonstrated that interaction between new immigrants and established residents and their assimilation to American life do not take place in some free-floating way, as if newcomers absorbed American values and patterns of behavior outside of an institutional context. By examining mediating institutions and the ways they are structured and shaped by larger political and economic forces, we can understand the relative lack of interaction between newcomers and established residents in many settings. Our critical tales also have revealed subtle ways in which newcomers are often peripheralized or displaced through tactical and structural uses of power despite their own reactions to that power.

Our conclusions underline the importance of class in relationship to power.

Upper- and middle-class newcomers are much more able to shape institutions to their benefit than new immigrants who have entered the American working class. Further attention needs to be given to the structure of workplaces, living arrangements, schools, and local governments in working-class neighborhoods and in communities with large populations of new immigrants from rural and working-class backgrounds. Only if these structures become more flexible and open to reform can the power and equality that are beginning to emerge for Chinese immigrants in Monterey Park also come to characterize the experience of other newcomers across the United States.

Conclusions

These examples indicate that the face of American cities is indeed changing. But what we have called "mediating institutions" often act to contain and peripheralize newcomers, keeping them in marginal English-as-a-second-language classes, in short-term, dead-end manufacturing and service jobs, and in separate apartment buildings within a complex. It is not an issue of traditional segregation. After all, Haitians and Cubans work side by side in the Miami garment factory. Vietnamese, Anglos, Mexican Americans, and Latino immigrants are all employed by IBP in Garden City, and Guatemalans, Anglos, and Mexican Americans rent from the same landlord at Arborland in Houston. The lack of interaction between newcomers and established residents is the product of subtle and micro-level structuring of the labor process at work, scheduling of classes and extracurricular programs at school, and landlords' policies in apartment complexes.

A newcomer's inability to speak English does create barriers to interaction, but language, we argue, cannot account for the amount of isolation and compartmentalization researchers have reported. There was little in the way of violent conflict, but neither was there a great deal of interaction. At best we see a kind of "parallel tracking system," with newcomers fitting into particular economic niches in urban areas, creating their own social networks and institutions for preserving their cultural identity while becoming Americans. The class composition of newcomer populations suggests that even in the second generation, it will be those immigrants from middle- and upper-class backgrounds (including some, but not all, Chinese, Cubans, and Koreans) who will succeed in America. Immigrants from peasant and working-class backgrounds may find that their children remain within the American working class, experiencing unemployment, lack of skills and education, and confinement to deteriorating urban neighborhoods.

Our analysis paves the way for a broader consideration of class and power in assessing the place of new immigrants in American society. The following chapters suggest that newcomers are relatively disempowered and will remain so unless the structures of mediating institutions are changed. Although we have found examples where boundaries have been crossed and institutions are in the process of transformation, we have been struck with the extent to which newcomers are not being integrated with established residents in the contexts of everyday life. There are still important and subtle boundaries that compartmentalize newcomers and established residents in the workplace, the school, the neighborhood, and the community.

References

Anderson, Grace. 1974. *Networks of Contact: The Portuguese and Toronto.* Ontario: Wilfrid Laurier University Press.

Anderson, Nels. 1923. *The Hobo.* Chicago: University of Chicago Press.

Aronowitz, Stanley. 1973. *False Promises: The Shaping of American Working Class Consciousness.* New York: McGraw-Hill Book Company.

Bach, Robert, Rodolfo de la Garza, Karen Ito, Louise Lamphere, and Niara Sudarkasa. 1991. Changing Relations Final Report. New York: Ford Foundation. Typescript.

Barth, Fredrik. 1969. *Ethnic Groups and Boundaries.* Boston: Little, Brown.

Bean, Frank D., Georges Vernez, and Charles B. Keely. 1989. *Opening and Closing the Doors: Evaluating Immigration Reform and Control.* Santa Monica, Calif.: RAND Corporation and Urban Institute.

Bluestone, Barry, and Bennett Harrison. 1982. *The Deindustrialization of America.* New York: Basic Books.

Bodnar, John, Roger Simon, and Michael P. Weber. 1982. *Lives of Their Own: Blacks, Italians, and Poles in Pittsburgh, 1900–1960.* Urbana: University of Illinois Press.

Broadway, Michael. 1990. Recent Changes in the Structure and Location of the U.S. Meatpacking Industry. *Geography* 75 (1): 76–79.

Browning, Harley L., and Rodolfo de la Garza. 1986. *Mexican Immigrants and Mexican Americans: An Evolving Relation.* Austin: Center for Latin American Studies, University of Texas.

Burgess, Ernest W. 1967. The Growth of the City. In *The City,* edited by Robert E. Park, Ernest W. Burgess, and Roderick D. McKenzie. Chicago: University of Chicago Press.

Castro, Max. 1989. The Politics of Language in Miami. Miami: Greater Miami United. Typescript.

Collins, Thomas. 1980. *Cities in a Larger Context.* Athens: University of Georgia Press.

Conquergood, Dwight, Paul Friesema, Paul Albert Hunter, Jane Mansbridge, Mary Erdmans, Jeremy Hein, Yvonne Newsome, and Yung-Sun Park. 1990. Changing Relations: Newcomers and Established Residents in the Albany Park Area of Chicago. Evanston, Ill.: Center for Urban Affairs and Policy Research, Northwestern University. Typescript.

Cressey, Paul G. 1932. *The Taxi-Dance Hall.* Chicago: University of Chicago.

Di Leonardo, Micaela. 1984. *The Varieties of Ethnic Experience: Kinship, Class, and Gender among California Italian-Americans.* Ithaca, N.Y.: Cornell University Press.

Drake, St. Clair, and Horace Cayton. 1945. *Black Metropolis*. New York: Harcourt, Brace.
Dwyer, Kevin. 1982. *Moroccan Dialogues: Anthropology in Question*. Baltimore: John Hopkins University Press.
Eames, Edwin, and Judith Goode. 1977. *The Anthropology of the City*. Englewood Cliffs, N.J.: Prentice-Hall.
Erickson, Ken C., and Donald D. Stull. 1990. Bovine Anthropology: "Pulling Count" in the Packinghouse. Paper presented at the American Anthropological Association Annual Meeting, Washington, D.C., 20 November–2 December.
Ford Foundation. 1987. Project Statement (manuscript authored by Changing Relations Project Board). New York. Typescript.
______. 1988. Press Release on Changing Relations Project, 28 January. New York.
Foucault, Michel. 1972. *Power/Knowledge: Selected Interviews and Other Writings*. Edited by Colin Gordon. New York: Pantheon Books.
Fox, Richard. 1977. *Urban Anthropology: Cities in Their Cultural Settings*. Englewood Cliffs, N.J.: Prentice-Hall.
Gans, Herbert J. 1962. *The Urban Villagers: Group and Class in the Life of Italian-Americans*. New York: Free Press.
Glazer, Nathan, and Patrick Daniel Moynihan. 1970. *Beyond the Melting Pot: The Negroes, Puerto Ricans, Italians, and Irish of New York City*. 2d ed. Cambridge, Mass.: MIT Press.
Glenn, Evelyn. 1986. *Issei, Nissei, War Bride: Three Generations of Japanese American Women in Domestic Service*. Philadelphia: Temple University Press.
Goode, Judith. 1989. Urban Anthropology in the United States. *La Ricerca Folklorica* 20.
______. 1990. A Wary Welcome to the Neighborhood: Community Responses to Immigrants. *Urban Anthropology* 19 (1–2): 125–53.
______. (N.d.) Service Encounters in Philadelphia. In *Labor, Capital, and Community*, edited by Guillermo Grenier and Louise Lamphere. Forthcoming.
Gordon, Milton. 1964. *Assimilation in American Life: The Role of Race, Religion, and National Origins*. New York: Oxford University Press.
Gulick, John. 1968. The Outlook. Research Strategies and Relevance in Urban Anthropology. In *Urban Anthropology*, edited by E. Eddy. Athens: University of Georgia Press.
______. 1984. The Essence of Urban Anthropology: Integration of Micro- and Macro-perspectives. *Urban Anthropology* 13 (2–3): 295–306.
Handlin, Oscar. 1974. *Boston's Immigrants: A Study in Acculturation*. Rev. ed. New York: Atheneum.
Hannerz, Ulf. 1969. *Soulside: Inquiries into Ghetto Culture and Community*. New York: Columbia University Press.
Hershberg, Theodore, Alan N. Burstein, Eugene P. Ericksen, Stephanie Greenberg, and William L. Yancey. 1979. A Tale of Three Cities: Blacks and Immigrants in Philadelphia, 1850–1880, 1930, and 1970. *The Annals of the American Academy of Political and Social Science* 441 (January): 55–81.
Horton, John. 1989. The Politics of Ethnic Change: Grass-Root Responses to Economic and Demographic Restructuring in Monterey Park, California. *Urban Geography* 10 (6): 578–92.

———. 1990. Changing Relations: Newcomers and Established Residents in U.S. Communities: The Case of Monterey Park, California. University of California at Los Angeles. Typescript.

Hymes, Dell, ed. 1969. *Reinventing Anthropology.* New York: Pantheon.

Keefe, Susan Emily, and Amado M. Padilla. 1987. *Chicano Ethnicity.* Albuquerque: University of New Mexico Press.

Keiser, R. Lincoln. 1969. *The Vice Lords.* New York: Holt, Rinehart, and Winston.

Kubat, Daniel, ed., with Ursula Merlander and Ernst Gehmacher. 1979. *The Politics of Migration Policies: The First World in the 1970s.* New York: Center for Migration Studies.

Lamphere, Louise. 1985. Bringing the Family to Work: Women's Culture on the Shop Floor. *Feminist Studies* 11 (3): 519–40.

———. 1987. *From Working Daughters to Working Mothers: Immigrant Women in a New England Industrial Community.* Ithaca, N.Y.: Cornell University Press.

LaRuffa, Anthony. 1988. *Monte Carmelo: An Italian-American Community in the Bronx.* New York: Gordon and Breach.

Leeds, Anthony. 1973. Locality Power in Relation to Superlocal Power Institutions. In *Urban Anthropology,* edited by Aiden Southall, 15–41. New York: Oxford University Press.

Liebow, Elliot. 1967. *Tally's Corner: A Study of Negro Streetcorner Men.* Boston: Little, Brown and Company.

Lopata, Helena Znaniecki. 1976. *Polish Americans: Status Competition in an Ethnic Community.* Englewood Cliffs, N.J.: Prentice-Hall.

Lynch, Owen. 1984. Rationale and Romance Reassessed. Paper presented at the 83d annual meeting of the American Anthropological Association. Denver, 14–18 November.

March, Kathleen. 1991. Words and Worlds of Tamang Women. Typescript.

Markusen, Ann, Peter Hall, and Amy Glasmeier. 1986. *High Tech America: The What, How, Where, and Why of the Sunrise Industries.* Boston: Allen and Unwin.

Moore, Joan, and Harry Pachon. 1985. *Hispanics in the United States.* Englewood Cliffs, N.J.: Prentice-Hall.

Moynihan, Daniel Patrick. 1965. *The Negro Family: The Case for National Action.* Washington, D.C.: Government Printing Office.

Mullings, Leith, ed. 1987. *Cities of the United States: Studies in Urban Anthropology.* New York: Columbia University Press.

Park, Robert. 1916. The City: Suggestions for the Investigation of Human Behavior in the Urban Environment. *The American Journal of Sociology* 20. Reprinted in Sennett 1961, pp. 91–130.

Peattie, Lisa, and Edward Robbins. 1984. Anthropological Approaches to the City. In *Cities of the Mind,* edited by Lloyd Rodwin and Robert M. Hollister. New York: Plenum.

Peterson, William. 1971. *Japanese Americans: Oppression and Success.* New York: Random House.

Portes, Alejandro, and Ruben Rumbaut. 1990. *Immigrant America: A Portrait.* Berkeley: University of California Press.

Portes, Alejandro, and Alex Stepick. 1985. Unwelcome Immigrants: The Labor Market Experiences of 1980 (Mariel) Cuban and Haitian Refugees in South Florida. *American Sociological Review* 50 (August): 493–514.

Redfield, Robert. 1941. *The Folk Culture of Yucatan*. Chicago: University of Chicago Press.
______. 1947. The Folk Society. *American Journal of Sociology* 43:293–308.
______. 1955. *The Little Community*. Chicago: University of Chicago Press.
Redfield, Robert, and Milton Singer. 1954. The Cultural Role of Cities. *Economic Development and Cultural Change* 3:53–73.
Rodriguez, Nestor P., Jacqueline M. Hagan, Janis Hutchinson, Nanette Navarre, Patricia L. Schadt, and Carlos Quirino. 1990. Evolving Relations in Houston: Established Residents and Latino Newcomers. University of Houston. Typescript.
Sanjek, Roger. 1988. *The People of Queens for Now to Then*. Flushing, N.Y.: Asian/American Center, Queens College.
______, ed. 1989. *Worship and Community: Christianity and Hinduism in Contemporary Queens*. Flushing, N.Y.: Asian/American Center, Queens College.
______. 1990. Urban Anthropology in the 1980s: A World View. In *Annual Review of Anthropology*, 151–86. Palo Alto, Calif.: Annual Review Press.
Sawers, Larry, and William K. Tabb. 1984. *Sunbelt/Snowbelt: Urban Development and Regional Restructuring*. New York: Oxford University Press.
Sennett, Richard, ed. 1969. *Classic Essays on the Culture of Cities*. New York: Appleton-Century-Croft.
Shelton, Beth Anne, Nestor P. Rodriguez, Joe R. Feagin, Robert D. Bullard, and Robert D. Thomas. 1989. *Houston: Growth and Decline in a Sunbelt Boomtown*. Philadelphia: Temple University Press.
Spradley, James P. 1970. *You Owe Yourself a Drunk*. Boston: Little, Brown.
Stack, Carol B. 1974. *All Our Kin: Strategies for Survival in a Black Community*. New York: Harper and Row.
Stepick, Alex, Max Castro, Marvin Dunn, and Guillermo Grenier. 1990. Changing Relations among Newcomers and Established Residents: The Case of Miami. Typescript.
Stull, Donald D., Janet E. Benson, Michael J. Broadway, Arthur L. Campa, Ken C. Erickson, and Mark A. Grey. 1990. Changing Relations: Newcomers and Established Residents in Garden City, Kansas. Final report to the Changing Relations Project Board. Lawrence: Institute for Public Policy and Business Research, University of Kansas, Report 172.
Thernstrom, Stephan. 1973. *The Other Bostonians: Poverty and Progress in an American Metropolis, 1880–1970*. Cambridge, Mass.: Harvard University Press.
Van Maanen, John. 1988. *Tales of the Field: On writing Ethnography*. Chicago: University of Chicago Press.
Wirth, Louis. 1928. *The Ghetto*. Chicago: University of Chicago Press.
______. 1938. Urbanism as a Way of Life. Reprinted in Sennett 1969, pp. 143–64.
______. 1945. Human Ecology. Reprinted in Sennett 1969, pp. 170–79.
______. 1956. Rural-Urban Differences. Reprinted in Sennett 1969, pp. 165–69.
Wolf, Eric. 1990. Distinguished Lecture: Facing Power. In *American Anthropologist* 92 (3): 586–96.
Wong, Bernard. 1982. *Chinatown: Economic Adaptation and Ethnic Identity of the Chinese*. New York: Holt, Rinehart, and Winston.
Yanagisako, Sylvia. 1985. *Transforming the Past: Tradition and Kinship among Japanese Americans*. Stanford, Calif.: Stanford University Press.
Yancey, William L., Eugene P. Ericksen, and Richard M. Juliani. 1976. Emergent Eth-

nicity: Review and Reformulation. *American Sociological Review* 41 (June): 391–403.

Zavella, Patricia. 1987. *Women, Work, and Family in the Chicano Community.* Ithaca, N.Y.: Cornell University Press.

Zorbaugh, Harvey W. 1929. *The Gold Coast and the Slum.* Chicago: University of Chicago Press.

1 THE PRICE OF A GOOD STEAK: BEEF PACKING AND ITS CONSEQUENCES FOR GARDEN CITY, KANSAS

DONALD D. STULL, MICHAEL J. BROADWAY, AND KEN C. ERICKSON

He is a beef-boner, and that is a dangerous trade, especially when you are on piece-work and trying to earn a bride. Your hands are slippery, and your knife is slippery, and you are toiling like mad, when somebody happens to speak to you, or you strike a bone. Then your hand slips up on the blade, and there is a fearful gash. And that would not be so bad, only for the deadly contagion. The cut may heal, but you never can tell. . . . There are learned people who can tell you out of the statistics that beef-boners make forty cents an hour, but, perhaps, these people have never looked into a beef-boner's hands.

UPTON SINCLAIR,
THE JUNGLE (1906)

You have to be real careful. Everywhere you walk through or move you can either slip or get hit by something, or if it's not that, somebody else with a knife can cut you, or run into something. . . . One time I slipped and hit myself, but I have that metal apron and it stopped it, but I feel weird in there. . . . I used to cut gloves every day. I have the mesh glove under, but the plastic glove that I had on top, I would always cut it by accident, not on purpose. But I was glad I was wearing that mesh glove, boy, because every day I would have had an accident.

SLAUGHTER WORKER, JUNE 4, 1989

Modern meat-packing plants are a far cry from those described by Upton Sinclair at the turn of the century. Still, with all their impressive innovations—

We wish to acknowledge funding and support services from the Ford Foundation's Changing Relations project, the University of Kansas General Research Fund (allocation 3104-XO-0038), and the Institute for Public Policy and Business Research. The maps in Figure 1.1 are slightly modified from ones which first appeared in *Urban Anthropology* 19(4):306. Our sincerest thanks go to Louise Lamphere for encouraging us to tell this tale, for her many helpful comments on earlier drafts, and for constantly pushing us to "get it out the door." And above all, we wish to thank the many Garden Citians who shared of their time and knowledge.

ergonomics, robotics, computerization, laser technology—the knife, the meat hook, and the steel remain the basic tools of the trade. Today's plants, like the ones they have replaced, are rigidly organized, labor-intensive factories. And as when Sinclair wrote *The Jungle,* immigrants are still attracted to packinghouse jobs because command of English is not required and because wages are relatively high. But instead of the German, Irish, Lithuanian, and Polish workers of Sinclair's day, packinghouses are now crowded with Southeast Asian refugees and Mexican immigrants, with blacks, Latinos, and Anglos from American farms and cities. Plant conditions continue to shape interrelations not only on the kill floor and processing line but within the communities that are home to their workers as well. Thus, knowledge of the working conditions, organization, and interethnic dynamics in the plants is crucial to a full understanding of relations among and between newcomers and established residents in packinghouse communities.

For packers, accidents and turnover are like death and taxes—they are inevitable, or so the packers believe. Record fines imposed by the Occupational Safety and Health Administration (OSHA) have forced them to search for ways to reduce on-the-job hazards, and a shrinking labor pool has led them to search for ways to retain their workers longer. But ask any packer—from the top executive to the hourly line worker—and he'll tell you it's a dangerous business in which few intend to make a career.

With profits of less than 1 percent of total sales, consumer resistance to higher prices, and shrinking demand for their product, packers have only two ways to make money—increase productivity and cut costs. The packers take steps to achieve these twin goals both at the industry level and on the floors of their plants. Their strategies to increase productivity and cut costs have a direct impact on relations among and between workers, and they have ramifications for the larger communities in which the plants are located as well.

At the industry level, new packing companies have sought to lower costs by locating large-capacity plants close to feedlots in right-to-work states. Within the plants, productivity has been increased by the development of a disassembly line and the simplification of the meat-packing process, so that highly skilled (and well-paid) butchers can be replaced by unskilled and semiskilled laborers. The repetitive motions associated with many tasks contribute to the industry's high injury rate. In Kansas, for example, over 17,000 work-related injuries occurred in meat-packing plants from 1980 to 1988 (Austin 1988b). The distasteful and dangerous nature of many packinghouse jobs combines with the stress of working in such an environment to produce high employee turnover and inhibit the establishment of ties between these workers and the rest of the community.

Previous research on meat packing has focused either at the macro- or the micro-level. Richard Carnes (1984), for example, examined the effects of restructuring on productivity, and Michael Broadway (1990a) has documented the locational strategies of the new packers. At the micro-level, Robert Slayton

(1986) tells of life Back of the Yards at the turn of the century, and Hardy Green (1990) gives an insider's view of the protracted strike against the Hormel plant in Austin, Minnesota, in 1985–86. But descriptions of what it is like to toil on the chains and lines of modern meat-packing plants are almost nonexistent. Dorothy Remy and Larry Sawers (1984) offer a glimpse of the floor at the "Square Deal Packing Company" in their analysis of the consequences of retrenchment for women and blacks, but only William Thompson (1983) has described work in a modern packing plant.

In the pages to follow we offer a "critical tale" (Van Maanen 1988) of the meat-packing industry and how it shapes workers' lives and community relationships. Its tellers stand on a "middle ground" and look both ways. From such a vantage point, we hope to provide a much-needed addition to the scant literature on meat packing. But more important, we seek to transcend what has gone before by illuminating the interlocking connections between economic forces and their consequences both for workers and for the communities in which they live. We hope to demonstrate how closely intertwined are the processes of industrial restructuring and rural industrialization—how company policies, driven by market forces, can set in motion processes that go beyond the plant gates to recast the configuration of whole communities. This is not, then, just a tale about the meat-packing industry. Instead, it is a tale about community dynamics and how they got that way, of how relations on the job mold relations between social and ethnic groups.

John Van Maanen (1988:127) reminds us that in all societies, but especially in industrialized ones, ethnographic research and micro-level analysis are no longer sufficient (if they ever were) to explain social arenas and the actions of those within them. Yet ethnography remains necessary to full and proper understanding of both social systems and social processes. By linking macro- and micro-approaches, our tale relates how the restructuring of this industry affects the nature of relations not only within the meat-packing plant itself but also in the wider community. Specifically, it reveals how the packers control the nature of work in the meat-packing plants. The nature of the job limits interactions between workers and fosters mobility, which in turn restrict community relations between new immigrants and established residents in the packinghouse town of Garden City, Kansas.[1]

Structural Change in the Meat-packing Industry

The American economy since the end of World War II has undergone a rapid transformation in *what* it produces and *how* and *where* it produces. There has

1. This "tale" is but one in a larger "tale cycle." By combining macro-level data and analysis with micro-level ethnography, we present, for the first time, a detailed account of today's meat-packing industry and its impact on the lives of both workers and communities. For more tales in this cycle see Stull and Broadway 1990; Broadway and Stull 1991; Broadway 1990a, 1990b, n.d.; Erickson n.d.; Stull n.d.; and Benson n.d.

been a decline in the relative importance of manufacturing and agriculture to the overall economy. Individual sectors of the economy are increasingly characterized by oligopoly, as a result of corporate mergers. The distribution of industry has changed too, as corporations have sought new areas of comparative advantage (Knox 1988).

Meat packing is representative of these changes. Its employment fell by a third from 1967 to 1987, while at the same time red meat production came to be dominated by three companies—IBP, ConAgra Red Meats, and Excel. The biggest declines in employment were in the manufacturing belt, in states with high levels of unionization, while increases in employment occurred in right-to-work states (Broadway 1990b). In Kansas, for example, meat-packing employment increased by over 80 percent from 1967 to 1987. In contrast, Pennsylvania, Ohio, Illinois, Wisconsin, Missouri, and Minnesota all experienced reductions of over 25 percent. Within this overall pattern, the biggest reductions in employment were in major urban centers such as Chicago, St. Louis, and Philadelphia, while the new meat-packing plants have generally been built in small towns. This transformation from an urban to a rural base is part of an overall cost-cutting strategy by the new packing companies.

Beef packing is a high-cost industry—$93 out of every $100 in sales is eaten up in direct production costs (of these costs, $87.27 is for livestock and raw materials, while only $3.39 is spent on production labor). Profits are minimal—an average of 81 cents for every $100 of sales in 1986—and depend on high-volume sales and strict attention to cost cutting (Austin 1988a). IBP is the recognized leader in the movement to lower costs, and since the company's founding in 1960 it has acquired approximately one-third of the U.S. market for boxed beef, with sales of over $9 billion.

IBP, unlike the old meat-packing companies, avoided negotiating master contracts with the Meat Cutters Union, which established industrywide standards and benefits. In the company's plant in Dakota City, Nebraska, which was organized by the Meat Cutters, labor-management relations have been marred by several long and violent strikes. For example, in 1982 the union called a strike after IBP asked for a four-year wage freeze. A year later, following violent clashes between strikers, the Nebraska State Police, and the National Guard, union representatives signed a contract that reduced pay by $1.05 an hour. The packers' overall success in lowering wages is evident in the fact that in 1960 meat-packing wages stood at 121 percent of the average manufacturing wage; by 1988 this figure had fallen to 84 percent (U.S. Department of Labor 1985, 1989).

Labor costs have also been lowered by the development of a disassembly line, which, in management's eyes, eliminates the need for highly skilled (and well-paid) butchers. In their place, laborers perform simple, repetitive tasks at high speeds. The constant repetition associated with this work frequently leads to various hand, arm, and wrist disorders, such as carpal tunnel syndrome. Employers mitigate costs of these injuries to themselves by restricting workers' eligibility for health care benefits until they have worked up to six months.

Other cost-cutting strategies include locating large plants close to feedlots. This eliminates the need for middlemen and shortens transportation distances, which in turn minimizes the shrinkage and bruising of cattle. Large-capacity plants are much more economical than smaller ones. For example, in 1986 the estimated slaughter cost for a plant that operates at 25 head per hour was $41 per head; the corresponding figure for a plant operating at 325 head per hour was $22 per head (Miller 1986:19). The movement of packing plants to rural areas has been facilitated by the innovation of boxed beef, first developed and marketed by IBP in 1967. Fat and bone are removed at the plant, so that transportation costs are reduced as well as the need for retailers to employ highly skilled butchers.

Meat packing is clearly representative of structural changes in the wider U.S. economy. Technical innovations and capital mobility have enabled the new packing companies to locate in rural areas close to feedlots in right-to-work states and away from unionized urban areas. Kansas has experienced a boom in meat-packing employment as a result of this overall process.

The Kansas Beef-packing Industry: The Packers Come to Garden City

Beef packing in Kansas has undergone structural changes similar to those at the national level. Plants have closed in Kansas City and Wichita, and new plants have opened in small towns in southwest Kansas. The packers moved to southwest Kansas for several reasons. The introduction of center-pivot irrigation in the mid-1960s allowed farmers to tap water from the Ogallala Aquifer and successfully cultivate a variety of feed grains. The widespread availability of water and feed led in turn to the introduction of commercial feedyards. Plenty of fat cattle and water, Kansas's status as a right-to-work state, and the lower costs of operating plants in rural areas all helped attract the packers. Communities also offered them incentives. To help convince IBP to build near Garden City, the Finney County Commissioners provided $3.5 million in property tax relief for ten years and helped finance the construction of the plant with an issue of $100 million in industrial revenue bonds.

Although southwest Kansas has excellent physical resources to support the packing industry, it lacks a traditional attraction for a manufacturing plant—an available labor force. Unemployment in the county was 3.2 percent the year before IBP opened its Finney County plant west of Garden City (Kansas Department of Human Resources 1988).

Garden City is 215 miles west of Wichita and 309 miles southeast of Denver (see figure 1.1). At 2,900 feet, it sits on the semiarid short-grass and sandsage prairie of the southern High Plains. With a population of almost 25,000, it is the

A large feedyard near Garden City. (Photograph by Michael J. Broadway)

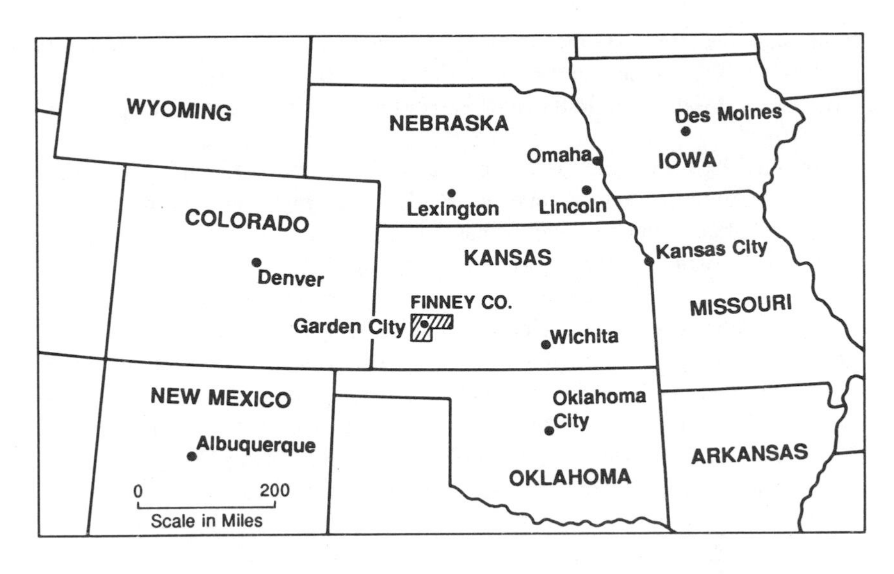

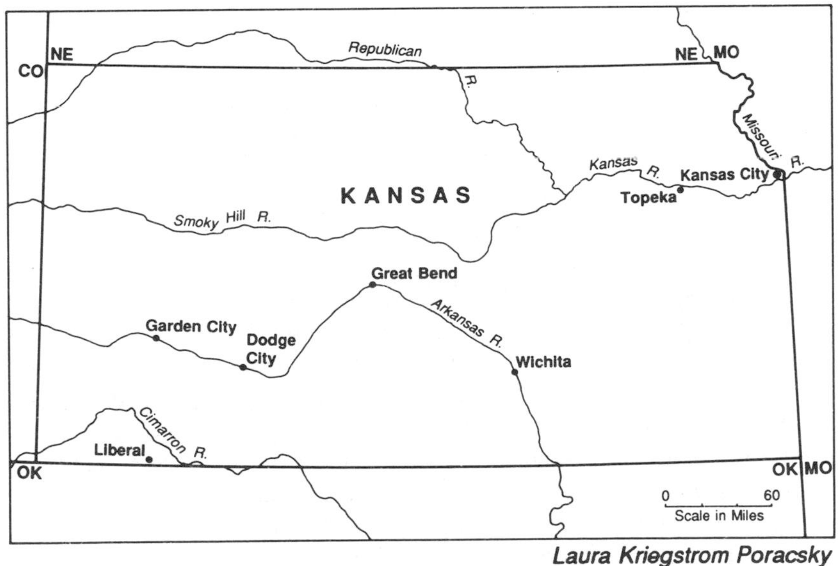

Laura Kriegstrom Poracsky

Figure 1.1. Location of Garden City, Kansas

Finney County seat and a trade and service center for small agricultural communities and unincorporated rural hamlets in a five-state area (Garden City Planning Department 1989).

In 1980 Garden City's population was 18,256, and in many ways the town typified the so-called heartland. Its citizens were predominantly Anglo (82 percent). Hispanics, who first came in the early 1900s to work on the railroad and in the sugar-beet fields (Oppenheimer 1985), were the only substantial minority (16 percent). One percent of the population was African American, and 0.5 percent each was American Indian and Asian (Garden City Planning Department 1989:16).

But the 1980s witnessed rapid change. In December 1980, IBP, Inc. (formerly Iowa Beef Processors), opened the world's largest beef-packing plant ten miles west of Garden City, near the hamlet of Holcomb. It added a second shift to become fully operational in the recession year of 1982. Lacking an adequate local labor force, IBP recruited far and wide, running newspaper advertisements and television commercials in other packing towns and sending recruiters to areas of high unemployment. In 1983, Val-Agri, Inc., purchased Garden City's idle Kansas Beef Processors plant, modernized it, and doubled its capacity. This plant was later sold to Swift Independent Packing Company and is now owned by Monfort, a division of ConAgra Red Meats Companies.

The "push" of a sustained recession combined with the "pull" of "good" wages in an expanding industry (starting between $6.00 and $6.40 an hour for production workers) lured many people to Garden City. These new jobs, requiring few previous skills—not even a command of English—drew more than two thousand Southeast Asians. Over half came from nearby Wichita, which was suffering from layoffs in its meat-packing and aircraft industries. Southeast Asians were also being "pushed" by shrinking federal and state assistance to refugees. Many Hispanics, primarily Mexicans, as well as Anglos came seeking work.

In five short years, Garden City was transformed from a bicultural community of established Anglos and Mexican Americans to a multicultural community, as Southeast Asian refugees and Hispanic migrants came to work in the beef plants. By the late 1980s, the minority population had doubled, from 18 percent in 1980 to about 36 percent by 1989 (Stull et al. 1990:83). Today the two plants employ approximately 4,000 workers and have a daily slaughter capacity of 8,400 head. In 1987, they combined to slaughter and process 2,400,000 cattle (Laudert 1988).

Most newcomers are young; the median age in Garden City is twenty-six. And they are mobile—monthly turnover in the packinghouses is 6–8 percent (Wood 1988:76). Many are single men, but the numbers of women and children are increasing. The demographic profile of the migrants, combined with their sheer numbers, severely strained the community's capacity to provide basic services such as housing, health care, and education.

While Garden City experienced the problems of rapid growth, early and concerted efforts on the part of the clergy, news media, schools, police, and social service agencies kept negative consequences to a minimum. Its growing ethnic diversity has given Garden City a cosmopolitan quality that seems unusual for a community its size, especially one that sits as it does in the heartland.

The Garden City Changing Relations Project

Garden City's ethnic diversity, rapid growth, and reputation for successfully accommodating new immigrants drew five anthropologists and a social geographer to study the town for more than two years. Our investigation was designed to produce an ethnography with emphasis on four arenas—work (especially packinghouses), school (particularly the community's one high school), neighborhoods, and community structure. We tried to balance ethnography with quantitative data from documents and questionnaires and to divide our time between participant observation and in-depth interviews. Each member of the team was assigned primary responsibility for specific arenas and populations, although we consciously attempted to overlap with and assist one another. Broader reports on our findings appear elsewhere (Stull et al. 1990; Stull 1990).

Interest in beef packing and beef-packing workers emerged naturally out of our research and practice. After all, most of Garden City's newcomers come to work in the packinghouses, and we wished to learn how men and women of such diverse ethnic and cultural backgrounds interacted on the job.

Stull's research focused on work and interethnic relations in the packing plants and feedyards. IBP and Monfort declined his invitation to participate directly in our study, so that we were forced to rely on indirect methods of data collection. Stull (and other team members) conducted formal interviews with a cross section of packinghouse line workers and supervisors and with feedyard managers and others familiar with cattle feeding and beef packing. He took every opportunity to go on tours of the plants; enrolled in a meat and carcass evaluation class at the community college to learn more about the industry, make contacts, and gain regular entry into "the cooler" where carcasses are graded; and occasionally assisted his meats instructor in tagging cattle on the kill floor. He regularly attended monthly worker's compensation hearings and spent countless hours as a patron and sometimes bartender at Tom's Tavern, a favorite with many packinghouse workers.

Broadway examined the economic processes that brought beef packing to southwest Kansas and the consequences of rural industrialization for Garden City. He also pulled off our only interview with a top executive of a major meatpacking firm.

Erickson was the state refugee services coordinator in southwest Kansas. His job required frequent contact with plant management and offered periodic opportunities to enter the plants. In the summer of 1988 it brought a call from the owner of the Dupaco plant in Norfolk, Nebraska, looking to "hire some Vietnamese." Although he declined the offer to become a bounty hunter, Erickson did conduct telephone interviews with the plant's owner and managers, was on site for six days, went through orientation with a small group of new workers, and worked on the fabrication floor two days to develop suggestions for training and retention.

On the Floor

Having shown how the packing industry has reduced its costs by restructuring, let us now turn to the plants themselves. Most modern beef plants are divided into Slaughter, Processing (or Fabrication), Offal, and Hides divisions. Cattle arrive at the plants in "bullwagons"—trucks holding about fifty animals each—to be weighed, given a lot number, unloaded, and held for only a few hours before being slaughtered. Animals are stunned ("knocked") before they are killed; the carcasses are then skinned, gutted, and trimmed as they move along the "chain" or "line." They leave the kill floor about an hour later as hanging sides of beef. Meanwhile, tongues, hearts, and other viscera travel on hooks and conveyors to Offal for final processing, while hides are transported to an area where they undergo the first stages in the tanning process before being shipped out by rail. Carcasses cool in the "hotbox" for twenty-four hours or so; then government inspectors grade them before they move on to the Processing floor.

In IBP's Finney County plant, twelve processing lines break the sides down into subprimal cuts. On each line, hourly workers—"whitehats"—face one another across plastic cutting surfaces and a moving conveyor. Their work is supervised by a "yellowhat," assisted by two "lead persons" or "bluehats." "Orangehats," or "QC," are there to ensure quality control of the product.

Workers share tasks as the meat moves along the conveyor. On the tenderloin

At dawn, feedyard workers load cattle for shipment to a nearby packing plant. Cattle trucks, or "bullwagons," can be seen in the background. (Photograph by Donald D. Stull)

line alone, there are twelve tender pullers, two saw operators, ten tender trimmers, two quality control retrimmers, three flat bone pullers, five flat meat trimmers, nine scale operators and packagers, and an "8300" (shrink-wrap machine) operator—forty-three persons in seven task groups, each depending on others for product flow. Beef leaves the processing floor shrink-wrapped and boxed for delivery to restaurants and retail stores. From Processing, the boxes (weighing up to one hundred pounds each) go for a ride on the computerized Material Handling conveyors to be "palletized" (grouped in stacks of twenty-four boxes), then stored on refrigerated shelves attended by robotic lifts.

On the south side of the plant, shaggers maneuver refrigerated trailers into position at the loading docks. The personnel director says that the company moves "one truckload of boxed beef every twenty-two minutes of every day, seven days a week"—sixty-five truckloads each day (Stull field notes 7/22/88). One truckload of beef contains about ninety-five head of processed cattle (Erickson field notes 4/26/90).

On the plant floor, management makes every effort to cut costs and increase productivity. Both are absolutely essential in a business where profit margins are so low that even the industry leader, IBP, claims it made only 0.04 percent return on sales in 1989 (Kay 1990). The strategies used to achieve these goals affect the nature of the work itself and the relations among and between workers. And as we will see in the concluding section, the nature of the workplace has consequences for the community as well.

Cutting Costs

Strategies for cutting costs include low wages, minimum benefits, limited and often inadequate training, and insufficient staffing ("short crewing"). We have discussed these measures elsewhere (Stull and Broadway 1990; Stull n.d.; Erickson n.d.) and will allude to them only briefly in the pages to follow.

Around Garden City one often hears that the packinghouses pay "good wages." And by regional standards they do, especially for unskilled workers who cannot speak English. But the hourly wage is deceptive. Estimated gross annual income for a full-time Processing line worker at IBP ranges from around $15,500 for a Grade 1 job (lowest level) after one year to about $22,000 for a Grade 7 job (highest level) after two years.[2] However, demand for beef is seasonal, and workers' hours are increased or cut back with fluctuations in cattle supplies and consumer demand. As we have already pointed out, in the 1980s

2. The wage levels, working conditions, availability and characteristics of the work force, and plant organization described in this paper are for 1988–89. Since then, starting wages at IBP have increased by 20 cents per hour and changes have been implemented on the floor. The Monfort plant has expanded its slaughter capacity and work force. Knowledgeable informants say they are witnessing declines in the number of Southeast Asians and a concomitant increase in Hispanics, most of whom are coming from Mexico.

Trucks carrying boxed beef leaving IBP's Finney County Plant. (Photograph by Donald D. Stull)

packers cut wages while they increased production (Skaggs 1986:204–8; Stanley 1988:9).

If wages are not as good as they first appear, neither are benefits. It is true that packers provide health and life insurance, paid vacations, and yearly bonuses, but workers are not eligible for such benefits for several months—many do not make it that long. And injured workers may be dismissed for failure to perform their jobs.

"Getting It out the Door"

Productivity, in the eyes of management, means "getting it out the door." Productivity is measured by "chain speed"—the number of carcasses processed in an hour. Between 350 and 400 head are killed, bled, skinned, gutted, sawed, boned, cut, trimmed, shrink-wrapped, boxed, and loaded every hour. If the workers are really "humping," and nothing breaks down, they may even get 425–50 head an hour. Chain speed is regulated by those in management—they can speed it up or slow it down. This frustrates workers, who often sacrifice safety and quality to keep up. But they must keep pace and do the job right, or face reprimand or termination.

> So far I have never heard anybody complaining. I just know I don't have time to sweep my sweat from my face, but I haven't heard anybody complaining about how fast it's going. We know it is going fast, and they want to still go faster. But . . . [we] just take it, I guess. I don't know. A good way to slow it down would be to do a bad job . . . but then they catch you, they watch you, and you can get written up for that, they take you to the office, and three times, they [fire you]. (Stull interview with Slaughter worker 6/4/89:47)

The packers have been very successful in increasing productivity—up 21 percent from 1980 to 1986 (Austin 1988b). They get more out of each worker in part through technological innovations that allow machines to do more of the work. But when the chain speeds up, each worker must produce ever more product just to keep up—and to keep a job. Fast chains have their price: worker turnover and high rates of injury.

Turnover

Worker turnover is a problem throughout the industry. All the beef plants in southwest Kansas report average *monthly* turnover rates of between 6 and 8 percent (Wood 1988:76). Turnover is said to decline, and worker longevity to increase, the longer a plant is in operation. Turnover at IBP's Finney County plant, the largest in the world, remains fairly constant at about 7 percent a month, and approximately one-third of its workers have been at the plant for two or more years. But when it first opened, turnover reached levels as high as 60 percent a month (Stull field notes 6/17/88:9, 7/22/88:9, 5/6/89:23).

Packers decry their "turnover problem" but accept it philosophically as part of the price of doing business. Managers and workers alike agree that working on the line is hard—not everyone can "pull count." You must learn to do your work right, and quickly, to make it on the line. Working conditions are often poor, and the work is distasteful. Workers must "hang with it" or quit. It is a tough business, and little sympathy is given to those who cannot pull their count. As the safety director at one plant put it: "We don't change their Pampers for 'em."

Industry critics and many workers say that high turnover benefits the packers, and they encourage it.

> What you get in this business . . . is that because they make so much money on turnover, you don't really give a shit about the employee except to manipulate him. . . . So you don't spend any money on supervisory training that teaches human relations. . . . You spend as few dollars as you can on that aspect of the business. And so most of the supervisory people that you see come out of the gang. . . . That's where they learned how to be a boss, by watching what the boss did. If you don't train him and change him, they're not going to be any different. So that's what you have. You have an inbred industry, with very few innovative thinkers.
>
> **Q:** Do you think it pays the packer to turn over the work force rapidly?
>
> **A:** It must or he wouldn't do it. . . . The tradeoff there is that the packer is paying a tremendously high cost in workman's compensation claims. So you take his workman's comp claim experience and add that to lost product and slower chain speed if he suffers that, or damaged product by inexperienced people. I mean, once you damage a cut of meat it's damaged, you can't hide it. I think the packer would be better off to work more toward a stable work force, but then of course you get into the problem of the higher wages. (Stull interview with respondent with wide industry experience 3/30/89:29, 25–26)

Industry executives deny such charges:

> I've heard the old song that high turnover benefited packers because . . . people didn't stay long enough to where they had two weeks' vacation, etc. If there was that thought ten years ago, there sure as hell isn't now. Surely now, particularly as labor is getting harder to find, I don't think anyone thinks they benefit from high turnover. . . . [But] I think the tendency is for most employees, even those that don't mind their job . . . to feel this is an eight- or

> ten-year job. Then they'll move on. (Broadway interview with meat-packing executive 4/29/89:9, 11)

Safety

Meat packing has always been a dangerous business. Today's workers wear hard hats, earplugs, stainless-steel mesh gloves, plastic wrist guards, chain-mail aprons and chaps, leather weight-lifting belts, and/or baseball-catchers' shin guards. Still, meat packing is America's most hazardous industry, with an annual injury rate of 33.4 per 100 workers (Glaberson 1987). It is also the most dangerous industry in Kansas. From 1980 to 1988, 17,000 Kansas meat-packing workers were injured on the job; more than one-third of these lost work time—eight died. One-third of the injuries involved cuts and punctures; almost one-quarter were due to carpal tunnel syndrome or cumulative trauma disorder (Austin 1988b).

Record OSHA fines for underreporting injuries and unsafe practices, coupled with declines in the meat-packing labor pool, have forced packers to pay more attention to safety. Ergonomists try to improve equipment and tool design, new workers receive training and conditioning to protect them from injury, supervisors are held accountable for accidents on their crews, and incentives are offered for reducing accidents.

But "getting it out the door" is still the order of the day. Packers readily admit that injuries cost them money—but the cost is minor, and apparently acceptable. Industry wide, payment for workers' compensation benefits, insurance, and hospitalization averaged $1.47 per $100 of sales in 1986 (Austin 1988c).

The threat of being written up or fired is always there. Supervisors, with production quotas for their crews, are constantly under pressure to get it out the door. When the chain speeds up, or when the product does not meet the standards of Quality Control, supervisors have little recourse. And if a supervisor has it in for a worker, it is not hard to find a reason to "write him up."

> "Bill" says there are plenty of ways that a supervisor can find to fire you if he wants. He knows them all because when he first started working there three years ago, his supervisor took a liking to him and taught him the ropes. For example, you are allowed six minutes for a "piss break." But there is no way you can get to the bathroom, take off all your gear, take care of business, wash up, put your gear back on, and get back on the line in six minutes, especially for women during their period. But the supervisor can enforce that rule and hound the person out or easily build a case for termination. (Stull field notes 1/27/89:5)

Management, from line supervisors to plant managers, want workers who will work efficiently and compliantly, workers who will do as they are told.

> They want somebody that naturally will work hard. I think everybody looks for someone like that. But they want somebody that will follow—I mean true-to-the-line follow. Whatever they say, you do. . . . I mean that in terms of they don't want you to think or bring up other ideas or anything or question their ideas or question their methods or anything. . . . they want you to work blind. You just do what they tell you to do, and that's all they want. And if you don't, then they try and make it rough for you. (Stull interview with Maintenance worker 5/9/89:31)

Interethnic Relations on the Floor

It is within the context of unpleasant surroundings, dangerous work, and constant pressure to increase productivity that supervisors and workers interact. This environment has much to do with the amount and kind of interaction between workers from diverse backgrounds who labor on the kill floor and processing lines.

Immigrants, minorities, and women have always found work in meatpacking plants. They are a natural labor pool from which packers recruit heavily. Once hired, workers are assigned to whatever job is vacant, though they may express personal preference. Current company records are unavailable, but in early 1987 approximately 900 of IBP's 2,400 workers were Southeast Asians (Erickson 1988); the remainder were believed to be Hispanics and Anglos in roughly equal numbers.

Table 1.1 presents the gender and ethnicity of workers at the Monfort plant in Garden City for 1986–88 (Bustos 1989).

Table 1.1. Gender and Ethnicity of Monfort Workers, 1986–88

		White		Hispanic		Asian		Black		Native American		Total Workforce
		M	F	M	F	M	F	M	F	M	F	
1986	N	299	74	566	132	38	12	25	8	—	—	1,154
	%	26	6	49	11	3	1	2	<1	—	—	
1987	N	268	67	554	117	47	13	20	7	—	1	1,094
	%	24	6	51	11	4	1	3	<1	—	<1	
1988	N	308	273	616	189	20	5	28	7	1	2	1,449
	%	21	19	43	13	1	<1	3	<1	<1	<1	

This table makes two important points. First, contrary to local stereotypes, all Monfort employees are not Hispanics. Most Hispanics are believed to be immigrants, and they make up the majority of workers, but their share of the work force may be declining. This leads us to the second and more important point. Increasing numbers of women now work with hooks and knives alongside men, skinning and trimming in Slaughter, boning and trimming in Fabrication. In 1986, one in five Monfort workers was a woman; in 1988 that figure jumped to one in three. Even more interesting, perhaps, is the changing ethnicity of female workers. While female workers have increased among both Hispanics and Anglos, they have risen dramatically among Anglos—from 6 percent in 1986 and 1987 to 19 percent in 1988.

Changing attitudes offer one explanation for this demographic transition. As one executive told us:

> When we started [in the 1960s], we had no women in the plant. It wasn't because I was a sexist, I tell my wife, it's because we didn't used to think that was fit work for women. That sounds bad, but hell, we couldn't anymore begin to staff our plants if we didn't have women, and we get quite a group. . . . I hope we can get them to stay longer because they probably aren't as mobile. I mean . . . [our] average [employee in another state] is a twenty-four-year-old divorcee with two kids. And she needs the work. (Broadway interview 4/29/89:11)

He also points to another important reason that women are "manning" meat-packing lines and chains in increasing numbers: packers are facing a labor shortage caused by lower pay, faster chain speeds, and high risk for serious injury, along with "high" national employment and reduced demand for beef (Kay 1989:46, 48). Native-born women, many with small children, often have less freedom and fewer job options and are thus more stable than their male counterparts.

This trend is confirmed by plant managers at the IBP beef plant that opened in Lexington, Nebraska, on November 8, 1990. They project that 60 percent of the Processing employees will be women and that many will be Anglo wives from nearby small towns and farms; these women, they believe, are often unemployed or underemployed. In an effort to attract and hold female workers, the Lexington plant offers day care on its premises. IBP hopes that this service, along with some ergonomic refinements on the floor, will ultimately reduce turnover to 3 percent. If day care proves successful in Lexington, IBP executives intend to take similar steps at their other plants (Stull field notes 6/28/90).

The possibilities for interethnic contact depend largely on where you work. Southeast Asians made up only 2 percent of Monfort's workers in 1988, down from 5 percent the previous year. The potential for interaction also depends on whether you work in Slaughter or Processing (called Fabrication at Monfort). In the summer of 1989, approximately 82 percent of the A shift (day) line workers on the IBP kill floor were Hispanic (mainly Mexican immigrants), 12 percent Anglo, 2.5 percent African American, and 1 percent Vietnamese; 14 percent of the total were women. Supervisors were all male at the time, although until recently one line supervisor had been a Vietnamese woman. The floor supervisor was Anglo, the general foreman Hispanic. The three lines (skinning, drop heads-gut table, and trim line-head table) were supervised by two Hispanics and one Anglo; their bluehats (assistants) included one Anglo, one Vietnamese, and one of unknown ethnicity. (These data are derived from repeated interviews with one worker.)

These figures offer at least partial support for the generally held beliefs that Hispanics more often work in Slaughter and Vietnamese in Processing, and that Vietnamese are more commonly found on B shift (nights). On the other hand, they dispel the notion that Anglos dominate the ranks of supervisors. Indeed, these data confirm other evidence that bilingualism offers an important path to upward mobility, one not readily open to most Anglo workers.

Ethnic awareness is very much a part of the culture of the floor. Workers know the ethnicity of others on their crew and at other work stations as well. Despite official company policy, which does not assign workers by ethnicity, clustering often occurs.

> There aren't too many Vietnamese on my shift. In the night shift there used to be a bunch . . . but little by little, man, when I started four years ago, they have been disappearing. There are only a few now. . . . All of them have been replaced by Mexicans, Anglos, anybody. When I first got [the job here], I was working "first hang-off," and right in front of me there were two Vietnamese, and they're nice. And for the longest time, man, there were Mexicans all the way in the line. I used to count everybody, and in the line I could just find one or two Anglos, no Vietnamese. . . . I'll say that in the skinning [line] . . . there have been only five Anglos at all times. Like around five, and maybe one black. The rest are Mexicans.
>
> **Q:** How about Asians?
>
> **A:** I have [been on this shift] for at least one year, and no Asians have been in the skinning line. There used to be two of them that worked side by side . . . they used to joke a lot and . . . they got fired over one fight. So they got into a fight with another Mexican guy, and they got fired. (Stull interview with Mexican Slaughter worker 7/31/89:44, 7/16/89:9)

Although workers from one ethnic group or nationality often work in close proximity, there is no evidence that this represents a conscious policy on the part of management. New hires are placed in jobs according to vacancies and prior experience. Company spokesmen say that training is a major investment, but many workers say it consists merely of watching the person you are replacing for a day or two and doing the work with increasing frequency. Then you are on your own. They say the company does not want to pay two people to do the job of one. New hires have a ninety-day probationary period, as do current employees who bid to a new job. There are seven different job classes at different pay scales. At six months, workers receive an automatic raise and insurance benefits. After one year they receive an additional raise and become eligible for the year-end bonus. Thereafter, workers receive only infrequent cost-of-living increments unless they bid to better-paying jobs.

Once off probation, line workers may bid on other jobs in the same division as they become available (Slaughter workers cannot bid on jobs in Processing, for example). People bid on a job for several reasons: to move from one shift to another, to move to a better-paying job, to move to a safer or easier job, or out of boredom. Some workers prefer to remain in one job, while others move around. Those who change jobs get to know more people and are more likely to develop cross-ethnic relationships.

Communication must be quick and to the point; workers have little time for idle conversation—or even work-related discussion—when carcasses or boxes are whizzing by at four hundred or more an hour. When communication does take place, it is only among workers at the same or nearby stations, or with yellowhats or bluehats.

Interaction with coworkers is a function of proximity. Material Handling has only a few widely scattered employees, who monitor boxes as they roll along metal causeways to be sealed, labeled, and sorted by computers and lasers. In contrast, line workers in Processing work elbow to elbow and face to face wielding hook, knife, and steel. Interaction is also a function of the job itself—how demanding it is and how many people do it. Once a job is mastered, especially if several workers share the task, there may be time for a bit of conversation and rest, even horseplay.

Sound also interferes with worker interaction. Earplugs, which often dangle unused down the workers' backs, suspended from the headbands of their hard hats, are supposed to block the constant, deafening sounds of conveyors and saws. When the plugs are removed, workers can yell brief messages to a nearby worker or supervisor; conversation is impossible.

> In the inspection working areas we have a decibel range of 85–92, that's a constant, so you have to wear hearing protection. And so if you're going to talk to one another you have to shout. Learn how to read lips.
>
> **Q:** How much communication is really required? Can you go through most of the day and not have to communicate very much?
>
> **A:** Yeah, you really can, if you tend to your own business. . . . now if you want to socialize there's time for that, but you're simply required to do your work. [Conversation] is mostly work related. There's also some other conversation as in any nor-

> mal workplace, but it's just not a place to talk, too damn hard to get it done and do your job too. (Stull interview with respondent with wide industry experience 3/30/89:9)

Interaction among workers is largely confined to those at the same or a nearby work station. Workers are allowed two scheduled breaks a day—one of fifteen minutes approximately 2.5 hours into their shift, and thirty minutes for lunch after about 5.5 hours. Breaks, as well as starting and quitting times, are staggered down the line.

> One thirty-minute lunch, one fifteen-minute break a day, that's it.
> **Q:** And what about bathroom runs? Do they get those, or do they just have to hold it?
> **A:** If they can find someone to spell them out, yeah. That's what the bluehat is supposed to be for, to take care of that. I've seen people shit their pants, in that plant, on more than one occasion, because no one would spell them out. (Stull interview with respondent with wide industry experience 3/30/89:10–11)

To the outsider, IBP's Slaughter lunchroom appears segregated by ethnicity and gender. Mexican immigrants occupy the northeast and southwest corners; Southeast Asians sit at a couple of tables in the middle of the room; an Anglo couple sits across from each other near the south wall. There are exceptions—an Anglo sitting with Hispanics here and there, an Asian and a Hispanic woman sitting at a center table. When only a few workers are on break, they quietly watch the color television that runs continuously atop its perch at the southeast corner. When the lunchroom is crowded, most pay little attention to it. Instead, they visit among themselves, often sharpening their knives or rubbing down their steels.

This clustering is only partly explained by workers' preferences to socialize with others of the same sex or ethnic group. Those from the same station also congregate together. For example, workers from the cooler always sit at a table in the northeast corner—the part of the lunchroom closest to their station. In Slaughter, fifteen or twenty workers at a time go on break, in Processing many more. Whom one sits with is thus determined by a *combination* of ethnic and personal bonds *and* work station proximity. While those of the same ethnic group will sit with one another if they have the opportunity, ties developed on the line may take precedence.

With such severe restraints on the amount and quality of interaction between workers, their ideas about members of other ethnic groups are often highly stereotyped.

> Xuan, a bilingual worker in the refugee program, says that he has heard that Mexicans are lazy. When I bristle at this ethnocentrism, he replies "but that is just what I have heard. They don't stay on

> the job. When they get tired they just quit and go home to Mexico."
>
> * * *
>
> After three days on the line, Thien works alone, without his trainer beside him. There are four people on his work station. Two *nguoi me* ("Mexico people") and one *nguoi my* ("America people"). Thao says in Vietnamese: "Those Mexicans really work hard. They work as hard as Vietnamese Communists. The Americans don't work so hard. The Americans are the tall ones with the things like this" (he pantomimes a supervisor writing on a clipboard). "But those Mexicans really work well."
>
> I protest mildly, saying there are *nguoi my* at various jobs in the plant, but Thien persists—the Mexicans work harder. "The Americans are very tall, the Vietnamese are very short, and the Mexicans—right in the middle. Just right for the job." (Erickson 1990:8)

Stereotypes about members of other groups may be positive, negative, or mixed. Language differences and prejudice, as well as barriers to communication inherent in the workplace, often contribute to conflict.

> You don't see a lot of socializing between Southeast Asians and Anglos or the Hispanics. . . . There's a lot of barriers between us—language and everything. . . . I've never seen a lot of blatant prejudice. . . . You see some of it but it's mainly groups of people that sit there, and they'll talk about the gooks, what they're eating and things like that. But I never saw much face-to-face confrontation between any particular ethnic group out there. I noticed a lot more confrontation between the Southeast Asians themselves than anybody else. You know, I've seen fights between them, but I've never seen a fight between a Southeast Asian and an Anglo or an Hispanic.
>
> **Q:** What does IBP do if people get in fights?
>
> **A:** Fire them, no questions asked.
>
> **Q:** So does that mean people carry the fights somewhere else?
>
> **A:** I saw that a few times. . . . But you don't see much of it. You know, everybody out there is an adult and you don't see much of that. There was a lot of shouting matches. That just has to do with, you know, the pressure gets too much sometimes. One guy thinks the guy next to him is not pulling his count or doing his share of the work, and so they get a little shouting match there. But I think management overall does a pretty good job of keeping things under control out there. Mainly I would see fights in the cafeteria, and it would be before work generally. And usually between Southeast Asians. (Stull interview with an Anglo former Material Handling supervisor 5/29/90:30–31)

Despite the pressures of the chain and the watchful eyes of supervisors, or perhaps because of them, workers find time to joke with and tease each other. Sometimes the joking is good-natured; at other times it is malicious. New hires bear the brunt of such mischief and must prove their mettle. But supervisors and bluehats are not the only ones who exert power on the floor. Whitehats (hourly workers) may contest for power among themselves. They also let their supervisors know they can't be pushed too far.

> "Thelma" was mad when she came into Tom's. As several of us—Hispanic and Anglo—sat around the table, she angrily recounted how earlier that evening some workers had intentionally caused her to injure her finger—pushed something down the line, I think. She is an orangehat, training to be a yellowhat. She said that they were Mexicans, and much of the conversation that followed centered on how it is always Mexicans who are mean and resentful on the floor, never the Asians.
>
> Thelma is "half-Spanish"—her mother is from Spain, her father somewhere else. She speaks Spanish. She grew up in the Southwest. She started work "squeeging the floors, the lowest job out there." Mexicans would throw scraps on the floor intentionally so she would have to pick them up, or throw them directly at her. You're not allowed to confront other workers directly. If you have a complaint you must go to your supervisor, who will take it to Personnel, who will take it up with the accused's supervisor. It boils down to one person's word against another's, unless there are witnesses. And people that are out to get you will just deny it.
>
> When she threw back the meat scraps, she earned the respect of those who were testing her to see what she was made of. That she spoke Spanish helped as well. The event earlier in the day seems to be the same thing. Workers who will eventually have to work under her authority are testing her and showing her that she is no better than they are. They may also be pushing her because she is a woman.
>
> Quite a bit of this goes on. You do something to goad or injure someone else—of a different race, a different sex, a newcomer on the line, or someone you just don't like. You do it so you can deny that it was you or that it was intentional, but then you make eye contact with the victim to let him know it was you. Then the victim may retaliate—Thelma threw back the meat, another time she turned up the water on the boot wash so they all got wet. (Stull field notes 8/7–8/8/89:14–15)

When I recounted this incident to "Estevan," he replied:

> We Mexicans have that tendency of really getting to somebody, once they see that that person won't do anything. See, like, they

> push and push and push to see how far they can go, you see what I mean?
>
> It's like, I mean, there is no end to it unless a person really stops and puts an end to it and says, "Look, this is as far as you are going. And either you stop it right here, or we can settle it some other way. But I don't want that to happen, you know." That's the only way. And that's the way that it has to be. Test the bounds. Because over here, man, it's just more Mexican than anybody down there [in Mexico].
>
> **Q:** Do you think they were doing it to her because she's a woman?
>
> **A:** They will do it because she let them. She will give in to anybody, that's why. . . . They will do it with anybody, even a guy, another guy that lets them, or another girl. I think that all that happens because they give them a little chance. They might start joking a little bit, but then things get joking heavier. They are joking, and that's when somebody's going to feel it, is when the others complain. Yeah, the best way to be . . . is not to joke, just to be so serious practically not to talk to anybody. (Stull interview 8/13/89:36)

The packinghouse floor is a place apart. When workers enter it, they must subject themselves to a different environment with a different set of rules from those that govern their lives on the outside. But the boundaries are not always easily crossed; the floor is not quickly left behind at the end of the day. According to Estevan's wife,

> [In] the packinghouses is a different world from this world. They are changed people when they go in there. They're aggressive; they're hostile; they look out for Number One. People who are the nicest people in the world outside, when they go in there, they're the most bigoted people you'd ever want to meet. It's the packinghouse and that environment that does that. [My husband] comes home from work, shoo[t] man, he's like a totally different person. He is real hostile. He wants to pick a fight with me. He's got everything figured out and whether I like it or not, you know, he's not willing to discuss it. After a while . . . when he gets out of the mood he gets in, in there, in the packinghouse, then he becomes the man I know and love. But that type of environment—hot, dirty, hazardous—everybody looking out for Number One, because if you help a friend out, it's going to be your job too, you know. (Stull interview 7/26/89:75)

Estevan's wife is right: the plant floor is a different world. It is one where interaction with others is highly circumscribed: by a rigid hierarchy, by the very nature of the work and the speed of the chain, by the deafening noise of machinery. Workers have little opportunity to get to know those beyond the immediate confines of their own line; they have little incentive to do so anyway. After all, chances are that their fellows, if not themselves, will soon be gone. Why then go beyond first names and nodding acquaintanceships?

The plants' employees come from far and wide; most have not grown up together, sharing the common geography and history of southwest Kansas. What they may share are commonalities of language, culture, ethnicity, and gender. And it is to those of their kind that they cleave. In spite of company policy that assigns workers according to job vacancies, ethnic and gender concentration are readily apparent. Few Southeast Asians choose to work at Monfort. They are a rarity on IBP's kill floor. Mexicans, on the other hand, predominate there. Southeast Asians hold sway on B shift Processing. Women are far more likely to work in Processing than in Slaughter or Hides. So even in an ethnically diverse plant, opportunities to mingle with those of other backgrounds may be limited. Yet even when such opportunities do exist, there are formidable barriers to significant communication—language differences, the ever-present noise, demands by supervisors to pull your count or else.

Regardless of heritage, whitehats do share a common work experience—and it forms a bond between them. But it is not sufficient to forge significant links between those of different backgrounds once they leave the floor and head home.

Consequences for Community Relations

The newcomer–old-timer relations that Upton Sinclair so poignantly described almost a century ago were relations of exploitation. Immigrants were exploited by foremen, landlords, shopkeepers—many recent arrivals themselves. While beef now moves along chains and workers no longer run from table to table making their cuts, relations between workers and managers in the packing plants, and between groups in the larger community, are much the same in Garden City today as they were in Sinclair's Packingtown. Coexistence—and social distance—between ethnic groups, between packinghouse workers and those who look down upon yet tolerate them, and between newcomers and established residents, regardless of ethnicity, dominate group relations. Inter- and intragroup relations are diverse and complex. They are enhanced or limited by linguistic, cultural, and religious similarities and differences. However, the primary social force in Garden City is population mobility, fueled by high turnover in the packing plants.

Newcomers, especially packinghouse workers, come to Garden City to find work. Their attachment to the community is fragile.

> I don't think they feel part of Garden City, but then again Garden City could be anyplace. I don't think they would feel part of Marshalltown, Iowa, or Chicago, or anyplace. . . . I think it is because of the transient attitude they have. . . . they were not

> born here. They were not raised here. It's not their home. They don't really have any ties here. (Stull interview with Anglo wife of a Mexican packinghouse worker 7/26/89:78, 80)

It is not surprising that the workers feel little attachment. They work long and grueling hours on the line—six days a week during much of the year. Many work the B shift from 3:00 P.M. till midnight; still others work cleanup on the C shift (midnight till 6:00 A.M.), or swing shifts. Little time is left to meet and socialize with people outside of work. Socializing is often limited to having a beer or two after work; playing in a softball or bowling league with coworkers; shopping, doing laundry, or going to the park on Sunday—the only day off when the plants are running at capacity. Many workers live in trailer courts on the outskirts of town, in apartment complexes hastily constructed to meet the demands of rapid growth, or in run-down residential motels—their neighbors most often line workers like themselves. Often they speak little or no English and must rely on their children or friends to translate when they do business in the majority community. And as in any packinghouse town, packers carry a certain stigma, regardless of income or ethnicity.

High turnover on the job translates into high mobility in the community. Monthly turnover at IBP and Monfort averages 6–8 percent. Using the lowest figure, 6 percent of the approximately 4,000 workers at the two plants amounts to about 240 persons a month, or 2,880 persons per year, who leave the industry. Many do not remain in Garden City, because there is a lack of other jobs and they have little attachment to the community. They in turn are replaced by 2,880 new workers, most of whom are new to town. Thus, as many as 5,700 workers move into and out of the community each year—more than one-fifth of the town's population. And this estimate does not take into account members of the workers' families.

Further evidence of high mobility is to be found in school records. To determine how long newcomers stay in Garden City, we focused on the most readily identifiable group—parents with children of school age. They may not be representative of all newcomers, since families with children can be expected to be less mobile than single adults. But single adults are harder to identify and trace.

Newcomer households ($N = 241$) were identified for the 1986–87 academic year from student listings provided by the Garden City School District; records for earlier years were unavailable. We then traced these households for two academic years to determine length of residence in the community. Within one year, 44 percent of the cohort had left the community; a year later, another 20 percent had gone—so that two years after arrival only a third of the newcomers remained. Surprisingly, there was no statistically significant difference in the length of stay between Anglos, Hispanics, and Southeast Asians. Nor did it matter whether they were beef packers. It appears that for a majority of newcomers, Garden City is just a place to stop and work for a year or two before moving on. This view is supported by the results from a random-sample survey of Southeast Asian males in Garden City (Broadway 1986). Asked, in 1985, whether they thought they would remain in the community, over 60 percent said no. In a follow-up a year later the percentage had risen to 75 percent, and a fifth of the original sample had left.

There appear, then, to be two Garden Cities. One is a stable community of established residents, many from families who have lived there for generations. The other Garden City is highly mobile—people who come seeking work, and who stay only as long as they have a job. Their attachment to the community is a tenuous one. And when this mobility is coupled with the barriers inherent between peoples of different ethnic, cultural, and linguistic origins, stable and meaningful intergroup relationships never really form.

Relations between newcomers and established residents, between ethnic groups, and between packers and others are in many ways influenced by the packing industry. As Thompson (1983) notes for another Midwest packinghouse town, work in the beef plant is "dirty work," and line workers are looked down upon by the larger community. While the shared stigma—and pride—of their work can build bonds that cross ethnic and language boundaries among the packers, the nature of the work and of the workplace offsets such bonding. Interaction and communication on the line are kept to a minimum by the noise and the speed of the chain, and each worker has a specialized or even unique task. While workers are expected to "pull their count," to be part of a team, they do so because "they are looking out for Number One." Thompson, who carried out his research by working on the Offal crew on the kill floor of a large packing plant, calls this "uncooperative teamwork" (1983:223). Assembly-line work by its very nature fosters anonymity among workers, and this tendency is exacerbated by cultural and linguistic diversity.

Yet it is the mobility of the workers and their families that has the greatest consequence for the community. They come to the community seeking work, not expecting to put down roots, but wanting to make enough money to start a small business, or buy a fishing boat and move to Texas, or go home to Mexico when times are better there. Maybe they'll move on to California or go back to Alabama if things don't work out here. And they do move one, some because they have saved enough money, others because they can no longer pull their count, having been used up by an industry constantly seeking to lower its costs.

This mobility disrupts the community and at the same time allows many to tolerate rapid growth and ethnic diversity. School administrators are unable to plan rationally for next year's enrollment, as they watch pupils come and go throughout the school year (Grey 1990). The incidence of violent and property crime has risen steadily, as have other indices of social disruption such as child neglect and abuse (Broadway 1990b). There is, however, little evidence of significant overt conflict between newcomers and established residents. This seems to be in large part because newcomers are not seen as competitors for

Children dressed in traditional costumes of their families' country of origin at the First Annual International Children's Parade, International Festival, St. Mary's Catholic Church, Garden City, June 1989. (Photograph by Donald D. Stull)

scarce economic resources; in fact, they serve a "dirty" but necessary economic function in the community (see Meara 1974). Many in the established community view the newcomers as transient and believe the packinghouses will one day close and the workers will move on. While there is little likelihood of the plants' closing, or of Garden City's newcomer populations' departing, individuals do come and go at an amazing rate. And their attachment to and influence on the community are little felt.

Garden Citians often say that people "get along" in large part because the different ethnic groups "don't mix." As one Anglo packinghouse worker succinctly put it: "People get along here because they don't [mess] with each other; whites don't [mess] with Mexicans and Mexicans don't [mess] with Vietnamese" (Stull field notes 5/25/89:1). So Garden City still belongs to the sedentary old-timers; the newcomers, especially Hispanics and Southeast Asians, live and work in the community but never become fully part of it.

The peaceful coexistence of the different ethnic groups in Garden City can be attributed to the fact that newcomers are not in direct competition with the established residents for scarce resources. More important, most newcomers do not stay in Garden City long enough to demand their "fair share" of community resources and political power. For most newcomers, whether they work in the packinghouses or elsewhere, Garden City is just a place to work for a time before moving on. The beef plants, with their high levels of employee turnover and dangerous working conditions, help foster this attitude among the work force. As a result, many newcomers avoid anything more than superficial interaction with established residents. And established residents maintain their distance. After all, the workers, if not the work, will soon be on their way.

References

Austin, Lisa. 1988a. "Rich Potential for Kansas Carries Risk." *Wichita Eagle-Beacon,* 11 September.

———. 1988b. "Packers Put Everything But the Moo Up for Sale." *Wichita Eagle-Beacon,* 12 September.

———. 1988c. "Riskiest Job in Kansas Escapes Close Scrutiny." *Wichita Eagle-Beacon,* 4 December.

Benson, Janet E. (N.d.) The Effects of Packinghouse Work on Southeast Asian Refugee Families. In Lamphere and Grenier n.d.

Broadway, Michael J. 1986. The Social Adjustment of Adult Male Vietnamese Refugees in Garden City, 1985–86. Garden City: Report to the Kansas Department of Social and Rehabilitation Services. Typescript.

———. 1990a. Recent Changes in the Structure and Location of the U.S. Meatpacking Industry. *Geography* 75 (1): 76–79.

———. 1990b. Meatpacking and Its Social and Economic Consequences for Garden City, Kansas, in the 1980s. *Urban Anthropology* 19:321–44.

———. (N.d.) Beef Stew: Cattle, Immigrants, and Established Residents in a Kansas Beefpacking Town. In Lamphere and Grenier n.d.

Broadway, Michael J., and Donald D. Stull. 1991. Rural Industrialization: The Example of Garden City, Kansas. *Kansas Business Review* 14 (4): 1–9.

Bustos, Tony. 1989. Personal communication. Lawrence, Kans.: Changing Relations project files.

Carnes, Richard B. 1984. Meatpacking and Prepared Meats Industry: Above-Average Productivity Gains. *Monthly Labor Review,* April, pp. 37–42.

Erickson, Ken C. 1988. Vietnamese Household Organization in Garden City, Kansas: Southeast Asians in a Packing House Town. *Plains Anthropologist* 33 (119): 27–36.

______. 1990. Relations at Work. Typescript.

______. (N.d.) Plate Bone and Short Ribs: Short-Term Participant Observation in a Beefpacking Plant. In Lamphere and Grenier n.d.

Garden City Planning Department. 1989. *Garden City Community Information Profile Report.* Garden City, Kans.

Glaberson, William. 1987. Misery on the Meatpacking Line. *New York Times,* 14 June.

Green, Hardy. 1990. *On Strike at Hormel: The Struggle for a Democratic Labor Movement.* Philadelphia: Temple University Press.

Grey, Mark A. 1990. Immigrant Students in the Heartland: Ethnic Relations in Garden City, Kansas, High School. *Urban Anthropology* 19:409–27.

Kansas Department of Human Resources, Research and Analysis Section. 1988. *Finney County, Kansas Labor Force History.* Topeka.

Kay, Steve. 1989. Packers Play Musical Chairs. *Beef Today* 5 (8): 46, 48, 50–51.

______. 1990. You Can't Stand Still. *Beef Today* 6 (7): 24–26.

Knox, Paul L. 1988. The Economic Organization of U.S. Space. In *The United States: A Contemporary Human Geography,* edited by Paul L. Knox et al. New York: Wiley.

Lamphere, Louise, and Guillermo Grenier, eds. (N.d.) *Labor, Capital, and Community.* Forthcoming.

Laudert, Scott. 1988. Information on Feedlot Capacity, Annual Feed Needs for Fed Cattle, and 1987 Finney County Production. Personal communication to Mary Warren, Finney County Museum. Lawrence, Kans.: Changing Relations project files.

Meara, Hannah. 1974. Honor in Dirty Work: The Case of American Meatcutters and Turkish Butchers. *Sociology of Work and Occupations* 1:259–82.

Miller, Bill. 1986. Why the Packer Crunch Will Continue. *Farm Journal Beef Extra,* June/July, p. 19.

Oppenheimer, Robert. 1985. Acculturation or Assimilation: Mexican Immigrants in Kansas, 1900 to World War II. *Western Historical Quarterly* 16:429–48.

Remy, Dorothy, and Larry Sawers. 1984. Economic Stagnation and Discrimination. In *My Troubles Are Going to Have Trouble With Me: Everyday Trials and Triumphs of Women Workers,* edited by Karen B. Sacks and Dorothy Remy. New Brunswick, N.J.: Rutgers University Press.

Sinclair, Upton. 1985 [1906]. *The Jungle.* New York: Penguin.

Skaggs, Jimmy M. 1986. *Prime Cut: Livestock Raising and Meatpacking in the United States, 1607–1983.* College Station: Texas A&M University Press.

Slayton, Robert A. 1986. *Back of the Yards: The Making of a Local Democracy.* Chicago: University of Chicago Press.

Stanley, Kathleen. 1988. The Role of Immigrant and Refugee Labor in the Restructuring of the Midwestern Meatpacking Industry. Department of Sociology, State University of New York at Binghamton. Typescript.

Stull, Donald D., ed. 1990. When the Packers Came to Town: Changing Ethnic Relations in Garden City, Kansas. Special issue of *Urban Anthropology* 19:303–427.

———. (N.d.) "Knock 'Em Dead": Work on the Killfloor of a Modern Beefpacking Plant. In Lamphere and Grenier n.d.

Stull, Donald D., Janet E. Benson, Michael J. Broadway, Arthur L. Campa, Ken C. Erickson, and Mark A. Grey. 1990. Changing Relations: Newcomers and Established Residents in Garden City, Kansas. Final report to the Ford Foundation's Changing Relations Project Board, 5 February. Lawrence: Institute for Public Policy and Business Research, University of Kansas, Report 172.

Stull, Donald D., and Michael J. Broadway. 1990. The Effects of Restructuring on Beefpacking in Kansas. *Kansas Business Review* 14 (1): 10–16.

Thompson, William E. 1983. Hanging Tongues: A Sociological Encounter with the Assembly Line. *Qualitative Sociology* 6:215–37.

U.S. Department of Labor, Bureau of Labor Statistics. 1985. *Employment, Hours, and Earnings, United States, 1901–84*. Vol. 1. Washington, D.C.: Government Printing Office.

———. 1989. *Supplement to Employment and Earnings*. Washington, D.C.: Government Printing Office.

Van Maanen, John. 1988. *Tales of the Field: On Writing Ethnography.* Chicago: University of Chicago Press.

Wood, Anita. 1988. The Beefpacking Industry: A Study of Three Communities in Southwestern Kansas: Dodge City, Liberal, and Garden City, Kansas. Flagstaff, Ariz.: Final Report to the Department of Migrant Education.

2 ON MACHINES AND BUREAUCRACY: CONTROLLING ETHNIC INTERACTION IN MIAMI'S APPAREL AND CONSTRUCTION INDUSTRIES

GUILLERMO J. GRENIER AND ALEX STEPICK
WITH DEBBIE DRAZNIN, ALINE LABORWIT, STEVE MORRIS,
AND BERNADETTE COPPÉE

When Aileen started working at the apparel plant, her worst enemy became the "chopper." At 7:30 on her first morning in training, she was introduced to the machine that she would have to master to secure employment at Fairwood Wells. Every day during her six-week training she would have to work on the "chopper," a dangerous contraption that cuts the ragged sides off the seam that it simultaneously sews. And when her training period was over, she would take the "chopper" with her on the floor. During working hours, the machine, the function it performed, and Aileen would be one and the same. Her actions and her interaction with fellow workers and managers would be controlled by the machine and her ability to manipulate the portion of the men's jacket that the "chopper" was designed to cut and sew. Except for the two breaks and lunch period during her eight-hour shift, and the times her machine would break down, her time might easily be measured in watts; it was considered machine time.

Across town, Steve had clocked in with the rest of his carpentry crew at the largest construction site in the county. About two hundred carpenters parked their cars in the fenced-in lot next to the contractor trailers and outhouses and walked into the massive structure that would eventually become the new Miami Beach Convention Center. Plumbers, electricians, masons, laborers, roofers, cement workers, painters, and inspectors—all parked their cars in the same lot. Many of them walked in the same immense door, an unfinished wall half the size of a football field. Once inside, they disappeared into their work areas, each trade tackling a different portion of the gigantic structure.

Steve walked with them on his way to his task for the day, screwing ten-foot metal studs called J-brackets into the wall. That day he would be working in the "dusty, dark, humid, lonely and mosquito-infested second- and third-story

We would like to thank the other contributors to this volume, the Project Board for the Ford Foundation Changing Relations project, Max Castro, Marvin Dunn, and the anonymous reviewers for their criticisms and suggestions. The final results, of course, remain the responsibility of the primary authors.

level hallways." Chances were that if he did interact with anyone before break time, it would be with another carpenter, since each trade tended to work on a particular part of the building at a certain stage of its development. Chances were that he would look for any reason to take a break from the dangerous, tiring work. But he knew he had to stay on schedule. The J-brackets were one step in the elaborate choreography of construction that involved the activities and interactions of thousands of workers in dozens of trades.

Such is daily work in two industries in Miami, where large numbers of newcomers and a shrinking number of established residents earn their daily bread. The differences between these industries are striking: one is dominated by males, the other by females; work in the apparel plant is considered unskilled machine labor, while the carpentry is considered skilled labor; the apparel workers do not own their tools, while the carpenters must own theirs.

Yet the similarities are also striking. Both industries provide basic employment opportunities for new immigrant workers, and both have been fundamentally restructured by Miami's immigrants. Both are traditionally unionized industries that have, in the Sun Belt and elsewhere, suffered deunionization in the process of economic restructuring. And while unionism is relatively weak in Dade County, both industries are benefiting from the surging militancy of the Latin labor movement in the region. Workers in each industry labor at different levels of a massive hierarchy.

The restructuring that has occurred in Miami is in many ways consistent with historical patterns of apparel and construction industries in the United States. In apparel, new immigrants continue to be the preferred work force. In construction, ethnic segregation by trade inhibits incorporation of new immigrants. Moreover, immigration has contributed to the informalization of these industries, especially during the 1980s.

In some important ways, however, at least some parts of Miami's apparel and construction industries are different. While immigration has dramatically altered ethnic composition and the structure of ownership and management of both workforces, this is especially true in the construction industry, where Cuban-owned and -managed firms have become dominant. This has reinforced the tendency toward segregation of the workplace based on ethnicity and thus has limited interaction among newcomers and established residents.

But segregation at the workplace is not complete. Institutions that have adopted positive policies of integration and equal treatment include the two that are the focus of this chapter: an apparel plant that is a branch of a large national firm and the local Carpenters' Union. In these two cases, we can assess the nature of face-to-face relations among newcomers and established residents in social arenas where the nature of the work itself establishes the parameters, in form and content, for ethnic interactions.

At one level of analysis, then, we find that ethnicity is explained as a reactive phenomenon. The restructuring of the industries and the nature of the work itself both contribute to ethnic segregation, which, in turn, establishes ethnic boundaries among workers at a common work site.

But there is more. Informal social relations constructed and maintained by workers themselves reflect an element of ethnicity that is more than reactive. During free time, workers strongly tend to associate first on the basis of national origin, second according to race, and third according to language. Thus, for example, Cubans are most likely to associate with Cubans. Sometimes white Cubans associate with white Americans; somewhat less frequently, Cubans will associate with Nicaraguans.[1]

There are some countertendencies to ethnic segregation at the work sites we studied—particularly organizational policies to integrate newcomers and certain contexts and rituals that promote interaction and identification across groups. While these mitigate the predominant segregation and provide possibilities for other forms of self-identification and group construction, we found our multiethnic workplaces to be primarily existential worlds of ethnic isolation. Within such a world of social separation, there was a corresponding construction and maintenance of groups on the basis of national origin.

The Research

The apparel plant is a subsidiary of the largest U.S. clothing manufacturer, which purchased the plant in 1985. Previously owner-operated, it has been in existence since the early 1960s and presently employs approximately 250 operators, most of whom are older Cuban women. Haitians have been increasingly employed since the early 1980s, and more recently Central Americans, especially Nicaraguans, have been hired. There are sprinklings of Black Americans and other Latins.

Workers have been represented by the Amalgamated Clothing and Textile Workers Union (ACTWU) since this plant opened. The ACTWU has been associated with the company that owns this plant since the early part of the century, when the two organizations joined ranks to develop some of the most progressive collective-bargaining agreements of the time. Since that time the union has also been one of the most active organizers of immigrant and female workers—groups considered by many mainstream social scientists to be the least organizable. Perhaps because of this long tradition with female immigrants, all the

1. We use the term "established-resident whites" rather than "Anglos" or simply "whites," because in Miami most Latinos and particularly most Cubans are light-skinned and conceive of themselves as white. Moreover, a significant percentage of Miami's white population is Jewish and objects to the label "Anglo." "White" thus does not distinguish between native-born white Americans and immigrant Latinos and the term "Anglo" discriminates against the native-born Jewish-American population.

employees of the three ACTWU-organized plants in Miami belong to the union. This level of voluntary membership in a labor organization is a notable anomaly in a right-to-work state.

We conducted extensive interviews with all managerial personnel, interviewing the regional vice president and the regional division chief. The managerial interviews lasted from forty-five minutes to three hours each. We also participated in various plant rituals as well as regularly walked the floor, talked to operators, and visited the lunchroom during the three different lunch periods. In addition, two research assistants worked as operators in the plant: Bernadette is a middle-aged Haitian woman with some experience in the apparel industry, and Aileen is a Jewish American who speaks fluent Spanish.

Fieldwork in the Miami's construction industry was conducted on two fronts, primarily by two graduate assistants, Steve and Debbie. Steve, a Hispanic, worked as a union carpenter's apprentice during the summer, while Debbie, a Jewish American, worked out of the construction union hall (where she also had worked prior to the project during the summer of 1987). She accompanied construction-union business agents on their rounds of organized sites and organizers on their rounds of nonorganized sites.

Steve worked during the summer of 1988 and was officially designated as a dry-waller, although he never did any dry-wall work. His work included laying insulation, installing 75-foot vertical beams, applying studs, and a variety of other chores. The site, one of Miami's largest construction sites, was a half-million-square-foot addition to the Miami Beach Convention Center. During his time at the site there were between 120 and slightly over 300 workers. Workers from diverse trades participated, including electricians, plumbers, painters, masons, carpenters, and laborers. The diversity of trades at the site as well as the number of workers of various ethnicities—established-resident Blacks and Whites, newcomer Cubans and Haitians—made for a conglomeration rarely found at noncommercial work sites.

Steve was placed through the Carpenters' Union. The Carpenters' Union was one of the first crafts to admit Latino members. Today approximately 30 percent of the members are Latino, slightly less than the overall rate in the construction trades (see figure 2.2). Workers are somewhat segregated, however, by work site. Most Anglos work at permanent, indoor sites at such jobs as cabinet making, while most Hispanics work at outdoor sites, such as where our researcher worked. Most important, since early 1979 one of the most eloquent leaders in the South Florida District Council has been a Cuban. In addition, in the summer of 1988 a Cuban was elected to head the local AFL-CIO (American Federation of Labor–Congress of Industrial Organizations). This apparent ethnic succession in regional labor leadership has produced a reversal of ethnic tension in some unionized environments. White established members of the Carpenters' Union, for example, who once excluded and discriminated against the then newly arrived Cubans, now feel excluded and powerless, although they still constitute a substantial majority of the membership.

Immigrants and Miami

Since 1960 immigration has transformed Miami[2] as much as if not more than any other major U.S. city, recasting it from a southern U.S. retirement and vacation center to the northern capital of Latin America.[3] By 1980, Miami had the highest proportion of foreign-born residents of any U.S. city, proportionally 50 percent more than either Los Angeles or New York. In the late 1980s, Hispanics became Miami's demographically dominant group, surpassing established-resident whites (Anglos and Jews). Sometime in the 1990s Hispanics are expected to establish an absolute demographic majority—not just in the inner city, where the change is even more dramatic, but throughout the metropolitan area, including all of the suburbs and Miami's elite residential areas. Predominant among Miami's Latinos are Cubans, who began coming to Miami in the early 1960s in the wake of Castro's revolution. Miami contains more Cubans (approximately 750,000) than any other city in the world except Havana (Boswell and Curtis 1984; Portes and Bach 1985; Pedraza-Bailey 1985).

A second major newcomer group is African Americans from various Caribbean islands. By the early 1980s, Greater Miami had become one of only sixteen metropolitan areas in the United States with more than 300,000 African Americans. Between 1970 and 1980, Dade's African-American population grew by 47 percent—a growth rate exceeded only in Atlanta. In the 1970s, after the civil rights movement had abolished legal segregation, other Caribbean African Americans, many of whom had settled in the northeastern United States, began to move to Miami. The largest concentration is of Haitians, who number approximately 70,000 in the Greater Miami area. Between 1977 and 1981, approximately 60,000 Haitians arrived by boat in South Florida, with the peak coinciding with the 1980 Cuban Mariel inflow (Miller 1984; Stepick 1986; Grenier and Stepick n.d.).

The Industries

Apparel

Behind tall fences and barren walls in the northwest section of Miami are many small apparel firms, the epitome of Sun Belt industry. There are no smokestacks or old grimy buildings, just low-lying concrete-block rectangles joined by acres

2. The name Miami can have a number of referents. Most narrowly, it means the City of Miami. It also can refer to all of south Florida, including Fort Lauderdale and further up Florida's east coast. In this book, we use "Miami" to refer to the contiguous urban area in Dade County.

3. Garreau 1981; Levine 1985 even argues that Miami is the capital of all Latin America.

Little Havana: Latino patrons in need of a "cafecito" gather at one of the hundreds of Cuban run cafeterias that open to the street on Calle Ocho. Guarapo is the name of a drink made from sugarcane juice, a traditional Cuban beverage. (Photograph by Peggy Nolan)

Haitian Market. Although there is a reported unemployment rate among Haitians of 60 percent, Haitian small businesses are growing in the Little Haiti area. This bookstore is one of the longest residents of the recently renovated Haitian Marketplace in the heart of Little Haiti. (Photograph by Peggy Nolan)

Table 2.1. Apparel: The U.S. Picture

County	Number of Workers	Payroll (Millions)	Year Average per Worker
Los Angeles	85,727	$982,998	$11,467
New York	75,603	$1,326,779	$17,549
Dade	**19,546**	**$192,375**	**$9,842**
Kings (Brooklyn), N.Y.	17,908	$199,980	$11,167
Bristol, Tenn.	14,681	$173,954	$11,848
Hudson, N.J.	14,648	$227,446	$15,527
Philadelphia	14,211	$202,367	$14,240
Queens, N.Y.	12,341	$162,338	$13,164
El Paso, Tex.	12,332	$154,396	$12,250
San Francisco	10,527	$115,796	$11,000

Source: U.S. Department of Commerce, County Business Patterns, 1985.

and acres of pavement covered with thousands of automobiles. Inside the block buildings is the Sun Belt's most attractive economic asset: abundant, mostly nonunion, low-wage immigrant labor.[4] In Miami, nearly 20,000 women, almost all immigrants and primarily Cuban, cut and sew the latest in fashions (see tables 2.1 and 2.2).

Miami's apparel industry has its roots in the 1940s diversification of the local economy, but its biggest boost came directly from immigration. Many New York, primarily Jewish, manufacturers relocated in Miami, attracted by the low-wage labor force made available by waves of Cuban immigration in south Florida. Overall rates of employment in the apparel sector have held steady in Miami for the past twenty years, in marked contrast with the degeneration of the industry in other parts of the United States.[5] Miami's apparel firms are almost all small, family-owned enterprises. Of the nearly 750 firms, only 20 percent have more than twenty workers, and the average number of employees is thirty (see table 2.2).

While overall employment has been steady, the ethnicity of workers has changed dramatically. As figure 2.1 indicates, thirty years ago employees were nearly 95 percent non-Latin white; and many, although by no means most, were unionized. Today, the apparel workers are 85 percent Hispanic women, and far fewer shops are unionized. Moreover, Cubans have gradually moved into management and ownership positions. Cubans hold close to a majority of management positions, although established-resident whites still own most firms.

Miami manufacturers claim that they have had difficulty finding new workers to replace their aging and retiring female Cuban workers. The economic suc-

4. Low corporate tax rates are another attractive feature of Sun Belt states.

5. We are grateful to Robert Bach for this observation.

Table 2.2. Apparel: The Dade Picture

Employer	Number of Workers	Payroll (Millions)	Number of Firms
Women's outerwear	10,286	$106.2	487
Men's/boys' furnishings	2,572	$28.9	72
Miscellaneous fabrics	2,528	$28.8	111
Rubber/plastic footwear	1,669	$28.9	5
Children's outerwear	1,659	$21.6	41
Total	22,173	$2,499.2	787

Source: Florida Department of Labor and Employment Security.

cess of the Cuban community (see Portes and Bach 1985) permits the second generation of Cuban women to forsake the low wages of the apparel industry, while the virtual elimination of Cuban immigration has reduced new supplies of workers. Haitians and black Americans provide a potential solution, but manufacturers have been reluctant to incorporate them. In 1960, when the industry was still gestating, 5 percent of the workers were black. Twenty years later, the proportion had climbed only to 7 percent. In the early 1980s, Haitian women began to work in the apparel industry, but after the falsely based acquired immune deficiency syndrome (AIDS) scare (Cooley 1983; Durand 1983; Laverdiere et al. 1983), Haitian employment plummeted. Currently, a typical factory of twenty to twenty-five workers is likely to have only one or two Haitians.

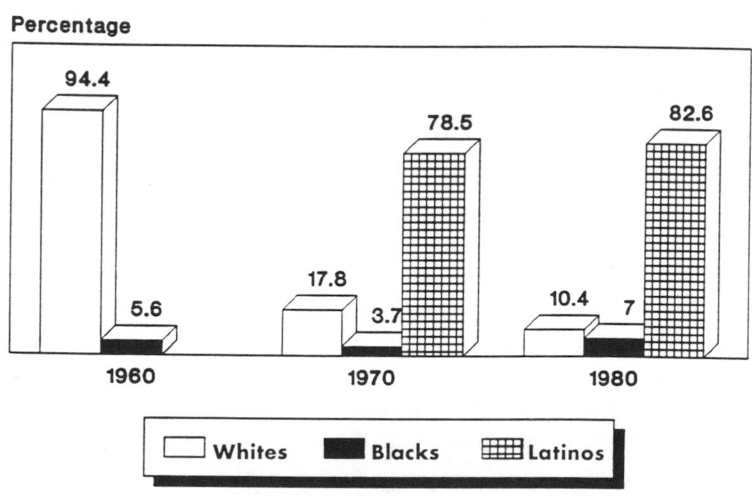

Figure 2.1. Ethnicity in Miami's apparel industry, 1960–80
Source: U.S. Census Survey of the Population, 1960, 1970, 1980

Instead of blacks' being incorporated into the labor force, the primary restructuring in Miami's apparel industry during the early 1980s was a rapid growth in home work, a practice illegal in the U.S. apparel industry.[6] Middle-aged Cuban women frequently preferred working at home, where they could take care of domestic tasks and work at their own pace. Some became successful enough to employ others, turning the living room or garage into a mini-sweatshop. If other women were employed, they were almost exclusively other Cuban women. This restructuring, thus, did not produce any interaction between new immigrants and established residents, or even between different groups of new immigrants.

The Nature of Relations: Resisting Technological and Bureaucratic Controls

According to management, the only difference between the company's other corporate plants and Miami is the ethnicity of the work force and their previous work experience under more flexible management. Because of these two differences, according to the quality control manager, "the people [at other plants] are more easy to control than here."

Because of this difference, management believes that its greatest problem, the most significant impediment to increased production, is interethnic conflict. Two aspects of the work process significantly determine the form of interethnic interaction: management's need to control labor and competition among workers who perform the same task along with a coordinate interdependence among workers with different tasks. In an industry where Taylorism is still practiced in its purest forms, it is not surprising that the new management attempted to implement a rigid, highly bureaucratized model of control. The chain of command is clearly hierarchical, and the union grievance procedure is presented as the method through which all workers must express their complaints.

Previous management was much more paternalistic and particularistic, and the union played no apparent role in worker-management relations. If a worker had a complaint, she or he presented it directly to the manager-owner, who resolved it usually immediately and individualistically. Workers were not encouraged to complain either to floor supervisors or to union representatives, although the plant was ostensibly unionized. One result was that the wage structure was extraordinarily complex. The manager-owner commonly would adjust a worker's wage in response to a complaint but would maintain the old wage rate for other workers engaged in the same task. The manager-owner also evinced a personal interest in the workers' lives outside the factory. If a worker needed a loan or medical attention, for example, the manager-owner would often help directly.

6. For a more extensive discussion of the informal sectors in both the apparel and construction industries, see Stepick 1989.

The management that assumed control in the mid-1980s assumed a remarkably different approach. The new management's parent company has been at the forefront of worker-management relations in the apparel industry since the early part of the twentieth century. Its managers have actively supported unions and urged the union to take a more active role in the Miami plant. The new management wanted to avoid becoming involved in workers' personal lives outside the workplace, and they further sought to rationalize the wage structure.

The new management has attempted to bureaucratize relationships between management and workers by forcing workers to work through channels. This has significantly enhanced the roles of both supervisors and the union. If workers have a complaint, they are now required to go first to their supervisor on the floor. If they cannot achieve satisfaction there, then they are supposed to go to the union representative, after which there is an explicitly delineated multistage process for dispute resolution. If a worker attempts to revert to the practice of the previous manager-owner by directly addressing the new plant manager, the worker is politely informed of the proper procedures and requested to address his or her concerns to the floor supervisor. Indeed, the plant manager views himself as one of the strongest supporters of the union at the plant, because he does emphasize the role of the union as a stabilizing force within the production and organizational structure.

This type of attitude toward bureaucracy and unions is not new. Bureaucratization of controls and the role of unionism in this process have had critics and proponents since the nineteenth century. Supporters view bureaucratization as the great equalizer, particularly when immigrants and minorities are involved: all workers are treated equally, because the bureaucratic process demands adherence from all. Critics see bureaucratization as the institutionalization of and an advance in managerial control of the work process, continuing the dehumanization and deskilling processes initiated by Taylorism at the turn of the century. As implemented in this plant, bureaucratization has had both of these contrasting effects.

On the one hand, at least from the position of the new management, all workers are treated equally. Rates are not adjusted to satisfy an individual worker, nor does anyone receive any more fringe benefits than anyone else. Similarly, floor supervisors and front-office personnel are explicitly instructed to treat everyone equally. Moreover, the management's commitment to the union has meant that this plant has *not* engaged in contracting out home work, an illegal practice that typified much of the apparel industry in Miami and the rest of the United States during the 1980s.

On the other hand, many of the workers complain about the decreased sensitivity and responsiveness of management. Haitian and some Central American workers allege that floor supervisors and front-office personnel discriminate in favor of Cubans.

As should be expected from an organization working toward a bureaucratized ideal, policies were implemented to reduce the individualism expressed during work hours by the workers. Indeed, it is the hope of management that strictly bureaucratizing the behavior of employees would eliminate personal expressions of ethnicity on the shop floor. Most of the policies were couched in terms of improving working conditions. Individual fans and radios were replaced by plantwide air conditioning and piped-in music. (According to the production manager, a station is played that alternates between American and Latin songs. "You can't please the Haitians on this one." Our own observations indicated that the piped-in music was virtually never played anyway.) Snacks at the machines, specifically the *bocadillos* brought by the Latina women, are no longer allowed, and neither are hot plates. The company put a new microwave in the lunchroom and encourages its use during breaks. While top management downplays the significance of these changes, complaints are still heard on the shop floor, three years after their implementation.

Managers' willingness to talk about "ethnic differences" in work behavior depends a great deal on the level and origins of the managers. From the perspective of upper Chicago management, the work force is homogeneous. Theirs is a work force of "immigrants" who need time to adjust to the new production demands of the company. Negative and positive attributes in production, interpersonal skills, or attitudes, according to upper management, are evenly distributed throughout the entire work force. When asked what characterizes a good worker, the plant manager emphasized timeliness, attention to detail, speed, reliability, and willingness to take direction and initiative. He also emphasized that no one group possesses more of these characteristics at the plant. Correspondingly, upper management's policy and practice make no ethnic distinctions. Supervisors have an explicit and well-developed ideology of ethnic equality. All supervisors claim that they treat everyone alike, although they may simultaneously assert that all workers do not act alike.

On the other hand, from the view of lower Miami management and the supervisors immediately in charge of particular departments, ethnic differences within the work force are critical. These supervisors and managers often maintain contradictory stereotypes of the various ethnic groups. Depending on whom one listens to, Haitians are either slow or fast; Cubans may talk too much or be extraordinarily dedicated workers. According to one Cuban woman who arrived in the 1960s, "The early employees, the earlier arriving Cubans, were much better people, better prepared, with more education. But the new workers are not like that. The new Cubans," by which she apparently meant 1980 Mariel Cubans, "and the new Haitians, along with Puerto Ricans, didn't care about their jobs. They didn't have good work habits and wouldn't stick with a job. They aren't *sensitivos*. Nicaraguans, on the other hand, are more like the earlier Cubans than they are like either new Cubans or Haitians."

Another Cuban supervisor states about Haitians, "You can't expect quality from them. . . . It's terrible to work with a Haitian. . . . all they want is money to send home." The one Haitian supervisor, however, describes Haitians thus: "They work hard. They talk less." Concerning Cubans, he claims, "For me, I don't see any best thing because they like money. That doesn't mean they don't make quality. The make and they talk. Sometime for the little thing they make a big problem. Sometimes when she talk this way she gets mad; she talk a lot. Some of them talk a lot."

The importance of upper management's ideology of ethnic equality is revealed when contrasted with the previous owner's flexible and individualized relationship with his workers. If workers had a problem, they dealt with neither their supervisor nor the union; they rather walked directly into the manager-owner's office. It is precisely this type of disruption that the new managerial bureaucracy was intended to control. According to the middle manager in charge of payroll, the policy has not been entirely successful. Haitians still storm into her office to question paycheck deductions or payment on benefits. According to her, "They don't seem to understand. Haitians are *muy brutos* (really stupid). Even the Cubans from Mariel will say, 'I don't understand but I will trust you.' Not the Haitians. I still have problems with them." She predicted that problems at the plant will increase as the number of Haitians continues to rise.

All managers share the belief that the new owners imposed their "northern, Anglo" management techniques too quickly and brusquely upon an immigrant work force that had been accustomed to and worked well under the more paternalistic, less bureaucratic approach of the previous owner. The highest management official we interviewed, the Chicago-based executive vice president, believes that for this reason the workers are self-consciously resisting change by work slowdowns. The on-site established-resident whites—that is, the new managers sent by the parent company—tend to recognize that they made errors in implementing changes, but they remain convinced that things would be better overall if the Latinos and Haitians became more like them; they do not advocate a return to the former paternalistic management styles. The Latino managers, on the other hand, believe not only that the established-resident whites made mistakes but that they have since changed and become much more like the Latinos. Now, at least, the plant manager has learned that he must talk to people at all levels to get them to work for him. During his first year, he seldom communicated with the workers and took little advice from the older middle-management group.

Structure of Work

While the bureaucracy was consciously implemented by management as a method of controlling the work force, it is also clear that the very nature of the work process serves to limit interaction between newcomers and established residents. As in all the apparel industry, interaction on the shop floor is rather limited and highly determined by the nature of the work process. Apparel work in general is characterized by an extreme division of labor. Each worker performs a minute task repeatedly, hundreds of times a day. Almost all workers are paid a piece rate: the more they produce, the more they are paid. Piece rates vary according to the difficulty of the operation. They are established with the intention that the "average" worker will earn the same "base rate," slightly under $5.00 per hour in this factory, regardless of the task. In this factory, over 80 percent of the workers earn less than the base rate. All workers believe that the supposedly "average" base rate is too difficult to obtain and that the piece rates are too low. Moreover, some types of material are easier and faster to work with, yet the piece rates have only one distinction, between plain and plaid materials. Workers vie to obtain bundles of easy materials that are paid at the same rate as slightly more difficult materials. It is the responsibility of the supervisor to regulate this competition among workers. While workers performing the same operation compete to obtain the easier materials, those at subsequent operations are dependent upon others to work efficiently enough to supply them with a constant stream of bundles for their own work. As one of our researchers reported, "There's a lot of discussion about whose job is the hardest and how fast people are working."

The new management sought to obtain high-quality feel with higher production by borrowing and adapting an Italian innovation that divides production into inner and outer shells for the coat. The company adapted the process by increasing the number of specialized tasks. Each worker would be responsible for a smaller proportion of the coat.

Considerable concentration is required to master the sewing operations and make money. Our research assistant, Aline, relates her initial experience with her machine, known as the "chopper."

> The "chopper" sews as it cuts, they said. Until I saw it work, I was completely baffled by the apparent paradox. But it does just that—it cuts off the ragged sides of the seam that is being made. I will be sewing an inside part of the shoulder of the jacket. . . .
>
> First, A. had me learn how to thread the machine, by watching her, then by doing it myself over and over again several times. Then she showed me the way to put the piece in the jacket. But she had me simply practice using the machine on pieces of plain cloth, without the chopper. I had a terrible time the entire day getting control over the foot pedal—it is delicate enough that with a not so delicate touch of the foot, the thing flies. All of the jokes from everyone not to get my fingers sewn together and not to get my fingers under any needles really weren't funny today. It all seemed very possible.

Even while in training, she described the work process as a demanding physical task. Operators are required to be at their machines when the break bell rings, "not running back." The constant reminder by her supervisor that she was working too slowly combined with the physical demands of the machine to make the production process "totally nerve-wracking. My shoulders are aching—and so is my ass from sitting on this hard chair the whole day." Talking and looking around were discouraged. All efforts focused on the task at hand: *dominar* the machine. The training director walked the floor, timing new and old operators, to "save the company money and help the workers."

Helping the workers meant to help them operate the machine faster to increase the piece-rate production. To this end, the workers were not taught to sew but to operate a specific machine that performs a specific task. Each machine has a different "personality" and it is the operator's job to learn it. After the training period is over, the operator and the machine are moved out to the floor, each knowing the other's quirks.

The job is learned as a series of distinct steps, each of which must be mastered. After two weeks on the job, Aileen had developed a list in her head of the "little shit" that had to be done perfectly.

> 1. Smooth the lining and continue to do so before each section is sewn.
> 2. Go around the little curve slowly at the top.
> 3. The piece that's being inserted is a little longer than the shoulder because it is supposed to make the shoulder full—so you have to push the piece gently to add fullness.
> 4. But it can't be pleated.
> 5. And going around the curve, the material can't be cut, just the leftover edges.
> 6. Sew in the middle of the foot, not too far to the edge or the inside.
> 7. Don't catch up the inside of the material as it rolls up.

Each step must be done perfectly, or the operation will not come out right. And if it does not come out correctly, "you have to do it again and again and again." To make money, you must also do it very quickly. While the training period allowed Aline time to chat as her quality was checked, such "down time" was almost nonexistent for the operators on the shop floor.

Bernadette, our Haitian research assistant, had worked previously in other Miami apparel plants, but she found this work more demanding.

> I will not have the time to talk to people because I am worrying about the job, so that I can make more. Well, I could do it. But, when I see people working, they are going fast. I would like to work like them, so that I can make a lot too. I am rushing, I want to make a lot too. But Fritz [the Haitian supervisor] said no. If you are rushing to make a lot, you are not going to make them well, because you don't know the work yet. . . . [Later I said to a coworker stationed beside me,] "The work is easy for you, but it

Garment Factory: One of the few male Haitian workers at the garment plant. The Cuban women surrounding him have been working at the site for over twenty years. Haitians have maintained a steady presence at the factory during the last seven years. (Photograph by Peggy Nolan)

> is difficult for me." She told me, "Don't worry, don't trouble yourself, because you are going to find that the work is not easy until you have three months." Until I have three months, that is when I will find it easy. I told myself, three months! Until three months?

In this intense production environment, conflicts occur. The most common form of conflict on the floor stems from competition over bundles. While the plant manager believes that there are fewer such disputes in Miami than in other plants within the corporation, he is certain that the incidents that do occur escalate to "big deals" much more often due to the ethnic nature of the conflicts. For example, the plant has a number of bundle boys, men whose job it is to carry the heavy bundles of partially sewn jackets to the individual sewing machines. One day a Haitian bundle boy, Jean, apparently ripped a bundle from the hands of an older Cuban woman, Angelina. Jean had evidently assumed the responsibility of trying to even out the "good" bundles. The two engaged in a shouting match and were referred to the plant manager's office. The plant manager first met with Jean and told him that he should not and could not take bundles out of peoples' arms. He also admitted that he believed Angelina purposefully tried to aggravate Jean. Then there was a meeting with the plant manager and both Jean and Angelina. Angelina became quite upset because she thought she was being blamed for Jean's pulling the bundle from her hands. Finally, the manager indicated that if it happened again they would both be fired. Angelina then asked to meet with the manager alone, apparently because she thought it was unfair that he had had a meeting alone with Jean. In this last meeting she said, "If you don't want me, why not fire me!"

This type of encounter exemplifies how the structure of the work process creates the potential for conflict. The very knowledge that the workers accumulate about the work process, the development of the skill required to perform the job, increases the potential for conflict. One of the Cuban supervisors presented an illustration of this point, as she discussed the types of communication she has with "her people." In her department two or three operators always work on the same operation. The bundles that are put on the benches come in different sizes, and while it is a heavier task to pick up a big bundle, it is the big ones that everybody wants. "Less time is lost cutting open a bundle if the bundle has a lot of work in it." The little bundles are, predictably, left for last. At the end of the month this causes a problem, because a new shipment, often a new style, is full of big bundles, and operators begin to work on these rather than finish the old. The supervisor was inevitably dragged into the midst of arguments and tugging matches, but she claims she has been somewhat successful in convincing the workers to cooperate and alternate bundles rather than always snatching the big ones. It is doubtful that asking the workers to cooperate in this matter will be successful. The fact is that the operators know that they will make more money, make fewer trips to the bench, and receive other measures of satisfaction if they continue to get the big bundles.

Social Groups

Workers strongly tend to remain within their ethnic group, and intergroup interaction frequently is characterized by tension and conflict. For example, during lunch virtually everyone eats and talks only with members of his or her own group. The company cafeteria contains seven-foot Formica-top folding tables with approximately eighteen chairs at each table, plus a food warmer, two refrigerators, and some vending machines, including one for espresso coffee favored by Cubans. Virtually everyone brings her or his own lunch, and most have some hot dish that they keep in the warmer.

The new commercial-style warmers were installed during the plant's 1988 summer break, after repeated complaints about the two toaster ovens that had been available to reheat food for lunch. Before work began the first day after the installation of the food warmers, two Haitians stood in front of the warmers. Speaking in Haitian Creole, one stated, "Oh, these are nice. Much bigger and better than the old ones."

The other replied, "Yes, they are nice, but they're only for Cubans."

"Really?" responded the first.

"Yes, I think so," said the second.

Gender segregation is common in the cafeteria. There are so few men at the plant (about a dozen) that they often sit alone or with any other man who has a break at the same time. Only rarely did our researcher Aline observe men and women sitting together. When they did approach each other, usually a man would stop by the table where the women were seated without actually joining them.

Many of the Cuban women have been working at the same plant for twenty years or more, and they have well-developed habits and rituals. Some sit in the same seat in the cafeteria every day for lunch. Aline reported that it took her and another new hire about a week to find appropriate seats in the dining room. Through looks, comments, and advice, she was made aware of the preferred areas of many of the older operators. Those who claimed the "best chairs"—molded plastic chairs that are more comfortable than the metal folding chairs—often brought large pieces of posterboard to save their place from the new hires.

On one occasion, a Haitian woman, apparently mistakenly, assumed one of these "reserved" Cuban seats. The Cuban woman politely asked the Haitian woman to leave, explaining that that was her customary seat. The Haitian woman assented, but another Haitian woman who was looking on objected somewhat quietly. The following day, however, the woman who had objected forced the issue by assuming the Cuban's seat. When the Cuban again requested her seat, not quite as politely this time as the first, the Haitian woman responded that it was a free country and there were no reserved seats in the cafeteria. As the argument progressed, she added that this was just another example of discrimination against blacks in general and Haitians in particular. The argument escalated into a shouting match, with interested onlookers sometimes adding their own opinions. It did not stop until one of the managers intervened. Both the Haitian and the Cuban were taken to the plant manager's office. Each attempted vociferously to present and defend her side of the dispute. But the plant manager indicated that regardless of who was wrong or right, they should not be so disruptive. He continued that it was not his responsibility to determine seating in the cafeteria. They were to settle that between themselves, and they could settle it however they wished, as long as they were not disruptive.

Harmonious intergroup interaction does occur in ritualized occasions, particularly for life-cycle and life-crisis events such as birthdays, birth and wedding showers, grave illnesses, and death. Such events are encouraged by management and promoted as a way to create a plantwide esprit de corps among workers and managers. As Louise Lamphere reported for a Rhode Island apparel factory, particular women tend to organize such events. In this Miami factory, these women are almost always Cuban. Apparently, until the twelve to eighteen months preceding our study, only other Cuban (and a few other Hispanic) women had participated. More recently, the Cuban organizers have taken to organizing such events for Haitians, too. The largest affairs are plantwide celebrations for Thanksgiving, Christmas, and just before the plant's two-week midsummer break. Workers are asked to come a half-hour early and to forgo their morning and afternoon recesses so that there can be one long midday break. While management cooperates with the organization of schedules, they do not organize or provide anything for the celebrations. Each of the plant's seven departments organizes its own celebration. Some go out to a restaurant; others order food that is brought into the plant; but most organize potlucks among themselves. One or two women take the lead and go around asking each worker what dish she wishes to contribute.

When the day comes, most dress up nicely, ready to have a real holiday. A couple of the women may leave their work ten or fifteen minutes early and begin setting up. The cafeteria will hold three or four groups, and another is allowed to use the management conference room.

Meanwhile, Haitian women organize similar events for Haitian coworkers. Haitians also commonly invite Cuban coworkers to attend outside life-cycle events, such as weddings. Two Cuban supervisors have attended such events, but no Cuban workers. Cubans do not invite Haitians to their outside social events.

Bernadette, our Haitian researcher, felt excluded from in-plant functions, too:

> They all went outside. But the other group of people went inside. They went inside. Then, some outside. Then, me, if they invite me to something, I go. But if they don't invite me, I don't go. My car was parked nearby. I got into the car; I was eating my lunch. I saw groups of Cubans and Haitians together. I see them in the backyard. But no one told me whether I had to give money or to help in any way. They did not tell me anything. I did not know anything about it. It was the first time that I saw them partying.

In some cases, the intergroup interaction begun in rituals extends beyond the plant. Our observations reveal, however, that this only takes place among Hispanics: for example, a Nicaraguan may become friends with a Cuban. The one exception was Aileen, our Jewish-American researcher, who did establish and maintain a friendship with a young Nicaraguan woman.

Thus, rituals partially overcome the distances among the different newcomer groups within the apparel factory. When they are successful, those involved usually alter their evaluation of the individuals from other groups, excepting them from the generally negative group stereotypes. Nevertheless, though such exceptions are made, the negative stereotypes are still generally maintained and social interaction remains primarily within one's own group.

Construction

As in other Sun Belt cities, construction in Miami has boomed in the postwar era. Between 1940 and 1960, Dade County's population increased by nearly 90 percent each decade. For the following twenty years, between 1960 and 1980, the rate declined but remained a significant 30 percent per decade. Until the late

1960s, unions controlled 90 percent of all housing construction in Miami. This changed, however, as the labor market was inundated with the first wave of Cuban labor.

A key factor influencing the development of the construction industry in Dade County is that from the 1960s until the mid-1970s, local building-trade unions refused to accept Cuban workers. The false security created from a near monopoly of the industry combined with nativistic sentiments to create an implicit policy of exclusion. One of our respondents emphasizes the importance of this strategy.

> A lot of the Cubans that came over were real pro-union. They went to the unions to get jobs. The answer they got was "we don't need you." So they went out and created their own companies. Now they are the strongest builders in Dade, and they are all nonunion.

This stance has been typical among the construction unions, which have been traditionally ethnically segregated. In Miami, however, the consequences have been more severe than elsewhere. The Cuban workers whom the unions refused to incorporate turned to work in the informal sector, operating out of the backs of pickups, charging less than the going rates, and receiving cash payments. As some Cubans gained positions in local banks, informal-sector construction workers began creating construction firms, many still partially informal—paying their workers in cash and not making any deductions for social security and other taxes. As Cuban immigrants began creating their own nonunion firms and competing for housing contracts, unionized construction workers focused on higher-paid jobs building condominiums in Miami Beach and office buildings in downtown Miami. Then the 1973 recession, which severely depressed the construction industry, impelled many non-Latino white construction workers to abandon Dade County altogether.

When the unions finally recognized their mistake of not attempting to incorporate the newly arrived Cuban construction workers, it was too late. The number of unionized carpenters, for example, declined from a high of 10,000 to a nadir of 3,000 in the late 1970s.[7] By the mid-1980s, Cuban firms, predominantly nonunion, controlled more than 50 percent of all Dade County construction and nearly 90 percent of new housing, the fastest-growing sector of the industry.[8] Larger construction firms controlled by established-resident whites virtually abandoned new home construction in Dade County to concentrate on the construction of high-rise office buildings in the city center.

The ethnic composition of the labor force, seen in figure 2.2, further reflects this transformation. The proportion of Hispanic construction workers doubled

7. By the mid-1980s, however, the number of union carpenters had increased to 5,000.

8. For an analysis of the forces that led to the growth of Cuban enterprises and the construction of an ethnic enclave, see Portes 1987.

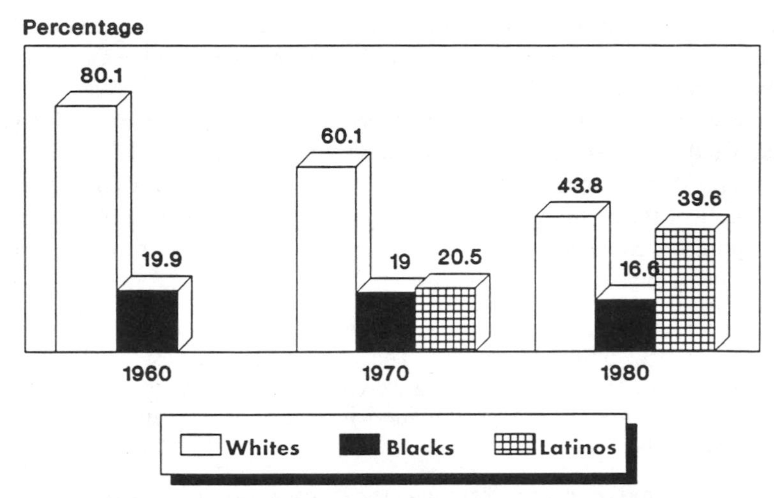

Figure 2.2. Ethnicity in Miami's construction industry, 1960–80
Source: U.S. Census Survey of the Population, 1960, 1970, 1980

in the 1970s, from 20 percent to nearly 40 percent. Hispanics achieved this relative growth primarily at the expense of non-Latino whites, whose numbers declined from 60 to 44 percent.[9]

Organized labor in the construction industry has experienced difficulties throughout the United States, and frequently nonunionized immigrants have played a role. In Miami, however, the union's decline was especially precipitous, and it was accompanied by the parallel growth of a new Cuban-controlled set of construction firms. Thus, not only was there a transformation in the work force (from primarily union to mainly nonunion) but the owners and managers also changed, from being exclusively established-resident whites to being primarily newcomer Cubans. The main impact of immigration on the structure of the industry has been the segregation of the industry into Cuban, nonunion firms and older established-resident white firms that are more likely to be unionized. As in the apparel industry, restructuring limits the interaction of established residents and newcomer immigrants. The exception in construction is among unionized firms, particularly in carpentry, which did reach out to newcomers during the 1980s.

The Nature of Relations: Ethnic Segregation and Occupational Cooperation

The nature of construction work directly affects construction workers' social relationships, especially those between newcomers and established residents.

9. While the proportion of blacks dropped from 19.4 percent in 1970 to 16.6 percent in 1980, the absolute numbers of both blacks and whites increased as the total construction labor force grew during the 1970s decade from 36,000 to almost 50,000 (U.S. Bureau of the Census 1973, 1983).

Unlike most employees in modern industrialized society, construction workers maintain a high level of independence and autonomy over their profession. Owning their tools, construction workers are freed from the technological dependence fostered by many other occupations. In Herbert Applebaum's analysis of construction-worker autonomy, independence among workers was found to extend through the entire process of construction work, including control over one's own managerial supervision, the ability to regulate which partners to work with, and sovereignty to decide whether to work in adverse environmental conditions (Applebaum 1981). In short, within the confines of construction-worker subculture, technological independence reinforces occupational autonomy.

Work at the Miami Beach Convention Center transformed individual autonomy into ethnic segregation. In Miami, different construction trades tend to be dominated by particular ethnic groups. They are also stratified in terms of prestige by race and as a result of previous political gains. The black tradesmen, Laborers,[10] are exclusively black American and Haitian and are viewed as the lowest. On the other end of the scale, those trades that require state licensing, Electricians and Plumbers, have the highest prestige. Not only are these last trades virtually all white, but they have also been the slowest to admit Latinos. Carpenters fall in the middle of this hierarchy, and they have the highest proportion of Latinos among the unionized trades.

The Carpenters working at the site were more or less evenly balanced between established-resident whites and Latinos, although among all the trade workers at the site established-resident whites dominated. Out of a maximum of seventy-five Carpenters working at once, there was only one black. In the entire site, there were about seventy blacks, nearly all of whom were Laborers. The Laborers themselves were further divided informally into black Americans (about three-quarters) and Haitians (about one-quarter). This trade/ethnic segregation significantly limits the possibilities for interethnic interaction.

This segregation was further emphasized by the spatial dispersion of workers across the massive site, which was larger than an average city block. Much of the progress of construction is sequential by trade. Interior walls cannot be erected until exterior walls are done. Electrical work must wait until most of the structure is roughed in. Thus, each trade tends to work by itself on a particular part of the building. Interaction among people of different trades is largely incidental to one's work.

This is not to suggest that Miami construction workers are not cooperative. By nature, building requires cooperation. Interpersonal and intertrade dependence

10. When referring to a particular union or member of that union, we have chosen to refer to it as a trade and to capitalize it—for example, Laborer and Laborers' Union. Some would not consider unskilled laborers to have a "trade," but our research reveals that they view their work, and especially union work, differently.

is a prerequisite to the successful completion of a project. This dependence, however, is governed by norms that ensure continued worker autonomy. Among the trades and individuals within trades, there are unspoken codes that ensure cooperation without jeopardizing worker sovereignty. The most important of these was succinctly summed up by one worker, "Do your own work and don't mess with anybody's shit."

When this norm is broken, racial and ethnic epithets are quickly hurled. A black American Laborer, for example, once broke this golden rule of construction work culture by "messing with another worker's equipment"—not only that of another construction worker, but that of a high-status established-resident white duct worker. The duct worker was furious. He came to the team's researcher, Steve, and asked whether he had seen anyone take his equipment. Steve said no and the duct worker left, screaming ethnic epithets. A direct confrontation did not take place, because the Laborer had left the area. If he had not, there probably would have been a physical confrontation.

Reciprocal access to craftsmen's tools, within a context of established trust, is the second most important workers' norm. When workers function in teams, trust is crucial. Cooperation between workers cannot take place if trust has not been established. Borrowing tools is a visible sign of acceptance among workers. Teamwork is assured when "reciprocity" is coupled with permission to borrow another's tools. During Steve's tenure as a carpenter's apprentice, he learned firsthand that to attempt to borrow another's tools without gaining his trust first would lead to conflict. While working on installing studs, Steve needed to replace a chop-saw blade but did not have the proper tools to complete the job. Consequently, he asked an established-resident white pipecutter whether he could borrow a set of channel locks. The pipecutter stared at Steve with a look of dissatisfaction and replied, "What would you do if I didn't bring my own tools with me—you'd have to go out and buy your own, now wouldn't you?" His statement reflected the general attitude that one should always be prepared to work, and a visible sign of "preparedness" is reflected in the possession of one's tools of the trade.

Adhering to these two rules, Cuban and established-resident white Carpenters generally enjoyed workdays free of conflict among themselves. On an individual level, relations were friendly. One established-resident white Carpenter said of his Cuban coworker, "I've known that son of a bitch for years, we're brothers in wood." Once one is accepted as a full-fledged member of a trade, one has the right to borrow tools from coworkers. In turn, the lender is expected to give the tool to one who asks, on the condition that it be returned in the same condition or replaced if lost or broken. This reciprocal sharing occurs regardless of individuals' ethnicity. Being a construction trade member, a coworker, who respects the norms of reciprocity and "not messing with anybody's shit" is all that is necessary. Thus, on an intratrade level, cooperation among individual workers of varying ethnicities and newcomer-established resident statuses was the norm. Cordial interethnic relations seemed to prevail.

On an intertrade level, however, this was not the case. Trade segregation obviously limits interethnic interaction. Though workers of diverse trades may come in contact at some time in the construction of a given project, these interactions are basically on a professional level and do not involve "free-time" encounters. Trade affiliation seems to be the strongest relational tie workers possess; during free-time activities, such as break or lunch, workers stay among members of their own trade.

The Laborers' Union is evenly divided internally between established black Americans and newcomer Haitians. Black American Laborers, usually characterized as being larger and darker-skinned, often function as scaffold assemblers and heavy task operators, while Haitians, usually smaller and lighter-skinned, serve as material suppliers.[11] The latter is less strenuous and often cleaner work. This intratrade hierarchy, the lack of English proficiency among the Haitian ranks, and the fact that the Laborers' foreman is Haitian contributes to newcomer–established resident isolation within the trade. This is manifest during breaks such as lunch, when black Americans and Haitians rarely sit together or speak to one another.

Previous studies of construction workers have indicated a high degree of worker solidarity reinforced by off-hours socializing, particularly in bars (Applebaum 1981; LeMaster 1975). In practical terms this means an integration of work and nonwork lives that transcends merely being friendly at work to include spending time outside working hours with one's workmates. In Miami, this is limited to a few workers who car-pool. Our research assistant, Steve, participated in a car pool that contained both established-resident whites and newcomer Hispanics. Interaction was always friendly, and on the way home from work a six-pack of beer was usually consumed. But relationships did not go beyond the car pool. Individuals never visited each other's houses or met in any place other than the work site and the car. When asked whether he "hung out and drank with the guys after work," an established-resident white Carpenter replied, "No way man, that's bad news. You're looking for trouble if you do that. There's things I got to do once I get out of here." His statement reflected the general perception that Miami is not geographically conducive to off-hours socializing. Isolated and dispersed, "waterholes" are not concentrated near construction sites. Moreover, workers at the site resided throughout southeast Florida—some living as far away as Palm Beach County, more than an hour's drive from the Miami Beach construction site. The integration of work and nonwork lives for construction workers in Miami is logistically impractical and difficult at best.

Despite the obstacles of trade affiliations, internal craft hierarchies, and spatial dispersion of workers throughout the site, instances of interethnic and newcomer–established resident interaction do take place. It is usually in the

11. Incidentally, Haitians are not always lighter-skinned than black Americans. The skin color of Haitians, both in Miami and in Haiti, spans the spectrum from dark black to white.

context of a joking relationship. For example, an established-resident white Carpenter may say to a Cuban coworker or black American Laborer, "Hey buddy, stop hanging around and get back to work, this ain't break time." The recipient of this "joke" usually smiles and goes on his way. This form of antagonism is within the behavioral limits of worker culture. Both parties know and accept this, so that conflict does not arise. Here joking is used to enforce the cultural norm of work expectations. The hidden message is, "Get back to work!"

In cases where conflict is a possibility, the "joking" takes the form of a release of unconscious prejudice, but in a way that avoids open aggression. On one occasion an established-resident white coworker told our graduate assistant, Steve, to watch out for Cuban insulators. "They carry big fucking knives and they'll use them." The insulator overheard the comment but did not act. This joking is similar to that observed among longshoremen (Pilcher 1976): insults that in any other context would express and elicit hostility will, in the joking context, express and elicit friendliness and solidarity.

With all these obstacles to interaction, it would seem that members of different groups could not possibly possess any form of collective consciousness. In actuality they do. It is expressed in its most successful form in times of tragedy. When any worker of any trade is injured, word travels around the site. The reaction is typical. Everyone asks about the condition of the injured. Concern for the fellow worker, despite ethnicity, race, or newcomer status, is genuine.

After the tragic event is over and forgotten, however, the ideal of "being in the same boat" fades. Internal hierarchies, positions of status, and ethnic identification are again important. Ethnocentric remarks made by Cuban workers, such as "The Cubans made Miami" are often heard at lunchtime and in "bull sessions." Stories of how things used to be better before the Cubans came are common parlance among established-resident white workers.

Despite this ethnocentric sentiment, there is a common mind-set that construction workers occupy society's lowest stratum. One worker recalled his experiences constructing the Hyatt Regency in Coral Gables. "They [the owners] wouldn't even let me go through the front door. Once we bust our balls and finish a building, the guys who own it think we are not good enough to walk in the front door. People might see us or something. What bullshit! They even told us we would get fired if we did." This feeling leads to a sense of job dissatisfaction among construction workers.

For established-resident white workers, however, the cause of their alienation is ethnically linked. One established-resident white coworker summed it up best. "When the union went Cuban, that was the end for us. The wages went down, contractors started hiring all those illegals. We lost control over our union." This sense of powerlessness is all the more remarkable since it comes in the face of an established-resident white majority in both union membership and among union contractors. This phenomenon, which we label psychological tipping, has meant a perception of helplessness among established-resident white workers. Cuban workers have in turn been motivated to "take over" the union because established-resident white workers are disinterested and don't participate.

Though groups may be perceived as "lazy Haitians" or "loud-mouthed Cubans," individual members of these ethnic groups can be more favorably evaluated. Damien, the only Haitian Carpenter, was praised by his coworkers for going to school and learning English and for saving money and investing it. Others who showed no signs of achievement were viewed as "worthless." For example, Bennie, a man of about sixty and one of only two black American journeymen Carpenters, was viewed this way. His coworkers claimed he was "as slow as molasses. He's gonna put the company out of business. They're really losing money with this guy on the job." Being a self-made man, getting an education, and making large sums of money are qualities that construction workers of any ethnic affiliation value. If someone demonstrates these traits, then others will suspend ethnic stereotypes of this one person—still maintaining them, however, for other members of the same group.

Summary and Conclusions

Newcomer immigrants have fundamentally restructured Miami's apparel and construction industries. Had it not been for immigrants, and specifically the low wages they have been willing to accept, Miami's apparel industry would be like that of Tampa—that is, nonexistent. During the 1980s, the presence of the Cuban work force further transformed the industry as an informal sector of home work arose. Similarly, if immigrants had been absent from Miami, the construction industry would have languished (since population growth would have been much lower) and unions dominated by established-resident whites would still control production. In these respects, restructuring in Miami is not too different from restructuring in other regions of the United States: it contributed to the lowering of wages, deunionization, and frequently an increased reliance upon immigrant labor. Miami's restructuring also contributed to the region's economic growth and its assumption of the role as the informal capital of the Caribbean.

Miami's restructuring is different, however, in at least one important respect. Not only has immigration changed the ethnic composition of the work force, but it has also transformed the ethnic structure of ownership and management. The exclusionary policies of the construction unions toward Cubans contributed to the emergence of a primarily nonunion construction sector in which both workers and owners were Cuban immigrants. This restructuring at the top of the industry affects social relations as much as the ethnic change of the workers.[12] Cubans work primarily in Cuban construction firms, and established residents work mostly in the older construction firms owned by established-

12. For a discussion of its impact outside of the workplace, see Mohl 1985 and 1987; Stepick et al. 1990; and Stack and Warren n.d.

resident whites. Thus, in Miami's construction industry segregation between established residents and newcomers is even more accentuated than in other parts of the United States, where top management and ownership of large firms remain largely among established-resident whites.

While the ownership and management structure in apparel have not been as dramatically transformed as in construction, the workers are overwhelmingly Hispanic, and among them Cubans are the majority. In the apparel industry's informal sector, Cubans are even more predominant.

Restructuring of Miami's apparel and construction industries, however, has not produced an absolute segregation at the workplace. As the two cases here show, some unionized firms have made efforts to integrate different workers. Despite these efforts, the nature of the work processes and informal social relations tend to maintain segregation among groups. The repetitiveness and speed of the tasks do not allow for much social interaction. Moreover, the work is competitively structured, so that interaction that does occur during work is likely to express competitive conflict. The integration of different groups that has occurred thus has produced work-related conflict that is likely to be interpreted ethnically, and often specifically in terms of the most recent newcomers versus earlier immigrants—for example, Cubans who came in the 1960s versus Nicaraguans or Haitians.

The structure of Miami's apparel industry, the nature of work in it, and the ethnic constitution of its work force are all similar to the patterns of the apparel industry throughout the United States, both contemporarily and historically. The significant difference in the plant we studied is that management has imposed a bureaucratic structure to control the work force by self-consciously ignoring ethnicity and admitting only that the workers are all newcomers who must learn the firm's American bureaucratic form. To what degree does this management policy make any difference? At a minimum, it has given work to Haitian and Central American women who might have not had it otherwise. The apparent shortage in the early 1980s of Cuban women willing to work in apparel required that individuals from some new groups be hired. Our Haitian workers' reports of apparent discrimination against Haitian applicants probably implies that without the firm's affirmative action policy, even fewer Haitians would be working there. Yet those complaints also suggest that those implementing the policy and facilitating informal social relations on the floor limit management's efforts to integrate new workers and treat everyone equally.

While informal social relations tend toward isolation of different groups, rituals such as birthday parties organized among coworkers partially overcome these social distances. While there is some individual variation, the events are usually open to everyone, regardless of newcomer status or ethnic background. Nevertheless, as revealed by our Haitian participant observer, Bernadette, the welcome is not always successfully conveyed or understood. Moreover, we found no cases of interethnic or newcomer–established resident relationships that began in the workplace and subsequently extended outside the factory.

In construction, as in apparel, the nature of the work further separates newcomers and established residents. The relative autonomy of construction workers and the sequential process of construction isolate the largely ethnically segregated trades from each other, and, to a lesser degree, even workers within a trade. Again, as with apparel, these aspects of Miami's construction industry are similar to what has occurred throughout the United States, but the Carpenters' Union efforts to incorporate newcomers provide an opportunity to assess how attempts at integration affect face-to-face relationships. And again, the nature of work and informal social relations tend to isolate. An unwritten etiquette, pithily summarized as "Don't mess with anyone's shit," along with strong norms of reciprocity, controls interaction that does occur. Moreover, the male-dominated construction industry does not have widely shared rituals that bring the various groups together. In contrast to descriptions of construction culture elsewhere, in Miami workers have little off-site interaction. While newcomer–established resident divisions probably limit off-site interaction, just as important is the broader urban environment: the workers' residences are so spatially scattered that workers spend much of their extra time commuting.

In short, the various levels of Miami's social and economic structure, from macro- to micro-, all tend toward limiting and controlling interaction between newcomers and established residents. Miami's peculiar form of restructuring, which includes newcomer Cuban owners and managers, makes social isolation more likely than in other U.S. cities. Moreover, informal social relations constructed and maintained by workers themselves reflect an ethnic isolation based first on national origin, second on race, and third on language. Thus, for example, Cubans are most likely to associate with Cubans; white Cubans may sometimes associate with white Americans; less frequently Cubans may associate with Nicaraguans.

There are some countertendencies—policies by some institutions to integrate newcomers and particular contexts, such as birthday parties in the apparel factory and car-pooling among construction workers, that promote interaction and identification across groups. Nevertheless, the workplace is primarily marked by isolation—not individual isolation but ethnic isolation.

References

Allman, T. D. 1987. *Miami, City of the Future.* New York: Atlantic Monthly Press.

Applebaum, Herbert A. 1981. *Royal Blue: The Culture of Construction Workers.* New York: Holt, Rinehart, and Winston.

Boswell, Thomas D., and J. R. Curtis. 1984. *The Cuban-American Experience.* Totowa, N.J.: Rowman and Allenheld.

Cooley, Martha. 1983. Haiti: The AIDS Stigma. *NACLA* (North American Congress on Latin America) 17 (5): 47–48.

Didion, Joan. 1987. *Miami.* New York: Simon and Schuster.

Durand, Guy. 1983. AIDS—The Fallacy of a Haitian Connection. *Bulletin de l'Association des Médecins Haitiens à l'Entranger* 19 (9): 17–20.

Garreau, Joel. 1981. *The Nine Nations of North America*. New York: Houghton Mifflin.

Grenier, Guillermo. 1991. Ethnic Solidarity and the Cuban-American Labor Movement in Dade County. *Cuban Studies* 20:29–48.

Grenier, Guillermo, and Alex Stepick. (N.d.) *Miami Now: Immigration, Ethnicity, and Social Change in America's City*. Miami: University Presses of Florida. Forthcoming.

Laverdière, Michel, Jacques Tremblay, René Lavallée, Yvette Bonny, Michel Lacombe, Jacques Boileau, Jacques Lachapelle, and Christian Lamoureaux. 1983. AIDS in Haitian Immigrants and in a Caucasian Woman Closely Associated with Haitians. *Canadian Medical Association Journal* 129:1209–12.

Lawless, Robert. 1986. Haitian Migrants and Haitian-Americans: From Invisibility into the Spotlight. *Journal of Ethnic Studies* 14 (2): 29–70.

LeMaster, Ersel E. 1975. *Blue Collar Aristocrats: Lifestyles at a Working Class Tavern*. Madison: University of Wisconsin Press.

Levine, Barry B. 1985. The Capital of Latin America. *Wilson Quarterly* 9: 46–69.

Loescher, Gilbert, and John Scanlan. 1984. Human Rights, U.S. Foreign Policy, and Haitian Refugees. *Journal of Interamerican Studies and World Affairs* 26:313–56.

MacCorkle, Lyn. 1984. *Cubans in the United States: A Bibliography for Research in the Social and Behavioral Sciences, 1960–1983*. Westport, Conn.: Greenwood Press.

Masud-Piloto, Felix Roberto. 1988. *With Open Arms: Cuban Migration to the United States*. Totowa, N.J.: Rowman and Littlefield.

Miller, Jake C. 1984. *The Plight of Haitian Refugees*. New York: Praeger.

Mohl, Raymond. 1984. Cubans in Miami: A Preliminary Bibliography. *The Immigration History Newsletter* 16 (1): 1–10.

———. 1985. The New Haitian Immigration: A Preliminary Bibliography. *The Immigration History Newsletter* 17 (1): 1–8.

———. 1987. Ethnic Politics in Miami, 1960–86. In *Shades of the Sunbelt: Essays on Ethnicity, Race, and the Urban South,* edited by Randall M. Miller and George E. Pozzetta. Westport, Conn.: Greenwood Press.

———. 1988. Immigration through the Port of Miami. In *Forgotten Doors: The Other Ports of Entry to the United States,* edited by M. Mark Stolarik. Philadelphia: Balch Institute Press.

———. 1988. The Politics of Ethnicity in Contemporary Miami. *Migration World* 14 (3): 51–74.

Pedraza-Bailey, Silvia. 1985. *Political and Economic Migrants in America: Cubans and Mexicans*. Austin: University of Texas Press.

Pilcher, Roy. 1976. *Principles of Construction Management*. New York: McGraw-Hill.

———. 1985. *Project Cost Control in Construction*. London: Sheridan House.

Portes, Alejandro. 1987. The Social Origins of the Cuban Enclave Economy of Miami. *Sociological Perspectives* 30 (4): 340–72.

Portes, Alejandro, and Robert Bach. 1985. *Latin Journey*. Berkeley: University of California Press.

Rieff, David. 1987. *Going to Miami: Exiles, Tourists, and Refugees in the New America*. New York: Little, Brown.

Stack, John, and Christopher Warren. (N.d.) Ethnicity and Politics in Miami. In Grenier and Stepick n.d.

Stepick, Alex. 1986. *Haitian Refugees in the United States*. 2d ed. New York: Minority Rights Group.

———. 1989. Miami's Two Informal Sectors. In *The Informal Economy: Studies in Advanced and Less Developed Countries,* edited by Alejandro Portes, Manuel Castells, and Lauren Benton. Baltimore: Johns Hopkins University Press.

Stepick, Alex, Max Castro, Marvin Dunn, and Guillermo Grenier. 1990. Established Residents and Newcomers: The Case of Miami. Center for Labor Research and Study, Florida International University, Miami. Typescript.

U.S. Bureau of the Census. 1963. *Census of Population, 1960.* Vol. 1, *Characteristics of the Population,* pt. 11, Florida. Washington, D.C.: Government Printing Office.

———. 1973. *1970 Census of Population: General Social and Economic Characteristics, Florida: Final Report PC.* Washington, D.C.: Government Printing Office.

———. 1983. *1980 Census of Population: General Population Characteristics, Florida.*

3 LIFE IN BIG RED: STRUGGLES AND ACCOMMODATIONS IN A CHICAGO POLYETHNIC TENEMENT

DWIGHT CONQUERGOOD

I have lived long enough amidst you to know something about your circumstances; I have devoted to their knowledge my most serious attention. I have studied the various official and non-official documents as far as I was able to get hold of them—I have not been satisfied with this. I wanted more than a mere abstract *knowledge of my subject. I wanted to see you in your own homes, to observe you in your every-day life, to chat with you on your condition and grievances, to witness your struggles against the social and political power of your oppressors.*

FRIEDRICH ENGELS
THE CONDITION OF THE WORKING CLASS IN ENGLAND (1845)

At 10:00 A.M. on August 16, 1988, Bao Xiong, a Hmong woman from Laos, stepped out the back door of her top-floor Big Red apartment and the rotting porch collapsed beneath her feet. All summer long I had swept away slivers of wood that had fallen from the Xiongs' decrepit porch onto mine, one floor below. Six households were intimately affected by Bao Xiong's calamity, because we shared the same front entrance and stairwell, and our respective back porches were structurally interlocked within a shaky wooden framework of open landings and sagging staircases that clung precariously to the red-brick exterior of the Chicago tenement. The six households included two Hmong, one Mexican, one Puerto Rican, one Mexican–Puerto Rican, and myself, a white male ethnographer from Northwestern University. Ethnically our wing represented much of the rest of Big Red, where other first-generation Hmong, Mexican, and Puerto Rican families were joined by refugees and migrants from Cambodia, Iraq, Lebanon, and Poland, as well as an elderly Jew and Appalachians and African Americans who had been displaced from gentrifying neighborhoods of the city, such as Uptown. Big Red mirrored the global forces of displacement and migration that had grouped such ethnically diverse working-class residents in one dilapidated building.

Although separated by language, ethnicity, and cultural background, the polyglot residents shared the commonplaces of daily struggle embodied in Big Red. By sharing the same crowded living space, they were forced to interact across ethnic lines and cultural traditions. The distinct smells of several ethnic

Front entrance to Big Red (photograph by Dwight Conquergood)

cuisines wafting from kitchens pungently accented the sounds of many voices and languages in the corridors and public spaces, collectively creating a richly sensuous experience of overlapping difference for anyone climbing up and down the back staircases. After reaching your landing, more often than not, you parted your way through damp clothing hanging from the clotheslines that crisscrossed back porches and extended the laundry of one household onto the threshold of another, your progress punctuated by the robust greetings, cries, and laughter of children.

Within minutes of arriving home on the day that the Xiongs' porch collapsed, I heard versions of the story from most of the neighbors whose back landings were structurally connected with Bao Xiong's. A Puerto Rican grandmother was relieved that her neighbor had come to no serious harm but worried about the future safety of the children, particularly her grandchildren. A young Mexican mother anxiously pointed out the loose and missing railing on her porch, and how her wash had been ruined by all the dust and falling debris. Then Bao Xiong joined us, uninjured but still shaken. She kept repeating to the small circle of neighbors: "Oh-h-h, very, very scared. Only me. Happen only to me. Why me? Oh-h-h, very scared." For her, the physical mishap was fraught with metaphysical meaning. She was not interested so much in why or how the porch collapsed. It is in the nature of things that they decay and fall. She sought explanation for the meaning-laden conjunction between the fall of the porch, and her stepping outside the back door. In her worldview, the precise timing of these two events was no mere coincidence, and she consulted the divination powers of a Hmong shaman who lived in another wing of Big Red.

Providing substandard housing to a mix of people from all over the world, Big Red became a highly contested site of convergence and friction between the forces of global resettlement and local redevelopment. More than an inhabited physical space, Big Red itself inhabited discursive space, became a site of cultural production and political struggle.

"Inhabited space—and above all the house," argues Pierre Bourdieu, "is the principal locus" for those socially constituted motivating principles that generate and coordinate cultural practices (1977:89). Bourdieu investigates the "premises"—both physical and figurative—on which people dwell and practice everyday life. His study of Kabylian housing demonstrates how the house is a threshold of exchange for both the incorporation and the objectification of a cultural ethos, those dispositions that enable and constrain practice (1990:271–83). He uses the terms "*habitus*" and "class *habitus*" to name these "durably inculcated" dispositions and tastes that are a consequence of one's position within socioeconomic space (see also Bourdieu 1984:169–225, 1990:271–83).

The house is a privileged site for Bourdieu because it is an enclosure with thresholds and openings, and thus epitomizes the "dialectic of the internalization of externality and the externalization of internality" (1977:72). Recently there has been a resurgence of interest among anthropologists in this inside-outside dialectic, in the interpenetrations between global forces and local particularities. George Marcus and Michael Fischer pose the challenge of "how to represent the embedding of richly described local cultural worlds in larger impersonal systems of political economy" and argue that these broader outside forces "are as much inside as outside the local context" (1986:77–78). Leith Mullings has called similarly for an anthropology of the city that complexly registers demographic, political, and economic pressures on urban lifeways (1987:9; see also Sanjek 1990).

Urban housing is just such an intersection between macro-forces and micro-realities. Housing encompasses intimate and collective as well as public space, and is situated between the deeply personal and the highly political.[1] Housing is both a physical structure and an ideological construction. It structures propinquity, shapes interactions, and provides a compelling issue around which people mobilize.

Big Red, a dilapidated tenement where I lived for twenty months in northwest Chicago's Albany Park neighborhood, intersects a distinctively local lifeworld with larger political-economic forces. In Albany Park, with its deteriorating housing stock—87 percent built before 1939—and a high density of four hundred large multiunit buildings, the issue of housing looms large (Royer 1984:37). This analysis begins by situating Big Red within the larger context of Chicago's Albany Park neighborhood, a port-of-entry for many new immigrants and refugees. It then explores the struggles of accommodation and tactics of resistance within Big Red, and concludes with the documentation of domination and displacement accomplished by agents of civil society through the rhetoric of transgression and redevelopment.

Big Red and the Transformation of Albany Park

Since the 1960s till now we've had everything moving in or moving out and I can't tell you "who," because there was no "who." The big buildings were deserted. There's a big building down there called Big Red. It's horrible. It was turned into a slum.

RUTH, LONGTIME RESIDENT OF ALBANY PARK

Most urban sociologists note that Chicago is "America's most segregated city" (Squires et al. 1987:94; Fremon 1988:124) and journalists echo this theme (Mc-

1. For an engagingly written study of the politics of housing and development in Chicago see Gerald D. Suttles, *The Man-Made City: The Land-Use Confidence Game in Chicago* (Chicago: University of Chicago Press, 1990). See also Gregory D. Squires, Larry Bennett, Kathleen McCourt, and Philip Nyden, *Chicago: Race, Class, and the Response to Urban Decline* (Philadelphia: Temple University Press, 1987). For an excellent study of the black migration to Chicago and its impact on the city, see Nicholas Lemann, *The Promised Land: The Great Black Migration and How It Changed America* (New York: Knopf, 1991).

Clory 1991:16). The South Side and the West Side of Chicago are primarily African American. Albany Park is located on the Northwest Side of Chicago, an area that historically has been predominantly white (see fig. 3.1). During the 1970s and particularly the 1980s the ethnic composition of Albany Park shifted, not from white to black but from white to an emergent third category in the racial and ethnic geography of Chicago, "immigrant" or "diverse." The extraordinary ethnic diversity of Albany Park parallels that of many Chicago North Side neighborhoods that have received substantial numbers of new immigrants and refugees from hemispheres of the South and the East. In the aftermath of the 1990 census, Albany Park is now a site of redistricting struggles to create a new ethnic ward for Asians or Latinos as a result of population growth through immigration (see Hinz 1991b; Quinlan 1991).

Housing has played a key role in the ethnic recomposition of neighborhoods like Albany Park. On March 25, 1964, Anthony Downs delivered a speech before the Chicago Real Estate Board titled "What Will Chicago's Residential Areas Be Like in 1975?" He forecast "many changes" in Chicago's residential neighborhoods, using three structural factors as causal predictors: the impact of rising real incomes, combined with the aging of the housing stock, and the impact of ethnic changes. "In older areas of the city," Downs explained, "older and less-well-maintained housing will become increasingly difficult to market to rising-income families. As a result, the housing in many of these so-called 'gray areas' will gradually shift to the market for either complete redevelopment or occupancy by lower-income groups, particularly nonwhites" (Downs 1964:4). His general predictions about neighborhoods with aging housing stock have come to pass, even though he did not foresee how the category "nonwhites" would expand significantly as a result of the 1965 Immigration Law and the 1980 Refugee Act.

Historical Processes and Demographic Changes

Back in 1907, the completion of the Ravenswood Elevated public transportation line that terminated at the Lawrence and Kimball intersection at the center of Albany Park stimulated a building boom, and the population grew at a stunning rate (see table 3.1). Population growth and housing construction continued apace into the "roaring twenties." The building boom was over by 1930 and the Great Depression of that decade: "by 1924 Albany Park reached residential maturity. Since 1930 there has been little residential development, and, in fact, after a slight increase in population during the 1930s, the community has lost population" (Albany Park Community Area 1982:17).

Throughout much of the twentieth century, Albany Park could be characterized, in the words of one resident, as "a step-up-and-then-out" community. After 1912 Russian Jewish immigrants augmented the original population of Swedes, Germans, and Irish. By 1930 Russian Jews were the majority among

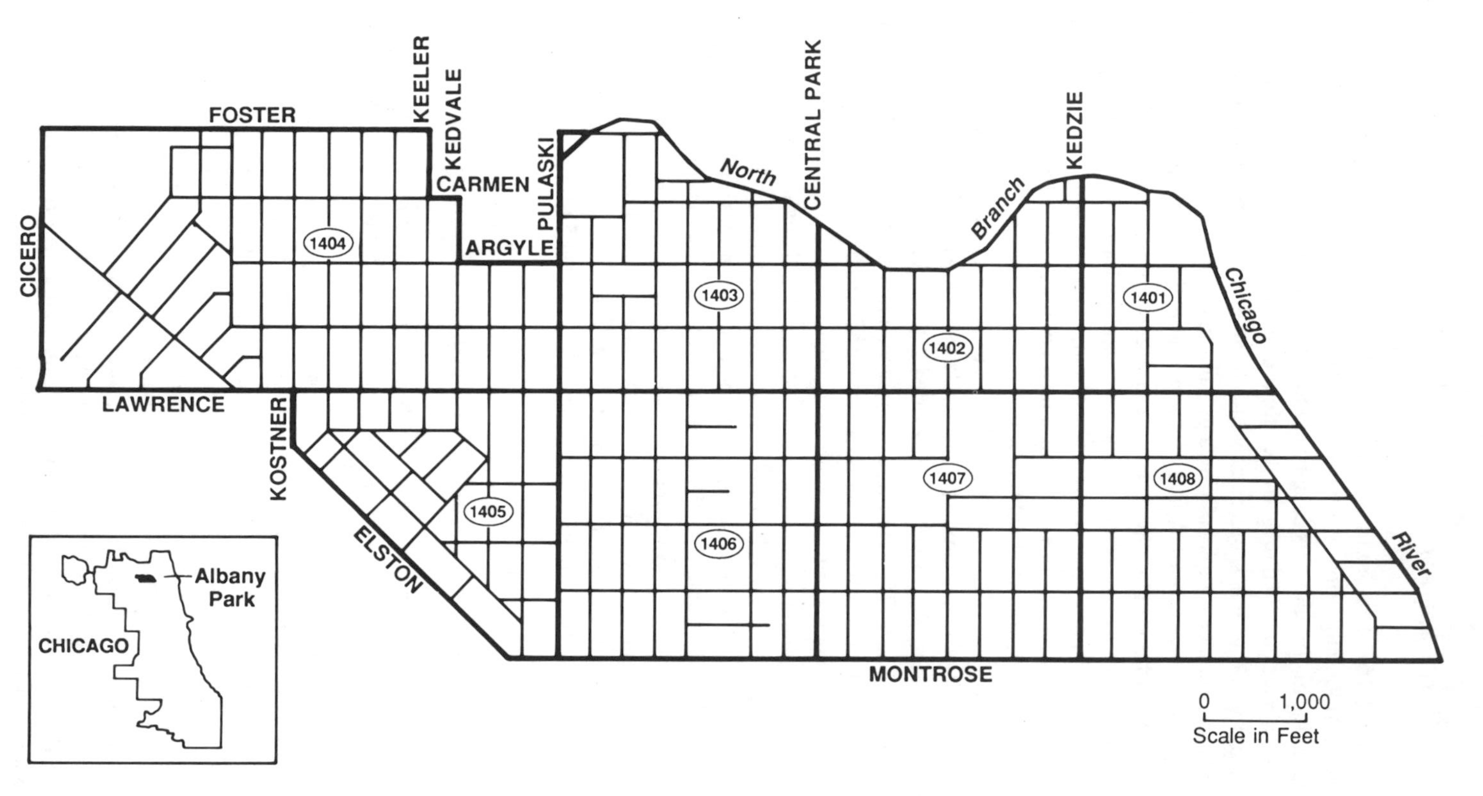

Figure 3.1. Community Area 14, Albany Park

Table 3.1. Albany Park Population, 1910–90

Year	Total Population	Year	Total Population
1910	7,000*	1960	49,450
1920	26,076	1970	47,092
1930	55,577	1980	46,075
1940	56,692	1990	49,501
1950	52,995		

Sources: U.S. Bureau of the Census; *Local Community Fact Book: Chicago Methropolitan Area, 1980.*
*Estimated

foreign-born whites. In 1934, when the population of 55,822 had almost reached its zenith (see table 3.1), it was almost 100 percent white. There were 43 listed under "Negro" and 43 listed under "Other." It was a community predominantly of first- and second-generation immigrants: 27.4 percent foreign-born white, and 43.8 percent native white of mixed or foreign-born parents, according to "Population and Family Numbers."[2]

An uncatalogued archival paper in the Albany Park Branch of the Chicago Public Library dating from the 1960s, "Changes in Population in Albany Park Area," interpretively summarizes the history of Albany Park's transitional population:

> Presently Alb Pk. [sic] is in the midst of the second population change since the war and its third in the last 40 years. Original settlement was Scandinavian, German and English. In the 1920's and 1930's a middle class Jewish population came in and was succeeded by a lower income Jewish population. Now a non-Jewish population is moving in and the Jewish population is moving away. Population is now mostly either middle aged or older. Few young families come into the area. . . . Between the years 1950 and 1960 Albany Park lost 30% of its child-bearing population. Community now has a larger number in proportion of older women. Young people are of high school and college age and will be marrying and moving away during the next few years. This makes an unstable community.

From 1940 to 1980 the population of Albany Park declined 18.7 percent, but during the 1980s it grew 7.4 percent (see table 3.1).

Moreover, the ethnic diversity of the neighborhood increased dramatically

2. Uncatalogued archival material, Chicago Public Library, Albany Park Branch. Scattered throughout the Albany Park Branch Library in file cabinets and desk drawers are minutes of committee meetings, North River Commission memoranda, old newspaper clippings and photographs, flyers and leaflets, and unpublished reports from key neighborhood institutions and groups. I am grateful to the librarians who helped me locate these materials.

Table 3.2. Albany Park Population by Race and Ethnicity, 1970–90

Year	Total	White	Black	Latino	Amer Indian	Asian	Other
1970	47,092	45,969	30	2,852	86	875	132
1980	46,075	34,070	279	9,074	257	6,502	4,967
1990	49,501	20,458	1,681	15,738	212	11,939	132

Source: U.S. Bureau of the Census.

during the decade of the 1980s. From an immigrant but overwhelmingly white neighborhood, Albany Park has changed to a neighborhood with a majority of nonwhites during the 1980s. At the same time that the total population of the neighborhood boomed 7.4 percent, the number of whites declined 40 percent, blacks increased 500 percent, Latinos increased 73.4 percent, and Asians increased 83.6 percent (tables 3.2, 3.3). According to the 1990 census figures, African Americans now make up 3.4 percent, Latinos 31.8 percent, and Asians 24.1 percent of the population of Albany Park (see Hinz 1991a). With twice as many Asians as in Chinatown on the near South Side, Albany Park is now the city's biggest Asian neighborhood (Quinlan 1991).[3]

The total population of Chicago declined 7.4 percent. The number of whites declined 20.1 percent, blacks declined 8.4 percent, Latinos increased 29.3 percent, and Asians increased 41.2 percent. Although in 1980 Chicago already had a majority of minorities, by 1990 whites had slipped from being the predominant group for the first time since the city was founded (see table 3.4).

Demographic data from the neighborhood schools vividly reflect the outmigration of the Jewish population in the 1960s and early 1970s and the arrival of new immigrants and refugees. In 1959 Roosevelt High School had been 70 percent Jewish; in 1965 it was still 60 percent Jewish ("Schools," n.d., uncatalogued archive, Albany Park Branch Library). By 1988, however, Roosevelt High School was 39.17 percent Latino, 24.01 percent white, 22.29 percent Asian, and 14.2 percent black.[4] This pattern intensifies at the level of a feeder elementary school. In 1959 Hibbard Elementary School had been 95 percent Jewish, and in 1965 it was 80 percent Jewish ("Schools," n.d., uncatalogued archive, Albany Park Branch Library). Although I do not have precise 1988 data for Hibbard, its students are overwhelmingly new immigrants, with more than fifty languages and dialects spoken.

The middle-class Jewish population has been replaced not only by immigrants and refugees from all over the world but also by a large number of Appalachian and working-class whites (Royer 1984:37). Public Aid statistics

3. The "Asian" category includes Middle Easterners.

4. "Racial and Ethnic Composition, Roosevelt High School," Chicago Public School System, unpublished report.

Table 3.3. Ethnic Composition of Albany Park by Census Tract, 1970–90

Census Tract	Year	Total	White	Black	Latino	Asian
1401	1970	3,762	82%	0.2%	14%	3.8%
	1980	4,096	28.4%	1.7%	27.6%	42.3%
	1990	3,987	23%	6.7%	34.9%	35.4%
1402	1970	5,270	88.9%	0%	8.6%	2.5%
	1980	5,499	44.5%	0.8%	20.5%	34.2%
	1990	5,873	31.3%	5.1%	27.8%	35.8%
1403	1970	6,217	93.1%	0.1%	4%	2.8%
	1980	6,352	66%	0.5%	16.2%	27.3%
	1990	6,944	37.8%	1.9%	25.9%	34.4%
1404	1970	6,123	98.4%	0%	1%	0.6%
	1980	5,467	91.2%	0%	3.5%	5.3%
	1990	5,479	78.2%	0.1%	9%	12.7
1405	1970	3,398	98.2%	0%	1.2%	0.6%
	1980	2,946	84.9%	0%	7%	8.1%
	1990	3,044	71.5%	0.6%	17.6%	10.3
1406	1970	7,326	92.1%	0%	5.7%	2.2%
	1980	6,904	59.1%	0.7%	17.9%	22.3%
	1990	8,011	39.3%	3.2%	34.5%	23%
1407	1970	7,724	91.2%	0.1%	6.4%	2.3%
	1980	7,640	40.1%	0.8%	28.2%	30.9%
	1990	8,782	29.8%	3.4%	47.1%	19.7%
1408	1970	7,272	88%	0.1%	8.5%	3.4%
	1980	7,171	44.5%	0.3%	27.9%	27.3%
	1990	7,381	39.1%	2.8%	40.4%	19.7%

Sources: U.S. Bureau of the Census; *Local Community Fact Book: Chicago Metropolitan Area, 1980.*

Table 3.4. Chicago's Population by Race and Ethnicity, 1950–90

Year	White	Black	Latino	Asian	All Races
1950	3,078,110	492,265	33,415	17,172	3,620,962
1960	2,602,748	812,637	110,000	25,019	3,550,404
1970	1,977,280	1,102,620	247,343	42,116	3,369,359
1980	1,321,359	1,187,905	422,063	73,745	3,005,072
1990	1,056,048	1,087,711	545,852	104,118	2,783,726

Source: U.S. Bureau of the Census.
Note: The total for all races is not necessarily the total for the other four categories since some individuals may be counted in two columns.

Table 3.5. Ethnic Composition of Chicago, Albany Park, and Census Tract 1401,* 1970–90

	White (%)	Black (%)	Latino (%)	Asian (%)
Chicago				
1970	59	33	7	1
1980	44	39	14	3
1990	38	39	19	4
Albany Park				
1970	91.5	0.1	6.1	2.3
1980	65	0.6	20	14
1990	40.7	3.4	31.8	24.1
Census Tract 1401*				
1970	82	0.2	14	3.8
1980	28.4	1.7	27.6	42.3
1990	23	6.7	34.9	35.4

Sources: U.S. Bureau of the Census; *Local Community Fact Book: Chicago Metropolitan Area 1980.*
*The "Little Beirut" area where Big Red is located.

show that whites living in census tracts dominated by nonwhites receive public assistance in disproportionate numbers to their percentage of the population. Three tracts illustrate this pattern: in Census Tract 1401, whites represent 20 percent of the population and 31 percent of Public Aid recipients; in 1403, whites represent 38 percent of the population and 57 percent of Public Aid recipients; in 1407 whites represent 27 percent of the population and 42 percent of Public Aid recipients.[5] Whites in Albany Park have a fertility rate of 70, compared to the citywide fertility rate of 52 for whites. Albany Park ranks ninth among Chicago's seventy-seven neighborhoods in the fertility rate of white women, and demographers connect high fertility rate among white women with low level of education (Bousfield 1989:16–18).

The northeast corner of Albany Park, Census Tract 1401 (known on the streets as "Little Beirut") has been the vanguard of Albany Park's demographic change (see map and tables 3.3, 3.5, 3.6). Little Beirut has the greatest population diversity, density, and residential deterioration in Albany Park. With its high concentration of large, multiunit apartment buildings owned by absentee landlords, it is the gateway for new immigrants into Albany Park. In 1970, Little Beirut was 36.1 percent foreign-born, compared to 22.2 percent for Albany Park as a whole. In 1980, 54 percent of the Little Beirut population was foreign-born, compared to 36.3 percent for Albany Park (Royer 1984:36). The Latino population of Albany Park—now quickly closing the gap with whites (table 3.5)—settled first in Little Beirut. Even though Census Tract 1407, the

5. I am grateful to Marie V. Bousfield, city demographer for Chicago, Department of Planning, for access to these unpublished data.

most populous in Albany Park, now has the highest percentage of Latinos, 47.1 percent, in 1970 it had only 6.4 percent, compared to 14 percent Latino in Little Beirut. In 1970, when Albany Park was only 8.5 percent nonwhite, Little Beirut was 18 percent nonwhite. Viewed in light of Albany Park changes over time, Little Beirut has been a bellwether more than an anomaly. Perhaps that is why it commands such interest from established residents; more than just a dramatic contrast, it functions as an augury of things to come.

Viewed within the "ethnographic present," however, Little Beirut appears to be the extreme case, even within a demographically interesting neighborhood like Albany Park. Whereas census figures for Albany Park reflect a fall in white population, from 91.5 percent in 1970 to 40.7 percent in 1990, whites in 1990 are still the largest group overall. In Little Beirut, however, whites, at 23 percent, are ranked third—behind Asians, who are the largest group with 35.4 percent, followed closely by Latinos with 34.9 percent of the 1990 population. Little Beirut has the largest concentration of African Americans, 6.7 percent of the population, compared to 3.4 percent for Albany Park as a whole (see table 3.5). Little Beirut had a higher percentage of Asians than any other census tract in the city, except two in Chinatown (Flores, Bousfield, and Chin 1990:19). According to 1990 census figures, however, Census Tract 1402, immediately east of Little Beirut, now has a higher percentage of Asians (see table 3.3).

Table 3.6. Census Tract 1401* Births by Ethnicity, 1979–87

Year	Total	White	Black	Latino	Asian	Am. In.	Unknown
1979	104	34	2	32	35		1
%		32.69	1.92	30.77	33.65		.96
1980	114	44	2	38	29	1	
%		38.6	1.75	33.33	25.44	.88	
1981	117	40	2	41	31	3	
%		34.19	1.71	35.04	26.5	2.56	
1982	108	31	5	32	39	1	
%		28.7	4.63	29.63	36.1	.93	
1983	128	41	8	42	36	1	
%		32.03	6.25	32.81	28.13	.78	
1984	129	33	11	34	49	2	
%		25.58	8.53	26.36	37.99	1.55	
1985	122	30	12	21	59		
%		24.59	9.84	17.21	48.36		
1986	115	30	10	19	55	1	
%		26.09	8.7	16.52	47.83	.87	
1987	104	22	13	28	38	2	1
%		21.15	12.5	26.92	36.54	1.92	.96

Source: City of Chicago, Department of Planning. I am grateful to Marie V. Bousfield, City Demographer, for releasing these unpublished data.
*The "Little Beirut" area where Big Red is located.

Little Beirut has the highest percentage of Public Aid recipients among Albany Park's eight census tracts: 13.19 percent, compared to 7.89 percent for Albany Park (see table 3.7). In 1980, only 15.9 percent of its housing units were owner-occupied, compared to 31.8 percent for Albany Park. The rate of overcrowding (more than one person per room)—perhaps the statistic most revealing of poverty—is 20.1 percent in Little Beirut, compared to 9 percent for Albany Park as a whole.

Middle-class white residents define Little Beirut as the alien, threatening "Other" of Albany Park. Here is the interpretive assessment of a young Jewish real estate agent, the grandson of longtime residents of Albany Park, who now works there:

> That's a war zone. That's the nastiest area in Albany Park. You don't even want to be there at night. Shit—that's the worst. All those big rental units—no one has a commitment to the property. I almost sold a two-unit on Ainslie. We were ready to close, a Vietnamese woman. But she had a brother who lived in the area. She said she just wanted to check with him before she closed on the deal. Oh man! He told her, "Don't even consider it. Don't even think about it. You don't want to even think about being here at night."

A municipal report describes Little Beirut thus: "Housing conditions . . . are poor, and this area has physically declined. Deferred maintenance, disinvestment and the deterioration of Kedzie Avenue have created the perception that this is not a good place to live. Gang related incidents and graffiti reinforce this image" (Albany Park Community Area 1982:40). A white policeman confided: "Let me put it to you this way: I'm carrying a gun, and I wouldn't come into this

Table 3.7. Percent of Albany Park Population on Public Assistance* by Census Tract, 1988

Census Tract	%	Census Tract	%
1401	13.19	1405	4.21
1402	12.85	1406	7.83
1403	7.21	1407	8.16
1404	2.12	1408	6.85
Albany Park		7.89%	

*Total Public Aid Cases.

Sources: I am grateful to Marie V. Bousfield, City Demographer for Chicago, for releasing the unpublished data on Public Aid Cases by census tract for 1988. The population estimates for 1988 were taken from *Areas at Risk: Chicago's Potential Undercount in the 1990 Census,* City of Chicago, Department of Planning, March 1990.

area after dark if I didn't have to." His partner described Little Beirut as "the armpit of the district."

Established residents cast their positive images of Albany Park against the negative Other of Little Beirut and, by extension, Big Red. Through synecdochic extensions, Little Beirut absorbs and intensifies most of the tensions reverberating around the historic transformations of Albany Park. Little Beirut is on the edge of Albany Park, literally and figuratively, and the edges, margins, and borders of a culture are always intensely contested zones charged with power and danger (Douglas 1966; Bakhtin 1986). People need concrete symbols through which they can grasp elusive meanings and discharge deep and contradictory feelings. Big Red is a particularly powerful symbol for the middle class, because it cathects property and people. The disturbing signifying powers of Big Red contradict other signs of neighborhood revitalization.

Commercial and Economic Development

Established residents formed the North River Commission (NRC)[6] in 1962 out of three powerful community institutions—Swedish Covenant Hospital, North Park College and Seminary (the Swedish Covenant Church), and Albany Park Bank—to forestall neighborhood decline and decay that was already evident. In the late 1970s, Albany Park hit bottom. In 1977 there was a 29 percent vacancy rate on the commercial strip, which included seven adult bookstores, three massage parlors, an X-rated movie theater, and a predominance of used-furniture and secondhand thrift stores. The number of home sales plunged from 1,122 in 1979 to 580 in 1980. In 1977, however, the Lawrence Avenue Development Corporation (LADCOR), an arm of NRC, invented the Streetscape Program and persuaded the city of Chicago to fund it. In 1978 Lawrence Avenue became the first commercial area in Chicago under this program to receive new trees, street and pedestrian lights, and benches without advertisements at a cost of more than $7 million to the city (Corral 1990:15).

In 1981 LADCOR spurred the city to launch the Facade Rebate Program. The plan provides a 30 percent cash rebate for property owners or tenants who renovate storefronts in accordance with guidelines set by LADCOR and the city. In Albany Park, 192 of 750 storefronts have been renovated through this program, representing $2.5 million in storefront improvements. No other neighborhood in the city even comes close to matching Albany Park's participation in the Facade Rebate Program. Other commercial strips such as Howard Street and Devon Avenue to the north have renovated ten to twenty storefronts through this program ("Looking Good Getting Tougher," *News Star,* 29 August 1989, p. 1).

Strategically planned large-scale commercial developments followed the success of the Streetscape and Facade Rebate programs. The Albany Park

6. For a history of NRC, see Suttles 1990:115–18.

Shopping Center at the run-down intersection of Lawrence and Kedzie avenues opened in February 1987, creating more than eighty jobs. In September 1988, two blocks west at the corner of Lawrence and Kimball avenues, Kimball Plaza opened with another eighty jobs. In February 1989 Dominick's Finer Foods opened at the corner of Lawrence Avenue and Pulaski Road (an area previously described as an eyesore), creating more than 350 jobs. In May 1990, Albany Plaza Shopping Center opened on the 4900 block of Kedzie, the block immediately north of Albany Park Shopping Center, bringing another eighty jobs (Corral 1990:16).

The revitalization of the Lawrence Avenue commercial strip has been a remarkable success. By 1988 the Albany Park community area was generating $8.3 million annually in federal income taxes, more than $900,000 in state income and sales taxes, and more than $180,000 in local taxes (Corral 1990:16). In 1987 there were 541 bank loans totaling $41 million. This level of bank lending compares favorably with those of three other ethnically diverse North Side neighborhoods: Rogers Park, 456 loans totaling $46.3 million; Uptown, 458 loans totaling $45.5 million; Lincoln Square, 455 loans totaling $36.3 million. There is a big difference, however, when one compares Albany Park to an affluent neighborhood like Lincoln Park: 1,655 loans totaling $229.8 million (Kerson 1990:88).

The annual number of residential sales has climbed 125 percent, from a 1980 low of 580 to a 1989 high of 1,307 (Corral 1990:27). The average value of an Albany Park house in 1990 is $94,976, a 62.54 percent increase over the 1980 overage of $59,395. Within Albany Park considerable variation in housing stock has developed, particularly if one looks at Ravenswood Manor, an insulated "yuppie" corridor in the southeast corner of Albany Park between Sacramento Street and the river; there the average value of a house jumps to $188,931, nearly double the rest of Albany Park (Meyers and DeBat 1990:41).

The dramatic turnaround of Albany Park's shopping district during the 1980s coincided with a startling climb in the number of jobs in the larger Chicago area. As reported in the *Chicago Tribune* on April 22, 1990, "Between 1986 and 1989, the Chicago area racked up a stunning increase of 12.8 percent in jobs, the region's longest and largest sustained upturn in employment in more than two decades" (Goozner 1990:1). The number of jobs in the six-county Chicago area reached just under 3 million in March 1989, an increase of 340,000 jobs since March 1986. The biggest gains were in the suburban counties, but Chicago added more than 56,000 jobs to bring city employment to 1.18 million, the highest level since 1981. This increase reflects a growth rate of 5 percent (Goozner 1990:1). Nearly half of all new jobs are concentrated in what is called the Super Loop, the downtown area and the areas immediately north along the river and Michigan Avenue (Goozner 1990:8).

Community leaders link the health of a neighborhood's commercial strip to the condition of its housing stock. The executive director of the powerful NRC explains the theory behind the redevelopment of Albany Park:

> Twelve years ago, the officers and volunteers of the North River Commission advanced a premise, then unknown and immediately ridiculed. That premise was that older, lower income, predominantly multi-family areas that suffer from slum and blighted conditions, do so beginning with the commercial strip or main street of the area. Up until then, the accepted wisdom was that decay began with deferred maintenance and ultimately abandonment of large multi-family buildings. . . . Our conclusion was that if you successfully change the look of the main street from decay to prosperity, and if you provide hundreds and even thousands of employment opportunities, then the housing market can be stimulated into rehabilitation. (Cicero 1988:8)

The NRC "premise" takes what a poststructuralist would call a social semiotic approach, which situates housing within a web of interactive signifying practices arising from and feeding back into a matrix of political-economic power. Altering the signifiers in one venue has consequences for another domain. Changing "the look of the main street from decay to prosperity" stimulates the "rehabilitation" of "slum and blighted conditions" along the residential side streets. "Every text, being itself the intertext of another text," Barthes affirms, "belongs to the intertextual" (1979:77; see also Hodge and Kress 1988).

Just one-half block north of the renovated facades of the commercially revitalized Lawrence Avenue, and only two streets west of affluent Ravenswood Manor, stands Big Red. Located on Albany Street, and officially named "Albany Apartments," the sprawling red-brick building opposes the official image of Albany Park. It belies the shopkeeper prosperity of Lawrence Avenue and threatens the "suburb within the city" tranquillity of Ravenswood Manor. Weighted down with history, Big Red is a drag on the development programs that attempt to disconnect or erase the past and to propel Albany Park towards a bullish future. Behind the incompletely and ambivalently achieved "streetscape" program, Big Red stubbornly presents other signs, other meanings about Albany Park. Big Red disrupts the discourse of success and revitalization. It challenges the ideology of progress and development. Its deteriorated structure overflows with a mix of poor Third World refugees and migrants alongside working-class African Americans and Appalachians. It stands as a document of the geopolitical and political-economic structures—of violence and oppression—that caused such a heteroglot group of people to ricochet from their multiple respective homelands and re-collect themselves in a dilapidated tenement side by side with this country's socioeconomically displaced and marginalized people. "Within an ever more integrated world," Eric Wolf observes, "we witness the growth of ever more diverse proletarian diasporas" (Wolf 1982:383).

Dwelling within Big Red

Everyday life invents itself by poaching *in countless ways on the property of others.*

MICHEL DE CERTEAU, *THE PRACTICE OF EVERYDAY LIFE* (1984)

I moved into Big Red in December 1987 in order to begin research for the Changing Relations Ford Foundation project.[7] At the time I moved in to the A2r apartment, previously occupied by an Assyrian family, I was the second white resident. An elderly Jewish man lived in C2L. The ethnic breakdown for the other 35 units was 11 Hmong, 10 Mexican, 10 Assyrian, 2 Sino-Cambodian, 1 Puerto Rican, and 1 Puerto Rican–Mexican mixed (see figure 3.2). During the twenty months I lived in Big Red, the ethnic mix was enriched by African Americans, Appalachian whites, more Puerto Ricans, and new immigrant Poles (see figure 3.3). I lived in Big Red until the end of August 1989, when along with all my A stairwell neighbors I was displaced and that wing of Big Red was boarded up. I rented an apartment just one block north of Big Red and continue to live in Little Beirut and interact with my Big Red networks at the time of this writing.[8]

Initial inquiries about renting an apartment pulled me immediately into interactions with other tenants. Beyond the "Apartment for Rent" sign, there was no formal assistance for prospective tenants: no rental office, telephone number, or agency address. Yet every vestibule and stairwell was unlocked, open, and filled with friendly people. All the business of renting the apartment was conducted informally, through face-to-face interactions with other residents. In twenty months, I never signed or saw a lease. It was a few months before I actually saw the absentee owner. The word-of-mouth way of getting information brought me into contact with a number of neighbors who graciously shared with me what they knew and ventured outside in the bitter chill of Chicago December nights to track down the janitor. Sometimes we would find the janitor, sometimes we would not: he held down another full-time job in order to make ends meet. Sometimes when we found him he would not have the keys.

From one perspective, the rental management of Big Red was highly ineffi-

7. The Northwestern colleagues with whom I worked on the Ford Foundation Changing Relations Project were Paul Friesema, Jane Mansbridge, and Al Hunter, assisted by graduate students Mary Erdmans, Jeremy Hein, Yvonne Newsome, and Yung-Sun Park. I wish to acknowledge support from the Ford Foundation, which funded the Changing Relations project through the Research Foundation of the State University of New York, Grant 240-1117-A. The Center for Urban Affairs and Policy Research (CUAPR) at Northwestern University facilitated the work of the Chicago team of the Changing Relations project, I thank the staff of CUAPR for their expertise and cheerful support. I am particularly grateful to my colleague Jane Mansbridge, who carefully read earlier drafts of this chapter and offered many helpful criticisms and suggestions.

8. The conditions and people of Big Red can be seen in segments of two documentaries: *America Becoming*, produced by Dai-Sil Kim-Gibson for the Ford Foundation, and *The Heart Broken in Half*, produced and directed by Taggart Siegel and Dwight Conquergood.

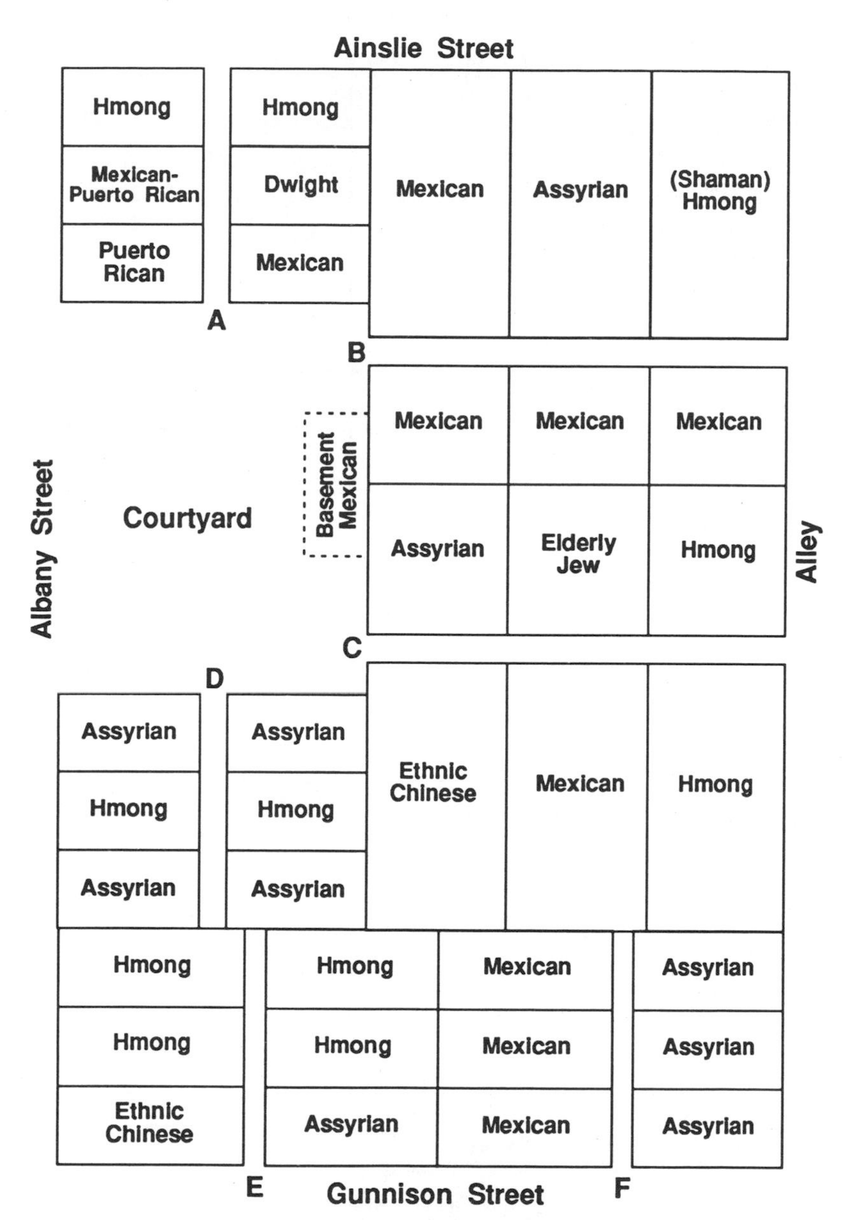

Figure 3.2. Big Red ethnic makeup, December 1988

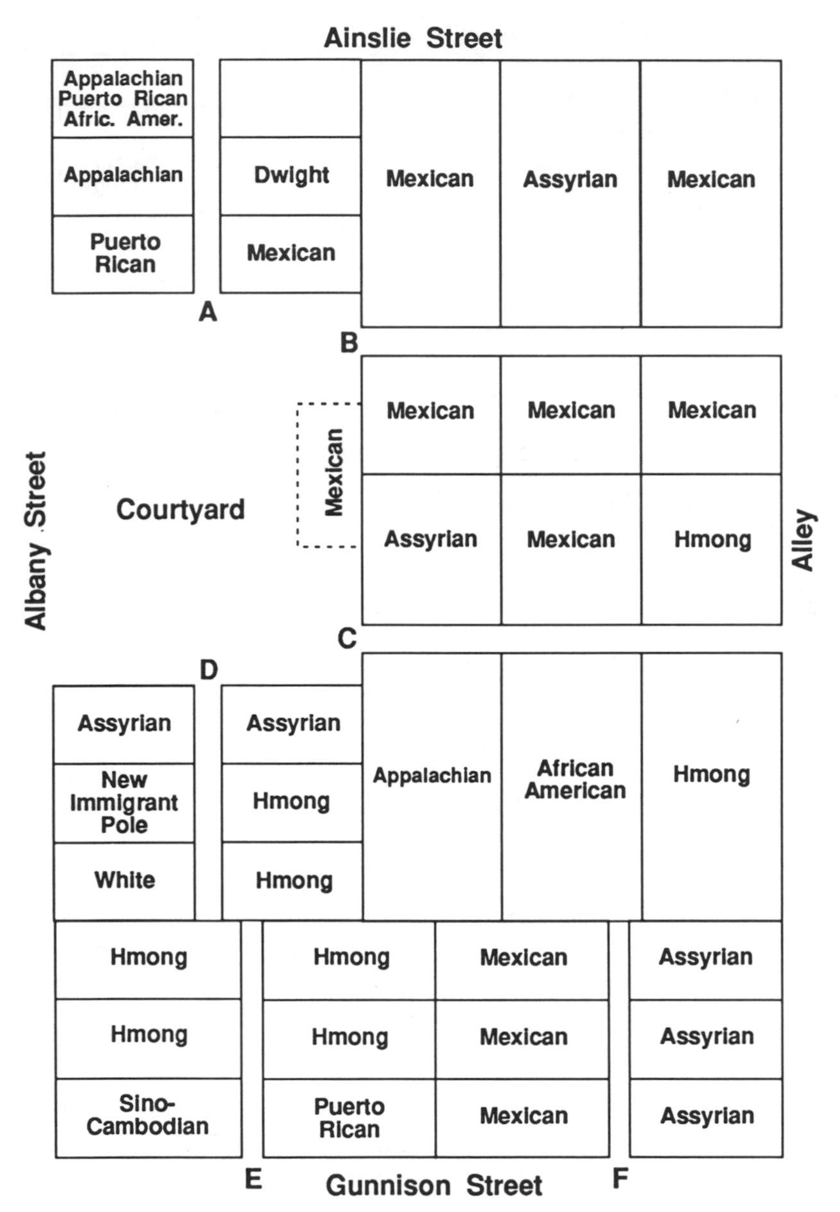

Figure 3.3. Big Red ethnic makeup, summer 1989

cient and required unnecessary trips, long waits, and delays. On the other hand, the absence of a managing authority made all the residents interdependent. By the time I was ready to move in, I was on friendly terms with several neighbors and had received offers of help with the move, including the loan of a car.

The physical dilapidation of Big Red is even more apparent from the inside than the outside, but it is mitigated by the warmth and friendliness of the people. Indeed, the chronic state of disrepair, breakdowns, and emergencies requires for survival a neighborly interdependence unheard-of in efficiently managed middle-class properties. Crises create community, but this is particularly true when the crisis relates to physical space that people share over time. When the plumbing on the third floor leaks through the second floor ceiling with every toilet flush, the residents of those two floors get to know one another in intimate ways.

It is the human quality of life in Big Red that eludes outsiders. The following NRC memo (1989) captures coldly the physical state of disrepair in Big Red. Even though it notes that "the building is currently fully occupied by low-income families," it discursively evacuates the human element, forgetting that people transform a tenement into a home:

> Due to neglect by the previous owners over the past 15 years, the property has declined into a critical state of deterioration. The building has suffered severely from a lack of any capital improvements. The mechanical systems are only partially operative or not performing at all. Prior attempts at building security have been feeble so that the apartments and common areas are open to abuse by anyone willing to gain access. The major apartment components are functionally obsolete and that, coupled with cosmetic neglect, greatly limits the marketability of the apartments and presents potential health and safety hazards. A few recent examples include a total lack of hot water, the collapsing of a back porch, rats and roach infestation, and small arson fires in the vestibules.

From the inside, one gets a more detailed experience of the building's deterioration, but that is complemented with a complex understanding of how people maintain human dignity within difficult structures. A casual inspection would reveal scores of housing-ordinance violations but might not capture their meaning in the day-to-day lives of the urban working class and under- and unemployed. The children complain of mice in their beds. Housewives trade stories of "roaches in my refrigerator." They make stoic jokes about this indignity, dubbing them "Eskimo roaches." They say that the roaches move more slowly but can survive in the cold, "just like Eskimos." One day I opened my refrigerator and discovered a mouse scurrying around inside. The refrigerator was decrepit, and the door did not always stay shut. There were jokes about "super-rats" so big that the traps would have to be "anchored." These and other vermin stories about aggressive mice and flying cockroaches resemble "fish stories."

Through exaggeration and shared laughter they made the situation more bearable.

Minor disasters related to the dilapidation of Big Red brought residents together across ethnic lines. In early July, 1988, Shajiba, an Assyrian mother of four from across the courtyard, stepped into her bathtub and the bathroom ceiling fell on her head. Not just some falling plaster, the entire ceiling rotted out and collapsed around her. Her husband, Daniel, ran to summon me. By the time I arrived, several neighbors had gathered in the bathroom to witness this most recent outrage. They asked me to take pictures of the bathroom with its debris-filled bathtub.

Almost every household had its own disaster tale. The neighbors did not search for small talk about the weather when they met in the stairwells, courtyards, and open back porches. They exchanged intimate, urgent concerns about shared hardships in Big Red. They inquired whether the Younans' (Assyrian) toilet still overflowed every time it was flushed, whether Bravo Xiong's (Hmong) ceiling had leaked during last night's rain, whether Mrs. Montalvo (Mexican) and her five children had a refrigerator yet. And there was the problem of the sweatshop operating out of the basement. When filling rush orders for surgical scrub suits, the Cambodian women worked all night, keeping some of the neighbors awake. Scraps from the sweatshop filled one of the two building dumpsters, aggravating the garbage-collection problem. The physical hardships and indignities of life in Big Red created a common experience and shared understanding that united the diverse ethnic groups. Coping strategies were the topics for talk among the residents of Big Red.

To limit the story of Big Red to appalling physical conditions would be misleading. Michel de Certeau in *The Practice of Everyday Life* investigates the creative and manifold "tactics" ordinary people use to resist the "strategies" of the strong—the hegemonic forces of governments, armies, institutions, and landlords. He illuminates the myriad ways vulnerable people "operate" within dominant structures and constraints, what he calls "the art of making do." To illustrate his intellectual project, he uses the metaphor of "dwelling":

> Thus a North African living in Paris or Roubaix [France] insinuates *into* the system imposed on him by the construction of a low-income housing development or of the French language the ways of "dwelling" (in a house or a language) peculiar to his native Kabylia. He superimposes them, and, by that combination, creates for himself a space in which he can find *ways of using* the constraining order of the place or of the language. Without leaving the place where he has no choice but to live and which lays down its law for him, he establishes within it a degree of *plurality* and creativity. By an art of being in between, he draws unexpected results from his situation. (de Certeau 1984:30)

Even highly vulnerable people are not simply contained by the structures, both physical and socioeconomic, within which they find themselves. Through imagination and human energy they contest and create "dwelling spaces" inside even forbidding structures.

The tenants of Big Red exploited the marginality, illegalities, and transgressive nature of Big Red in manifold ways. They turned the owner's negligence, which bordered on the criminal, to their advantage. While they suffered, to be sure, from the owner's neglect and lack of building maintenance, they also used his irresponsibility to circumvent typical middle-class restrictions, rules, and "tastes" pertaining to residential life, such as in the use of stairwells, courtyards, and alleys. Hmong women roped off a section of the front courtyard and planted a vegetable garden during the summer of 1988. The rest of the courtyard was an intensively used social space: the center was a playground for a group I will call the Courtyard Kids, while the fence between sidewalk and courtyard served as a volleyball net for teenage girls. The back area bordering on the alley was converted into an unofficial parking lot and open-air garage for working on old cars that were always in need of repair. Some back stairwells were used to sell drugs during the summer of 1989, when dealers set up operations in two Big Red apartments.

The back area also was used for weekend *bracero* alley parties. Whereas the courtyard and front sidewalk of Big Red were informally designated spaces for the evening sociability of women and children, the back alley, at night and on weekends, was a masculine space, so marked by one section of the back wall used as a urinal. This was the time when *braceros* shared the price of a case of beer, with a sensitively enforced code that those who were unemployed or newly arrived would be graciously exempted from any pressure to contribute. For those holding jobs, it was a source of esteem to assume a greater responsibility for financing these parties. This was a time for dramatizing the hardy manliness of their jobs by complaining about sore backs, tight muscles, blisters, and cut hands. Friendship networks of exchange and sharing developed at these alley parties. It was a sign of my acceptance when I first was invited to join these parties and then allowed, after initial protest, to contribute to the cost of a case of beer. Soon afterward, the three neighbors who worked at the Easy Spuds potato-chip factory began offering me free sacks of potatoes that they brought from work. Both the tools and the labor that helped me mount the steel security gate across my back door came from contacts made at the *bracero* parties. The front stairwells and lobbies were prime sites for display of gang graffiti, and during the winter the stairwells were used as spillover rooms for social drinking, talk, and smoking. In some respects, the residents had more autonomy and scope for use of Big Red than would have been possible within a better maintained, middle-class building.

The Courtyard Kids

De Certeau's discussion of spatial practices is eloquently apt for the Courtyard Kids: "To practice space is thus to repeat the joyful and silent experience of childhood; it is in a place *to be other and to move toward the other*" (1984:110, emphasis in original). Big Red lacks many material amenities but is rich in children. Its families typically are large. For example, I shared my stairwell with two families with six children each, two families with four children each, and another family with three children. Mrs. Gutierrez, who lived in my stairwell, had reared nine children in Big Red; all of them visited frequently with a retinue of grandchildren in tow. Across the courtyard, an Assyrian family had ten children.

Children naturally are threshold-crossers and boundary-blurrers. Curious, inquisitive, spared the self-consciousness that descends at adolescence, children are most open to others. Although there was a great deal of interaction among all the groups within Big Red, the free-for-all mingling of ethnicities was most intense among the Courtyard Kids, even when they played up the block at River Park.

The courtyard, extending into surrounding sidewalks and the street, was their space. There were no Nintendos in Big Red. As apartments were crowded and without air conditioning, the courtyard was far more inviting and exciting than any private apartment. In the shared public space of the courtyard, twenty to thirty kids, sometimes more, could organize games of dodgeball or improvise mud fights. Even in the cold Chicago winters, the courtyard was the place where the children of Big Red passed the time, throwing snowballs and building snowmen (see Suttles 1968:75–77).

What few toys or items of sports equipment the children possessed, they shared with the group. The one football in all of Big Red belonged to a little Hmong boy in my stairwell. This football was enjoyed by all the children in hotly contested courtyard games between "Assyria" and "Chinatown." Actually, the team on which one played had more to do with the time one joined the game than ethnicity. Mexicans, Puerto Ricans, whites, Cambodians, Assyrians, African Americans—all played interchangeably for "Assyria" or "Chinatown." Mothers served as courtyard monitors, using English to resolve disputes in the larger group and using their native language when checking their own children. The mothers clustered at the sidelines and chatted among themselves while observing the play of the Courtyard Kids. Sometimes a mother would join a game as a player, particularly if there were no other women in the courtyard with whom to visit. Often I saw Mexican, Hmong, Assyrian, and (later during my tenure) Appalachian mothers visiting among themselves while sharing child-supervision responsibilities. Mothers also cooperated in feeding the hungry children after a period of vigorous play. As a result, the Hmong children were introduced to pita bread from the Assyrian households, and this be-

The Courtyard Kids (photograph by Dwight Conquergood)

came one of their favorite foods. One white mother of three who moved into Big Red in 1989 was quickly absorbed into the nurturing network constituted around the Courtyard Kids. She proudly remarked how all the kids called her Mom.

When an African-American family moved into Big Red during 1989, no one commented except white families. At first, an Appalachian family made some racist remarks, and the white mother whom all the Courtyard Kids called Mom joked that her mother had said, "Those Black kids better not start calling me grandma!" But her son soon started playing with the African-American child, and that opened up relations between the two households. The white family helped their African-American neighbors find a new job. The white and African-American fathers began working together on back-alley mechanical repairs for their weather-beaten cars. One day the white mother saw the eight-year-old African-American son doing some mischief, and she took him by the hand and returned him to his mother's apartment, where both women scolded him. On another occasion, passing through the alley, I saw the teenage son from the white family carrying sacks of groceries up the back stairwell and inside the apartment for the African-American family.

During the summer of 1988, there was only one bicycle in Big Red, and it was broken. The Courtyard Kids often talked wistfully about owning a bicycle. One kid told me that his father said that maybe when he graduated from eighth grade the family could afford a bicycle. In the meantime, the Courtyard Kids made do with taking turns riding Tony's borrowed bicycle. Tony (Assyrian), who lived across the street, was called "rich" because he owned both a bicycle and a skateboard.

The sixteen-year-old son of the white family that moved into Big Red during the winter of 1989 had "street connections" that opened up a source for used bicycles priced at ten dollars or less. By May 1989, every Courtyard Kid owned a bicycle. That summer the courtyard became the site of much bicycle trading and dealing. The wheeling and dealing in used bicycles drew in East Indian and Pakistani kids from across the street and Cambodian kids from around the corner, as well as a large circle of Latino, white, African-American, Assyrian, and Hmong children. The Courtyard Kids developed and honed entrepreneurial and mechanical skills as they swapped bikes and borrowed tools from neighbors to tear down bikes, trade parts, and customize their purchases. It was an exciting time. The courtyard was abuzz with the talk of bike culture: "wheelies," "ollies," "bunny-hops," "cherry-pickers," and "mags." Not only did all the Courtyard Kids own bicycles, but it seemed that each one owned a different bike each week. By the end of the summer of 1989, ten-year-old Stevie (Assyrian) had owned seven different bicycles.

It is not easy to raise a large family in the conditions of Little Beirut. Parents seek, share, and welcome help from others, particularly with the counsel, caregiving, and even disciplining of the children. Mrs. Gutierrez, referring to

African-American kids from across the street, represents the community pattern of shared parenting: "I feel sorry for them. They don't have any money. I talk to them like a mother. When they ask me for money, I say, 'You be good, I'll give you a quarter! But if I see you do something bad, no more quarters!' "

My rapport with many of the households was established through the nurturing network constituted around children. Men are important participants in this network as well as women. The *bracero* alley parties, for example, were off-limits to women, but children frequently inserted themselves briefly into the circle for a hug or a whisper before scurrying off with change to purchase a treat from the musical ice-cream trucks that ply the streets in the evening. As I passed through the courtyard daily and became a more familiar figure, the Courtyard Kids began calling out to me for acknowledgment, attention, and advice. They announced the news of the day and shared their successes and concerns: "Hey Mr. Dwight, it's my birthday today," "These are my cousins—they're living with us now because my uncle died," or "Mr. Dwight, Frankie failed second grade." Parents told me time and again to help them watch their children: "You see my kid do something wrong, catch him—talk to him." Courtyard Kids asked me to accompany them to school on the day parents were required to pick up report cards, so that their parents would not have to take off half a day from work. Several times I accompanied a mother to the school principal's office when a child was in trouble. I also went to the police station with (and sometimes without) the parents to sign out teenagers who had been picked up for misdemeanors. This nurturing network expresses one of the strongest ethics of Little Beirut culture: children are cherished. Gang leaders in the area affirmed the community norm: "We look out for the little kids; we be watching that nobody messes with the little kids."

Not counting middle-class residents, only one person ever complained about the Courtyard Kids and challenged their access to the courtyard. This example underscores the power of this norm, while demonstrating the scrappy resourcefulness of the Courtyard Kids. In the spring of 1989 the absentee landlord hired an Appalachian man as the new on-site janitor for Big Red. He had been a day laborer before he moved into Big Red and lobbied successfully for the job of janitor. He seized this opportunity to make something out of the position. One of his first acts was to buy (with his own money) a flashing neon sign that said "Building Manager" and mount it in his window. As a way of undercutting his pretensions, the residents nicknamed him Mr. Jethro, after the television character from "Beverly Hillbillies."

Although in his income level, dress, speech, and apartment decor Mr. Jethro was as far away from the middle class as any other Big Red resident, he had aspirations for finer things. He soon announced to everyone that he was "taking the building back." By that he meant that he would introduce more middle-class standards of taste and notions of public space. Entirely on his own initiative, and out of his meager wages, he bought "Keep off the Grass" signs and strung them with ropes around the courtyard. Next he mounted "No Parking" signs for the back alley. He roped off the intensively used social spaces by the back stairwells and the sites of evening *bracero* parties for his announced plans of cultivating grass and shrubs.

Soon Mr. Jethro entered into battle with the Courtyard Kids in his attempts to "take back" the courtyard and transform it into a lawn. The kids did not surrender their playground without a fight. They threw eggs at his window, set his door on fire twice, broke all the windows of his car, then dropped marbles into the oil spout and ruined the engine. He was not seen for two weeks; his wife explained that he was in bed "with the nerves." Then he emerged from his apartment one day, rallied, and one more time attempted to chase the kids off the grass. All of a sudden, Pit Bull's brother (Pit Bull is a well-known Puerto Rican gang member), with his namesake dog, bounded into the courtyard and menaced Mr. Jethro. Pit Bull's brother and other gang members warned Mr. Jethro about what would happen to his "skinny ass" if he ever mistreated the Courtyard Kids again. Mr. Jethro was admonished to fight like a man, if he wanted to fight, and that no man worth anything would yell at little kids. The gang members shoved Mr. Jethro around a little bit to clinch their point, then left.

At that moment, Mr. Jethro dropped his beautification campaign and became quite conciliatory toward the Courtyard Kids. On one of the hot Sundays later in the summer he hooked up a water sprinkler in the middle of the courtyard for the kids to run and splash through. He brought a lawn chair out to the sidewalk, where he spent a pleasant afternoon watching the kids cavort around the sprinkler. For the July Fourth weekend he mounted a huge American flag outside his front window and clamped a spotlight on the sill so that the flag was illuminated at night. Next to the flag he positioned a menu-board sign that he had purchased at a flea market with this lettered message: "Have a Happy and Safe Fourth of July Weekend."

The Art of Making Do: On Kinship, Kindness, and Caring

Tenants stretched scant resources by "doubling up," a common practice enabled by the irregular management of Big Red. In order to save money on rent, two or three families shared a single apartment. The one-bedroom apartment directly above me was home to a Hmong family with three small children, and another newlywed couple with an infant, plus the grandmother. Nine people (five adults and four children) shared this one-bedroom apartment. The one-bedroom basement apartment sheltered two Mexican sisters. One sister slept with her four children (ranging in age from seven to sixteen years old) in the single bedroom, while the other slept with her three small children in the living room. The Assyrian family of twelve lived in a three-bedroom apartment. A Mexican family with six children shared a one-bedroom apartment. These "doubling up" arrangements probably would not be permitted in middle-class-managed buildings.

Perhaps the most vivid example of this practice is the large heteroglot household that lived above me during the summer of 1989. Grace, an Appalachian mother of six children with a Puerto Rican husband, lived with Angel, her Puerto Rican "business" partner, who brought along his girlfriend, his younger brother just released from prison, the brother's girlfriend, and his African-American friend (who before the summer was over went to prison), as well as a single pregnant mother and her best girlfriend—fifteen people in one three-bedroom apartment. The household was anchored by Grace's Public Aid check and Angel's street hustling activities. Two years earlier, Grace had been homeless, living on the streets with her six children; the girls had panhandled and the boys had stolen food and cigarettes from stores. She had a network with street people, and Angel was plugged into the prison culture, so three to five extra people would "crash" at the apartment at any given time. This household was the most multicultural one in Big Red, embracing whites and African Americans who cohabited with several Latinos and one Filipino. The illicit life-style of street hustling and drugs brought together these several ethnic groups in strikingly intimate ways. Their unruly household had many problems, but racism and prejudice never surfaced.

The gathering together of extended families and the creation of "fictive kin" (Rapp 1987:232) are primary tactics for "making do" within Big Red. A twelve-year-old Assyrian Courtyard Kid articulated this conventional wisdom: "It's good to have friends and relatives nearby so you can borrow money when you need it." Indeed, the culture of Big Red was characterized by an intimacy of interactions across apartments, expressing in part the kinship networks that laced together these households. When I surveyed the apartments at the end of my first year of residence, I discovered that every household but two (one of those being mine) was tied by kinship to at least one other apartment in Big Red. The young Mexican family with three small children directly below me in A1r, for example, had strong ties to the B stairwell. The husband's widowed mother lived in B1L, along with his sister, thirty-year-old single brother, and three cousins. His older brother lived across the hall from the mother in B1r, with his five children. Their cousins lived in B3r. Further, the three brothers and half-brothers all worked at the same place: the Easy Spuds potato-chip factory in Evanston. The families all ran back and forth from one another's back porches. Raul in A1r had three children, Salvatore in B1r had five, and two or three children always stayed with the single adults and grandmother in B1L, so there were many cousins to play with, circulate outgrown clothing among, share transportation, and collectively receive parenting from multiple care-givers. The grandmother in B1r had high blood pressure (one of the first things I was told when introduced) and was always surrounded by caring relatives. Maria, the daughter-in-law from A1r, spent so much time with her frail mother-in-law in B1L that it took me some time before I figured out in which apartment Maria actually lived.

The functional importance of this propinquity with immediate relatives became clear when Maria told me about her husband Raul's being laid off from work for seven months. One can get through such a crunch with immediate family close by. This supportive net of family is extended by several friendships with other Latino families in Big Red, as well as more friends and family in or near Albany Park. A more financially successful older brother who is a delivery-truck driver regularly visited from near Hoffman Estates. He had purchased a shiny new Ford truck with a camper cover that was shared with the Big Red kin for shopping trips.

Aurelio (Mexican), who lived across the hall from me in A2l, had a sister with a large family who lived in B2r. Over the summer, two of his younger brothers arrived from Mexico without papers, and they lived with his sister. Aurelio had eight sisters and seven brothers; all but the youngest lived in or near Albany Park. Three brothers and their families lived on Whipple Street around the corner; they and their children visited back and forth all the time. They pooled resources for major family celebrations. For example, Alfredo, Aurelio's baby boy, was baptized with four other cousins; a huge party and feast in the church basement followed for all the extended family and friends. All the working brothers and sisters cofinanced the *quinceañera* debutante celebration for Aurelio's niece; Aurelio bought the flowers. Thanksgiving 1989 was celebrated jointly with six turkeys. My first week in Big Red I could not find anyone with the key to get my mailbox unlocked. Gabriel, one of Aurelio's brothers from Whipple, passed by, pulled out a knife from his pocket, and forced it open for me. That incident represented the quality of life in Big Red, the back-and-forth visiting between households and the spontaneous offering of assistance.

Aurelio's family was also tied strongly to the financially strapped family (two sisters rearing their seven children together without husbands) in the basement of B. I think they were cousins, or maybe just good friends, but everyone in A2l looked out for the extended family in the basement because there was no father. The older sister did not speak English.

Alberto, the kid from C2r, practically lived with Aurelio. At first he told me that they were cousins, then later that they really were not blood cousins, but like adopted family because they had lived close together for so long. They had been at Whipple together and then had both moved to Big Red. The same is true for Raul and Hilda, directly below me, and their relatives in B stairwell: they had come from Whipple along with Aurelio. The president of the Whipple block club, a white woman, remembered Aurelio and his relatives; she had had an altercation with them that led to a court hearing and the breaking of all the windows on two sides of her house. She described the entire group negatively as "clannish."

Another example of a kin network in Big Red was the Assyrian family with ten children in D1r. They were on Public Aid with monthly rent of $450. Unable to afford a telephone or transportation, they were among the most needy, even by Big Red standards. In this case it was the wife who articulated the kinship lines. Her sister and husband lived two floors above them in D3r. The sister drove them to church, which was the hub of their social and economic sustenance (they obtained free meals there and clothes for the kids). The mother lived with the sister on the third floor, but every time I visited the family in D1r, the mother was there helping with caring and cooking for the ten kids, the oldest of whom was sixteen. The wife's brother lived just around the corner on the Gunnison side, in E1r. The brother's apartment was one of the more nicely furnished in Big Red. The D1r family depended on the brother for telephone use. The Assyrian family directly across the hall from them were cousins. The first time I was invited to this family's home for Sunday dinner, the children had picked leaves from trees in River Park; the mother stuffed the leaves with rice and served them with yogurt made from the powdered milk that is distributed once a month at the Albany Park Community Center.

The two ethnic Chinese families from Cambodia were intimately connected. The wife in E1L was the eldest daughter of the family in C1r, and both families helped manage the sewing shop in the basement.

The Hmong are noted for their kinship solidarity. Because they lived on the top floors, by and large, they could leave their doors open. Related families faced one another and shared back and forth, one apartment becoming an extension of the other. The kids ran from one apartment to the other, ate together, and blurred the household boundaries. The Hmong in the United States have not assimilated to the model of the nuclear family. My observations of the Latino and Assyrian families suggest the same, but the extended-family pattern was strongest among the Hmong. The Hmong neighbors directly above me had an apartment the same size as mine, one bedroom. It housed five adults—two brothers, their wives, and a grandmother—as well as the four small children of the older brother (the oldest child is eight) and the baby of the younger brother. They got along handsomely in this one-bedroom apartment. The kids skipped down to my apartment frequently for cookies. They were extremely happy children, polite and very well behaved.

This same Hmong family in A3r, the Yangs, demonstrated remarkably the importance of having kinfolk nearby. In December, when their Hmong neighbors across the hall moved to an apartment just across the street because they had suffered for a month with a waterless toilet (it was this same family whose back porch had collapsed in August), the Yangs could not bear to be alone on the top floor of our stairwell. Within two weeks they moved just across the courtyard to the D3l apartment in order to be close to their cousins living one floor below them in D2l. The mother explained that they had moved because she needed kin nearby to help with child care. This was the family's third move within Big Red in order to achieve close communal ties with relatives. Their understanding of "closeness" differed from that of white established residents. First, the Yangs' departing friends from A3l had only moved across the street, still in the 4800 block of Albany, within sight and shouting distance. Further, their cousins in D2l were in the same building, just across the courtyard. The Yangs, however, wanted a degree of intimacy that required side-by-side proximity to relatives or friends.

Even families from different ethnic groups expressed their friendship in "the idiom of kinship" (Stack 1974). The Mexican family in C2r told me that their new downstairs neighbors (Appalachian) in C1r were their "cousins." They claimed knowledge of a family tree that traced the Appalachians' family roots back to Spain, where the connection was made with the Mexicans' forebears. When I pressed the Mexican teenager who told me this, he did not know the specifics. But that did not seem to matter; he was delighted to have "relatives" living directly below him. He informed me that his neighbors—he calls them "hillbillies"—had told his family that they were also related to me, tracing their Irish side to my Scots background.

This interconnectedness with intimate others is highly functional for the people of Big Red. Carol Stack notes: "The poor adopt a variety of tactics in order to survive. They immerse themselves in a domestic circle of kinfolk who will help them. . . . Friends may be incorporated into one's domestic circle" (1974:29). Notwithstanding the unpleasant physical conditions, Big Red was an extraordinarily pleasant and human place to live because of the densely interlaced kin and friendship networks. My neighbors were not self-sufficient; therefore, they did not privilege self-reliance in the same way that the white middle class does. Sometimes they had difficulty making it from one paycheck to the next. They worked at connecting themselves to one another with reciprocal ties of gift-giving and the exchange of goods and services, as well as the less tangible but extremely important mutual offerings of respect and esteem. What Jane Addams observed almost a century ago still applies to Big Red: "I became permanently impressed with the kindness of the poor to each other; the woman who lives upstairs will willingly share her breakfast with the family below because she knows they 'are hard up'; the man who boarded with them last winter will give a month's rent because he knows the father of the family is out of work" (Addams 1910:123–24).

This ethic of care and concern for one another cuts across ethnic groups. The older sister of the Cambodian-Chinese family in C1r cut the hair of Latino neighbors, and the Latino youths in turn "looked out for" her family. I was amazed when the sixteen-year-old Mexican from the basement apartment walked through the courtyard on her way to the high school prom. She was beautifully dressed, with all the accessories. I knew that this household of nine sharing a one-bedroom apartment did not have the resources to finance such an outfit. I learned later that the dress had been borrowed from an aunt, the shoes from a neighbor, the purse from a cousin, and the hair-bow from another neighbor, and that her hair had been styled by the Cambodian neighbor.

This ethos of solidarity was expressed in the common greeting—used by

Latino, Hmong, Assyrian—"Where are you going?" "Where have you been?" "I haven't seen you for a while." They expected answers and explanations. They were interested in one another's business. It was from the Mexicans that I learned the Hmong paid $20 a month for their garden plots in the vacant lot down the street. An Assyrian man I had not yet met knocked on my door one day and asked me whether I could help him patent an invention. He explained, "I look through your window and see all the books and thought you must have a book on this."

Taking my cue from neighbors, I started a back-porch "garden" in June 1988. Within the first week of setting out the pots, I had gifts of seeds and cuttings from four of my immediate neighbors.

One of the poignant examples of interethnic sharing deserves a full transcription. Ching, a small eight-year-old Hmong boy from E3r, approached me one day in the courtyard:

> **Ching:** Mr. Dwight, do you know Julio [twenty-year-old Mexican resident of Big Red]?
> **DC:** Yes.
> **Ching:** [obviously troubled] Is he gang?
> [In order not to violate street ethics, I deflected Ching's question.]
> **DC:** Why are you worried about that, Ching?
> **Ching:** [staring at ground, voice sad] Because he's my friend.
> **DC:** He's my friend too. How is he your friend, Ching?
> **Ching:** Because he's nice to me. He always gives me lots of toys, the toys he used to play with when he was a kid.
> **DC:** Why do you think he's in a gang?
> **Ching:** Because people say he's gang.

As the example of Ching makes clear, people value the intangibles of friendship and caring as much as the tangibles of money, food, or toys that change hands. That is not to depreciate the real need for material support. Julio's hand-me-down toys are the only ones Ching has. Ching's family moved into Big Red because they had lost their savings on a house they bought. The house had been burglarized twice, and they had lost everything. The father told me that they had moved into Big Red to recoup, to start over again.

The other Courtyard Kids were as poor as Ching. One day as I was passing through the courtyard Azziz (Assyrian) came running up to me, calling out, "Hey Mr. Dwight. Today's my birthday. I'm thirteen. I'm a teenager. Tony [cousin who lives across the hall] and I have the same birthday. He's twelve. So my dad said that we can't afford to do two birthdays. So this year we will do his. And next year they will do mine." I spontaneously decided to take Azziz and his eleven-year-old brother for the treat of his choice. He chose McDonalds. Before placing his order, he conferred with me about the total price, worried that I might not be able to afford his Big Mac, fries, and small Coke. The boys told me that this was the third time in their life they had been out to eat.

All the Courtyard Kids were very conscious of the price of things. When I returned from shopping, they rushed to carry my grocery bags and ask the prices of items. Often one or two of them walked to the grocery store with me. They had a clear sense of price differentials at the local stores. Pao, an eight-year-old Hmong boy informed me: "Dominick's is cheaper than Jewel's, but Aldi's is the cheapest. Vanilla wafers are 79 cents and at Dominick's they're $1.09. But bags [at Aldi's] are 4 cents so we just carry the stuff in our hands." Observing me as I bought a newspaper, a Courtyard Kid remarked, "Newspapers is wasting your money, isn't it, Mr. Dwight? 'Cause you can get the news free from TV."

My neighbors have borrowed a variety of things from me: money for milk, newspapers, pliers, dustpan, toilet paper, flashlight, books, suitcases, hair dryer, Band-Aids, aspirin, toothache medicine, videocassettes, earache medicine, and clothes. Not everyone who borrows from me lives in Big Red. Propinquity affects the frequency and intensity of borrowings. The Mexican–Puerto Rican family directly across the hall from me borrowed the most costly items. The two teenage girls borrowed my camera. But that came after months of interaction. When Aurelio returned to Mexico for a short visit and Carmen's telephone stopped functioning, she borrowed my unit and plugged it into the outlet in her apartment. She did not directly ask to borrow it. She met me in the stairwell and asked me first whether I could fix her defunct telephone. Then she confided how frightened she was at night, being alone with six children. When I offered her the use of my telephone, she was appreciative but worried that sometimes I had to go out in the evening and she would be stranded. Finally, I recognized her indirect request and offered her my entire telephone. She protested but soon gratefully accepted the offer. This family also requested my services as a photographer at the joint baptism of their baby son Alfredo and four of his cousins, as well as the *quinceañera* celebration of Aurelio's goddaughter. Carmen asked me whether on washdays she could extend her clothesline across my back porch.

In return, the family did many favors for me. They kept an eye on my place when I was away. They gave my rent to the landlord, thus freeing me from having to stay home on rent-collection days. They offered me rides in their car when they saw me walking on the street. They cooked meals for me and shared their intimate family problems and life celebrations with me: baptisms, birthdays, cotillions. Aurelio invited me to the alley parties of the *braceros*. During the water shutoff in June, they began looking for another affordable apartment; finding a building that had two vacancies, they suggested that I could move with them. When they actually moved in November because of a fight with the landlord, I bought the floor-to-ceiling steel security gate Aurelio had installed on his back door. He and a nephew mounted it for me.

I was the recipient of manifold kindnesses from other neighbors throughout Big Red. The Hmong who lived directly above me gave me a hand-embroidered textile wall hanging and a beaded window hanging they had made. Mrs. Gutierrez (Puerto Rican), the "dean" of Big Red, was concerned about mail getting stolen from my mailbox with its defective lock. Consistent with her senior-woman-in-the-building status, she took charge of the situation. Without consulting me, she instructed the Puerto Rican mailman, whom she had known for years, to put all my mail in her box—she has one of the few locked mailboxes. Then she would espy me from her window as I walked through the courtyard and would station herself at the top of the stairwell, smiling grandly with my mail in hand. Until another neighbor showed me how to fix my lock, I was dependent on Mrs. Gutierrez for my mail.

The Big Red ethos of familiarity and reciprocity continues, for even though many of us have been displaced from the building, we still live in the area. In early July 1990, two teenagers (Assyrian and Mexican) hailed me as I carried a bag of groceries down one of the streets of Little Beirut. Consistent with local custom, they examined what was in my bag and said, "Thanks, Dwight," as they reached for two yogurts. There was no need to ask for the food. The nature and history of our relationship enabled them to assume this familiarity. Two days later, as they were riding around the neighborhood, they spotted me again and pulled the car over; the Assyrian fellow leaned out the window and offered me some of his food: "Hey Dwight, you want some of this shake?" These two incidents capture the quality of life in the Big Red area. At a micro-level, every day is filled with a host of significant kindnesses and richly nuanced reciprocities. To use a term from the streets, people are "tight" in Little Beirut (meaning tightly connected, not "tight" with their money). These micro-level courtesies provide a buffer against the macro-structures of exclusion and oppression. They enable people to experience dignity and joy in structures like Big Red, refashioning them into "dwellingplaces."

The fine-grained texture of the daily acknowledgments and courtesies that characterize life in Big Red provides a counterpoint to the blunter treatment the residents sometimes receive when they enter the system controlled by established residents and bureaucracies. Teenagers expelled from school have asked me to accompany their mothers to the principal's office for reinstatement because when the mother went alone, as one student put it, "they did not see her." In a communication system that required a different style of assertiveness, she was invisible. When I accompanied Mexican and Guatemalan mothers to school offices or police stations, all the attention and eye contact would be directed toward me, the white male. One time, after the high school principal had been persuaded to give one of my young neighbors a second chance, the mother gratefully extended her hand to thank him. But the principal reached right past her to shake my hand. Quite literally, he did not see her. A short, dark-complexioned Mexican woman, she had three factors that contributed to her invisibility: race, gender, and class.

Sometimes the erasure is not so subtle. While standing in line at the Perry

Drugstore checkout line, one of my Assyrian neighbors gave me an updated report on her finger, which had been bitten by a rat as she slept in Big Red. Although the bandage had been removed, the finger still looked as if it had been slammed in a car door. The cashier, a white woman in her late fifties, treated my neighbors very curtly at the checkout. Before the Assyrian woman was out of earshot, and as the cashier was ringing up my purchases, she began talking to the neighboring cashier, also an older white woman. Here is what the two of them said, in full hearing of the Assyrian woman, her husband, her granddaughter, and me:

> **Cashier 1:** Can you believe it? If my father were alive to see what's happened to the neighborhood!
> **Cashier 2:** I know. Don't get upset.
> **Cashier 1:** I hate getting upset first thing in the morning.
> **Cashier 2:** They're not worth it.
> **Cashier 1:** I know I shouldn't let them upset me.
> **Cashier 2:** They're not worth it. They're trash.

Tactics of Resistance

The residents of Big Red coped with their oppressive circumstances typically through circumventions, survival tactics, and seizing opportunities. They did not have the power and clout to confront the system head-on. They survived via connections, evasions, street-smart maneuvers, making end-runs around authority. De Certeau describes the "tactical" thinking of people everywhere who must find space for themselves within oppressive structures:

> The space of a tactic is the space of the other. Thus it must play on and with a terrain imposed on it and organized by the law of a foreign power. . . . It does not, therefore, have the options of planning general strategy and viewing the adversary as a whole within a distinct, visible, and objectifiable space. . . . It must vigilantly make use of the cracks that particular conjunctions open in the surveillance of the proprietary powers. It poaches in them. It creates surprises in them. It can be where it is least expected. It is a guileful ruse. (1984:37)

The Big Red tenants turned the "absenteeism" of the landlord to their advantage to enact spatial practices and temporal rhythms that would not have been tolerated in well-managed buildings. They had their tactics for dealing with the landlord. Mrs. Gutierrez from time to time would unleash a blistering tongue-lashing on him. She always announced to neighbors, days in advance, that she was going to "really shout at him this time." She would gather more complaints from the neighbors, gradually building up steam for one of her anticipated confrontations, and then, at the opportune moment, she would "really let him have it." Though none could match the explosive force of Mrs. Gutierrez, I overheard many women as they stood on back porches and denounced him.

Perhaps the best example of tactical resistance unfolded when the city shut off the water supply to Big Red because the landlord was $26,000 in arrears for payment. This action was taken at the end of June 1988, during a summer in which Chicago broke its previous record for days in which the temperature rose above 100 degrees Fahrenheit. During the three days of the water shutoff, temperatures soared to 105 degrees.

Attempts to work within the system were ineffectual. I contacted NRC, the powerful community organization, but it could do nothing to remedy the immediate crisis. I personally called several agencies and officials in the city, including the Water Department. It is legal, within the City of Chicago, to shut off water supply for a large building as a method of collecting debt payments. The only result my flurry of telephone calls produced was that a city inspector did visit Big Red during the time we were without water, wrote a report, sympathized with us, then drove away. We never heard from him again. If we had depended on his official intervention, Big Red would still be without water. What all the city bureaucrats told us was that they did not have the authority to turn the water back on until the debt was cleared, or at least a partial payment was deposited. The owner, of course, was unaffected by the city's action. Never easy to reach, insulated in his lakefront condominium, he did not even know that the water had been shut off.

By the third day without water, the situation was intolerable. The gross inconvenience, the outrage of having no water for drink, bathing, or flushing the toilet, intensified by the 105-degree heat, incited radical action. It is hard to say whose idea the final solution was, because I think we came to it collectively. I remember that we were all standing in the courtyard, quite bedraggled and exhausted. Mrs. Yang, the Hmong mother from C3l, kept insisting, "We have to do something!" Spontaneously, we decided to take action into our own hands, dig down to the water main, and turn the water back on ourselves. This action was not only unauthorized, it was illegal.

This plan required several steps of coordinated action across lines of ethnicity, gender, and age. The hue and cry raised during the first day of the water shutoff drew in the white Democratic precinct captain, who lived one block north of Big Red. He became involved in the day-to-day drama of the water crisis as it unfolded. He donated his tools and garage workshop for the Hmong smiths to fashion a custom wrench to turn on the water valve. Mexican, Hmong, and Assyrian residents of Big Red all took turns with the digging. This activity attracted several "sidewalk supervisors," many of whom were homeowners from across the street, others just passersby, including African Americans and whites. The diggers reached the water main only to find the valve sheathed in an eighteen-inch sleeve filled with dirt. A Puerto Rican woman volunteered her vacuum-cleaner hose, and extension cords were plugged into the nearest apartment outlet, which happened to be Assyrian. The Hmong ran back and forth with the white precinct captain to fashion the wrench that would turn the valve. This took several attempts. Once they got it to fit, the next problem to be solved was determining what manipulation turned the water on. A full turn? Half turn? To the right or left? The water company does not make it easy for unauthorized people to take control of their water supply. An elderly Assyrian woman was stationed in the window to check her sink and report the results of each trial turn: "Nothing yet—yes, a trickle, do that again—no, nothing—O.K., that's it."

It was close to midnight by the time the water flowed. Everyone was exhilarated. Several of the men went to the Mexican *bracero* bar down the street on Lawrence to celebrate. No one bought his own beer. Everyone crossed over and spent his money buying someone else's beer, although in the end there was an equal distribution of monies. There was much camaraderie, backslapping, handshaking, and clicking of bottles.

The audience of this drama was enlarged by a front-page story in the *Chicago Tribune,* "In Crisis, Immigrants Learn Who Their True Friends Are." Several follow-up stories and editorials appeared in the Lerner neighborhood newspapers, all supporting the pluck of the Big Red residents and condemning the conditions that allowed a building full of vulnerable people to go for a prolonged time without water during the worst of Chicago's summer heat wave. Spokespersons for the Water Department went on record to say that no legal action would be taken against the Big Red residents who circumvented the law to regain control of their water supply.

This crisis tightened the community. In a crisis, boundaries are suspended or become porous. The sixth month into the project, I had made headway in meeting my Big Red neighbors, but most of the meaningful interaction had been with neighbors sharing my stairwell. By the time the water was turned back on, I had been inside thirty-five of the thirty-seven apartments. The shared hardship of going without water during one of Chicago's most notorious heat waves threw Big Red into a "communitas of crisis," a heightened sense of "we-feeling" (Turner 1977:154). It was easy to approach anybody sharing that experience. Residents who had not previously met were greeting one another with warm familiarity by the end of the second day. This crisis transformed my position in the building from semi-outsider to an informal advocate of sorts. It accelerated trust and rapport with neighbors by a great leap.

The homeowners across the street and across the alley rallied in very kind and generous ways. These same people had been known to complain about the condition of Big Red and how this huge building overrun with children did nothing to enhance property values on the block. Nevertheless, one homeowner across the alley bought a connection for his garden hose so that it would reach into the first-floor windows and people would not have to lug buckets. Across the street, another family built a temporary brick walk across their yard to provide a more direct route for women and kids carrying heavy buckets of water from their outdoor faucet. One homeowner tried to charge people for the water, and he immediately became the scapegoat against whom everyone united in contempt.

The Big Red water crisis demonstrated clearly that even though marginalized people are highly vulnerable, they are not passive (Clifford 1988:16). This incident is only one dramatic example of myriad tactics and highly creative forms of resistance employed by the weak (Scott 1990).

The Rhetoric of Transgression and Redevelopment

We look at the material solidity of a building . . . and behind it we see always the insecurity that lurks within a circulation process of capital, which always asks: how much more time in this relative space?

DAVID HARVEY
CONSCIOUSNESS AND THE URBAN EXPERIENCE (1985)

On August 1, 1989, the president of Oakwood Development Company, who was also president of the Albany Park Landlords' Association, took control of Big Red. The absentee owner had failed to make his mortgage payments, and the building was being cited in criminal housing court because of building-code violations and physical deterioration due to his negligence. Notices had gone up warning of another water shutoff because of the owner's failure to pay the water bill. The court appointed Superior Bank as receiver. With NRC urging, the bank appointed Oakwood Development Company as manager of Big Red. Empowered by the state and allied with community organizations, an Oakwood Development crew used sledgehammers to break into the basement of Big Red to take charge of the utility meters and other facilities.

Almost immediately after the takeover, Oakwood and staff interviewed various residents and quickly pinpointed two drug-dealing apartments, the busiest one being the apartment above me that Bao Xiong and her family had formerly occupied. Oakwood used the crisis of drug trafficking as an excuse to evacuate the entire stairwell. With hindsight, I believe the drug dealers, who were real, became the lever Oakwood deployed to start emptying Big Red as quickly as possible.

When Oakwood took control in August, Big Red was fully occupied and still had a vital building culture and ethos of solidarity. Within four months, half of the Big Red households were displaced. One year later, thirty-one of the thirty-seven apartments were vacant (figure 3.4). Empty and boarded up, Big Red looms like a ghost building. The wrenching violence of this intervention was muted in the euphemisms that Oakwood and NRC used to describe their actions: "turning the building around," "turning the neighborhood around."

Oakwood, a multimillion-dollar company that specializes in managing low-income rental properties, works closely with NRC. The NRC director of housing development lives in an Oakwood building. Oakwood and NRC estimate that it will require a $1.5-million loan to purchase and rehabilitate Big Red. NRC Housing Development is working on getting a low-interest loan package through

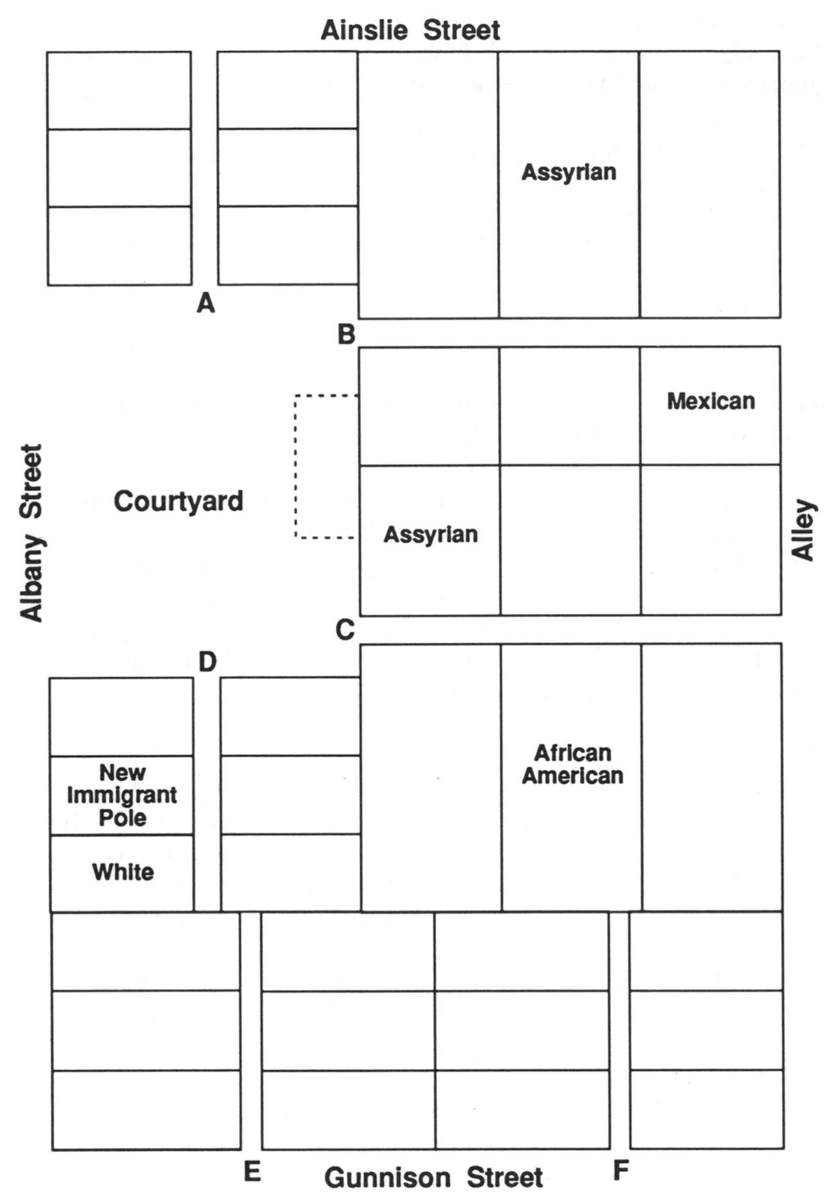

Figure 3.4. Big Red occupancy, summer 1990

Chicago EquityFund[9] and Community Investment Incorporation. The NRC Housing Development director explained the plans for Big Red: "We want to make it a community project—bring together Oakwood experience and profit-making know-how with NRC philosophy and provide quality rehab for poor people. Make it a good solid community, *but integrated with the rest of the community*" (emphasis mine). The partnership of Oakwood's "profit-making know-how with NRC philosophy," united against the market individualism of "slumlords" as much as the transgressive tenants, is a classic example of the complex way investment property mirrors "the internal tensions within the capitalist order" and anchors a coalition between private investment and the public sector in advanced capitalist societies (Harvey 1985:61). The absentee landlord of Big Red was displaced along with the residents: his locks were smashed with Oakwood sledgehammers on the day of takeover. The competitive tensions and profit-making dictates of capitalism are softened, elided, and simultaneously enabled by the moral rhetoric (NRC's "philosophy") of community organizations concerned with the public good. Community organizations like NRC produce strategic definitions of "the public good," "quality of life," and "good solid community" that are advantageous to capital development. "Community," David Harvey argues, "plays a fundamental role in terms of the reproduction of labor power, the circulation of revenues, and the geography of capital accumulation" (1985:252; see also 255–57).

NRC brought Big Red to the attention of a subcommittee of the U.S. Congress. Frank Annunzio, U.S. Representative for the district encompassing Albany Park, chairs the Subcommittee on Financial Institutions, which oversees the Federal Deposit Insurance Corporation (FDIC). In order to guarantee that Superior Bank would not sell Big Red to the highest bidder without a rehabilitation entailment—"slumbanger types who would rent to multiple families that would overrun the place," according to NRC staff—NRC pressured Annunzio, who was waging a tough reelection fight because of the savings and loan scandal. He needed the support of Patrick O'Connor, Fortieth Ward alderman; NRC worked through O'Connor, who then pressured Annunzio. Annunzio was reelected, but at the time of this writing Big Red still awaits repairs.

The NRC phrase "but integrated with the rest of the community" codes the middle-class anxiety about Big Red. Big Red transgressed the system by remaining outside it. With an unresponsive absentee landlord and an array of mostly new-immigrant working-class tenants, Big Red eluded middle-class strategies of containment and control. The plurality, fluidity, and openness that made Big Red accessible and accommodating to new-immigrant and working-class tenants were among the very qualities that the middle class finds forbidding. Situated in the center of Little Beirut, Big Red focused and displayed

9. Chicago Equity Fund is a not-for-profit loan company for low-income housing funded by a group of Chicago millionaires, who get a special tax break in exchange for the entailment that money go toward housing that will be designated low-income for fifteen years.

middle-class fears and ambivalences about difference, density, deterioration, and demographic change.

The domination and displacement of the residents of Big Red were underwritten by a rhetoric of redevelopment. Before the Big Red residents were physically vacated, they were discursively displaced. Drastic measures in the service of capitalism were discursively mediated as desirable and natural inevitabilities. Defined as dirty, disorderly, deteriorating, and dangerous, Big Red became ripe for redevelopment, making it "licit to intervene . . . in order to exercise the rights of guardianship . . . to impose 'the good' on others" (Todorov 1984:157). To legitimate the wholesale disruption and displacement of families, the community organizations, in league with real estate interests, defined Big Red as the alien, transgressive Other that threatened civil order and neighborhood stability (see Stallybrass and White 1986; Skogan 1990).

The rhetoric of transgression turns on a symbolic equation of dirt with danger. Mary Douglas helps us understand the symbolizing powers of dirt. Inspired by William James's insight that dirt is "matter out of place" (Douglas 1966:164), she argues: "Dirt is essentially disorder. There is no such thing as absolute dirt. . . . Dirt offends against order. Eliminating it is not a negative movement, but a positive effort to organize the environment" (1966:2). That which is out of place, marginal, different, and therefore dirty gets charged with danger and becomes subject to the moral imperative for correction, rehabilitation, development, all in the name of restoring order.

The rhetorical valences among these loaded terms can be schematized as a triangle with disorder at the apex and dirt and danger forming the base (figure 3.5). Density and deterioration are intensifying links in the extended causal chain that sets up development as a moral necessity. Underneath all these terms is difference, that which cannot be spoken without disrupting the discourse of liberal pluralism upon which the rhetoric of redevelopment draws. The president of Oakwood Development, for example, takes pride in being "a socially conscious real-estate developer" ("His Niche Is Low-Income Housing," *Albany Park News Star,* 27 February 1990, p. 1). Sanitized celebrations of "diversity" elide deep fears of difference. Local commercial boosterism promotes Albany Park's diversity as a "salad bowl," "mosaic," "orchestra," "symphony," and "bouquet" of cultures, but these metaphors invoke emblematic icons of the middle-class containment and taming of difference. Fredric Jameson critiques this form of "liberal tolerance":

> Much of what passes for a spirited defense of difference is, of course, simply liberal tolerance, a position whose offensive complacencies are well known but which has at least the merit of raising the embarrassing historical question of whether the tolerance of difference, as a social fact, is not the result of social homogenization and standardization and the obliteration of genuine social difference in the first place. (1991:341)

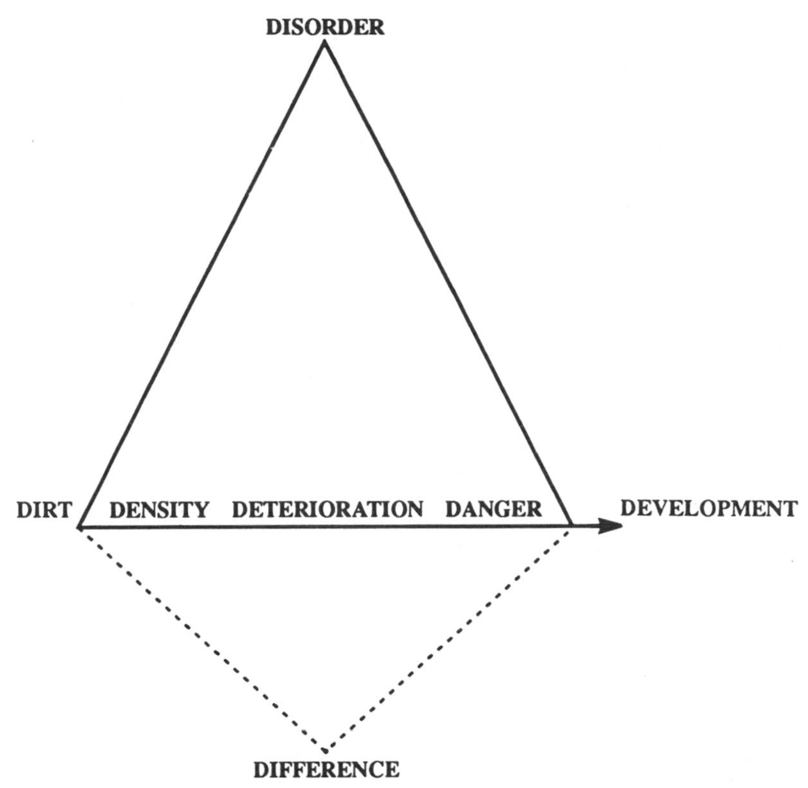

Figure 3.5. Configuration of key terms in the rhetoric of transgression

Anxiety about dirt and disorder sets the stage for the elimination of difference and mobilizes efforts to patrol boundaries and purge the environment.

The discourse of transgression legitimates official systems of surveillance, reform, enforcement, and demolition. A proposal from the Report of the Albany Park Planning Committee, an NRC group, vividly clarifies the connection between discourse and power (Foucault 1979): "We propose that the City use its powers of condemnation to inspect, acquire, demolish and prepare for redevelopment" (uncataloged archive, 1980:3).[10] The rhetoric of transgression features three definitional strategies for classifying buildings and areas as dirty,

10. For important studies of the relationship between discourse and power, see Edward Said, *Orientalism* (New York: Vintage, 1979); V. Y. Mudimbe, *The Invention of Africa: Gnosis, Philosophy, and the Order of Knowledge* (Bloomington: Indiana University Press, 1988); Christopher Miller, *Blank Darkness: Africanist Discourse in French* (Chicago: University of Chicago Press, 1985); Nancy Fraser, *Unruly Practices: Power, Discourse, and Gender in Contemporary Social Theory* (Minneapolis: University of Minnesota Press, 1989); John Dorst, *The Written Suburb: An American Site, an Ethnographic Dilemma* (Philadelphia: University of Pennsylvania Press, 1989); and Robert Scholes, *Textual Power* (New Haven, Conn.: Yale University Press, 1985).

dangerous, and therefore in need of redevelopment: (1) metaphors of disease and decay, (2) images of flux and instability, and (3) temporal retardation. These three strategies interact in complex and mutually reinforcing ways.

Community activists deploy organic metaphors of disease and decay to identify targeted buildings and urban areas with dangerous powers of pollution and contagion (Sontag 1979). The NRC Housing Development director called Big Red a "blight" on the neighborhood. Likewise, "cancer," "epidemic," and "plague" are frequently invoked terms of contamination. This trope is rhetorically potent because it imparts a sense of life-threatening urgency through images of rapidly spreading infection, debilitation, and death. The executive director of NRC unequivocally defined Big Red as casting a deathly presence over the neighborhood: "Big Red is the dead heart of the neighborhood. It's where it's situated. It's the dead heart of the neighborhood. It casts a pall over the entire neighborhood."

Gangs and drugs are particularly potent signs of urban disease that create re-

Back view of Big Red with decrepit porches facing alley. The graffiti on back walls and garage mark the contested turf of rival gangs in and around "Little Beirut." "Pee Wee RIP" is a "Rest in Peace" death mural that commemorates a fifteen-year-old Latin King who was killed the summer of 1990. Ten "RIP" death murals were inscribed on the walls of Big Red during the time I lived there. Gangs communicate in a complex code of symbols, icons, and acronyms. They invert and reverse the letters that stand for hostile gangs as a way of debunking rivals. The *R* and the *P* are inverted because they stand for the Royals and the Popes, two gangs currently at war with the Latin Kings (LK), the dominant gang in "Little Beirut." Whipple and Ainslie are the names of two streets whose intersection, one-half block from Big Red, is a popular "hang-out" for Latin Kings. (Photograph by Dwight Conquergood)

vulsion and dread among citizens. A civic report notes that "youth gangs and drug trafficking are the scourges of certain portions of Albany Park" and laments "the growing cancer of crime and drug activity" along the Kedzie corridor (Albany Park Community Area 1982:37,39). Oakwood Development initially used the fear of drugs and gangs to "clean out" Big Red. The A stairwell where I lived was the first to be evacuated, because it included a drug apartment and was covered with gang graffiti. I attended a meeting with the police and Oakwood staff. The police lieutenant described how drugs spread through a neighborhood like a metastasizing disease: "It infects the whole building, then the block goes, then the neighborhood."

The trope of contagious disease gathers resonance and intensity within a wider circulation of contemporary cultural meanings that connect the health of the body politic to the strength of the immune system. Donna Haraway has written brilliantly about the "semantics of defense and invasion" in "immune system discourse":

> My thesis is that the immune system is an elaborate icon for principal systems of symbolic and material "difference" in late capitalism . . . . the immune system is a plan for meaningful action to construct and maintain the boundaries for what may count as self and other in the crucial realms of the normal and the pathological. (Haraway 1989:4)

The boundary anxiety of "immune system discourse" renders confrontations with difference more acute. The symbolism of the vigilant immune system appeals to "the rules of purity, propriety and continuous production which govern bourgeois reason" (Stallybrass and White 1986:107).

This pathologizing of buildings and blocks as diseased bodies with dead hearts is an indirect way of stigmatizing the tenants, the socioeconomically least advantaged classes, caught in this "spatial entrapment" (Harvey 1985:40). In *The Politics and Poetics of Transgression,* Peter Stallybrass and Allon White insightfully discuss this "metonymic chain of contagion which led back to the culture of the working classes" (Stallybrass and White 1986:138). The associative link between perceptions of decay and class difference is patent in the following phrase: "older, lower income, predominantly multi-family areas that suffer from slum and blighted conditions" (Cicero 1988:8). Density, crowding, households' "doubling up" in Big Red and other "multi-family areas," and "bands of teenagers congregating on street corners" (Skogan 1990:2) are economically constrained spatial practices of the poor that affront middle-class norms of privacy, polite society, and property management. "Spatial practices," David Harvey argues, "become imbued with class meanings. . . . They take on their meanings under specific social relations of class, gender, community, ethnicity, or race" (Harvey 1989:223).

The rhetoric of transgression and redevelopment combines the bacterial metaphor of spreading contagion with kinetic images of flux and instability to depict dangerous disorder. An official report warned that the deteriorated conditions of housing in Little Beirut "will create a spill-over effect that will spread to the areas of good housing in Albany Park" (Albany Park Community Area 1982:42). A neighborhood "in transition" associated with "demographic change," dizzying "turn-over," and the "downward spiral" of property values is constructed as the dangerous, unbalanced Other that threatens the "stability" of "good solid" communities: "The single-family homes in Ravenswood Manor have served as *anchors* in keeping property values *stable* in Albany Park" (Pennelle 1989:1; emphasis mine). One of the stated goals of NRC is "to manage the demographic transition so that whole streets aren't turning over at the same time" (Albany Park Community Area 1982:44).

Topsy-turvy visions of upset and turnover are complemented by destabilizing imagery of ooze, spillover, and flood, particularly when applied to people, with the most commonly used descriptor of demographic change: "influx." In addition to property, the NRC is vigilant about people: "The attempt to stabilize the Kedzie corridor is also being fought on a different front—monitoring the influx of poor people into the area who are being displaced from other neighborhoods" (Albany Park Community Area 1982:44). Sometimes these migratory Others are discursively imagined as a "wave" that threatens to overwhelm an established neighborhood. An NRC spokesperson reassured the community: "The current wave of low-income residents will only be temporary; the long-term prospective is positive" (Pennelle 1989:2). Multifamily low-income courtyard buildings are described as "overflowing" with people, especially children.

Class difference gets constructed symbolically along the axes of stable/ unstable, solid/fluid, balanced/teetering, dry/wet, long-term/temporary, established/mobile. As I learned from living more than three years in Little Beirut (the first twenty months in Big Red), economically disadvantaged people, for a variety of reasons, have to move frequently. One of the most powerful ways of demeaning people is to call them "transient." Henry Mayhew opens his monumental nineteenth-century four-volume study, *London Labour and the London Poor,* with one grand binary opposition that proposes "wandering"—that is, instability, transience—as the universally defining characteristic of the poor:

> Of the thousand millions of human beings that are said to constitute the population of the entire globe, there are—socially, morally, and perhaps even physically considered—but two distinct and broadly marked races, viz., the wanderers and the settlers—the vagabond and the citizen—the nomadic and the civilized tribes. . . . Moreover it would appear, that not only are all races divisible into wanderers and settlers, but that each civilized or settled tribe has generally some wandering horde intermingled with and in a measure preying upon it. (Mayhew 1968 [1861]:1)

Wanderers, transients, nomads, migrants, and refugees are unattached to a "proper place" (de Certeau 1984) and thereby threaten order because they "transgress all settled boundaries of 'home'" (Stallybrass and White 1986:129). Nomination, the rhetoric of naming, is a strategy of containment for these drifters: "It is the task of nomination to fix a *locus proprius* for them, and to set limits for their drifting" (de Certeau 1986:72).

The NRC uses the stigma of transience to differentiate the "deserving poor" from the "undeserving poor." An expansive quote from a commission staffer is revealing:

> Our vice-president has an expression: "There are poor people and there are slobs." Well, we're not interested in the slobs. We're not interested in people who don't want to live between four walls. . . . We're interested in poor folks who need to live here because they're poor. We are concerned that they, in fact, will be a part of the community and observe property rights. But there are concerns about people who move in and out of the community, people who are floaters, who will take and will not give. We'd like to see them move in and out of the community. That's their problem; we're beyond the point where we're gonna sit and commiserate with them. (Albany Park Community Area 1982:44)

"Floaters" and "transients"—also named "slobs" and "trash"—embody the instability of the "transitional" neighborhoods they pass through and upset. No one wants to recognize that their nomadic practices are economically constrained.

It should be pointed out that the same kinetic imagery of circulation, movement, and mobility, when aligned with entrepreneurial interests, takes on a positive valence. The circulation of capital is construed as dynamic, and mobility is celebrated insofar as it is upward. Instead of "transient," nomadic capitalists are considered to be "on the fast track." Those in control of the production of images are able to play it both ways with the imagery of motion: dynamic and directional for the ruling classes, disintegrative and anarchic for the subordinate classes. The rhetorical deployment of kinetic imagery underpins a "politics of representation" (Shapiro 1988) that is used both to displace certain groups of people and to keep them in a subordinate place.

Like motion, time is strategically manipulated in the discourse of redevelopment. As a term, "development" has the same temporal ring as "growth," "progress," "modernization,"—a sense of advancing confidently through time toward improvement, fulfillment, and enlightenment. In *Keywords,* Raymond Williams charts the political career of "development" and notes that its late-nineteenth-century use in connection with industry and commerce was preceded by its eighteenth-century association with the new biology, when it became the virtual equivalent of "evolution," in the "specialized sense of *development* from 'lower' to 'higher' organisms" (Williams 1983:121; see also

102–4). Development becomes the temporal transposition of a moral hierarchy that is spatialized along a high/low vertical axis and a forward/backward horizontal plane.

Aligned with the forces of nature and fueled by trade and industry, the rhetorical power of development as an idea about time takes on quasireligious tones with the emergence, in the twentieth century, of "progress" as a "god term," a "rhetorical absolute." Richard Weaver argues: "By a transposition of terms, 'progress' becomes the salvation man is placed on earth to work out; and just as there can be no achievement more important than salvation, so there can be no activity more justified in enlisting our sympathy and support than 'progress'" (Weaver 1953:212–13). Anything that impedes progress, any building or urban area that is labeled as in need of redevelopment, suffers the stigma of regression, temporal retardation. It is perceived as delaying and retarding the natural order and progression of time and therefore as a legitimate target for intervention.

The rhetoric of urban redevelopment, therefore, is a "temporal setup" (Clifford 1988:16) with strategies and consequences similar to those of the development programs imposed on the Third World: "an often generous idea of '*aid* to the *developing* countries' is confused with wholly ungenerous practices of cancellation of the identities of others, by their definition as *underdeveloped* or *less developed,* and of imposed processes of *development* for a world market controlled by others" (Williams 1983:104). In *Time and the Other,* Johannes Fabian analyzes how global policies of imperialism and colonialism "required Time to accommodate the schemes of a one-way history: progress, development, modernity (and their negative mirror images: stagnation, underdevelopment, tradition). In short, *geopolitics* has its ideological foundations in *chronopolitics*" (Fabian 1983:144). Urban redevelopment attempts the temporal reversal of areas that drag neighborhoods backward in time, in the direction of decay, decomposition, and death, away from millenarian renewal. Redevelopment erases and rewrites history on the urban landscape.

In its strategic manipulation of time, the rhetoric of transgression and redevelopment resonates with the puritan jeremiad, a classic American form of public discourse much studied by rhetoricians (Bercovitch 1978; Johannesen 1985; Murphy 1990). The secular discourse of urban "renewal," "revitalization," "redevelopment," and "restoration," like the puritan jeremiad, castigates the current state of decline and promises a shining future through correction and reform. As Richard Johannesen reminds us, the prophet Jeremiah used discourse "to root out, to pull down, and to destroy, and to throw down, to build, and to plant" (Johannesen 1985:159). The contemporary rhetoric of urban redevelopment participates in a discursive formation with a long history of instrumental force. The discourse of economic revitalization profits from the jeremiadic undertones of moral redemption and rebirth.

The "chronopolitics" of redevelopment plays out in other ways. Big Red has stood empty since summer 1990 while Oakwood Development and NRC wait for the best interest rate and loan package for rehabilitation. In the meantime, the former tenants have been forced to relocate to substandard housing nearby. "Those who can afford to wait," Harvey notes, "always have an advantage over those who cannot" (1985:23). The president of Oakwood Development stated this time-based philosophy in a press interview: "And that's our philosophy; it's long-term. We own about 12 properties and we've sold two since 1975. We're hanging on for long-term gain" ("His Niche Is Low-income Housing," *Albany Park News Star,* 27 February 1990, p. 1). One of Oakwood's most effective methods of emptying Big Red was the five-day notice that warned tenants of eviction when their rent was late. Oakwood trapped and displaced the Big Red tenants with these "temporal nets" (Harvey 1985:29) while the company profits from "appreciation over time" ("His Niche," p. 1).

The people of Big Red have been displaced, but not erased. Victims of the bourgeois "will to refinement" (Stallybrass and White 1986:94) that purged the building, strained household resources, and dispersed the Courtyard Kids, most have redistributed themselves within Little Beirut with their friendship networks still intact. The culture of Big Red survives in remnants and fragments.

It is now starkly clear that all the initial talk from Oakwood and NRC about "making Big Red a safer and more pleasant place to live" did not include the people of Big Red in that vision. Indeed, my Big Red neighbors were perceived as part of the problem that had to be removed. The public statements of both Oakwood Development and NRC champion "the rights of poor people to decent housing." The people of Big Red, however, did not fit into the class of the deserving poor, a category that includes only those who embrace middle-class values.

Walter Benjamin's insight, "There is no document of civilization which is not at the same time a document of barbarism" (Benjamin 1969:256; see also Brenkman 1987:3), can be transposed in the case of Big Red to "There is no act of redevelopment which is not at the same time an act of violence and oppression." In the words of Harvey, "The perpetual reshaping of the geographical landscape of capitalism is a process of violence and pain" (1985:29). The sturdy tenants who had coped successfully with the gross negligence and greed of a slumlord, and made homes, reared children, and created an interdependent culture of warmth and neighborliness, were no match for the outside agents of middle-class order and stability who branded Big Red as a symbol of incivility, thus legitimating drastic measures of control and correction.

References

Addams, Jane. 1960 [1910]. *Twenty Years at Hull-House.* New York: Penguin.

Albany Park Community Area. 1982. *Chicago Comprehensive Needs Assessment.* Vol. 2. Chicago: Melaniphy and Associates.

Bakhtin, Mikhail M. 1986. *Speech Genres*. Edited by Caryl Emerson and Michael Holquist. Translated by Vern McGee. Austin: University of Texas Press.

Barthes, Roland. 1979. From Work to Test. In *Textual Strategies: Perspectives in Poststructuralist Criticism,* edited by Josue V. Harari. Ithaca, N.Y.: Cornell University Press.

Benjamin, Walter. 1969. *Illuminations*. Edited by Hannah Arendt. Translated by Harry Zohn. New York: Schocken.

Bercovitch, Sacvan. 1978. *The American Jeremiad*. Madison: University of Wisconsin Press.

Bourdieu, Pierre. 1977. *Outline of a Theory of Practice*. Translated by Richard Nice. Cambridge, U.K.: Cambridge University Press.

———. 1984. *Distinction: A Social Critique of the Judgement of Taste*. Translated by Richard Nice. Cambridge, Mass.: Harvard University Press.

———. 1990. *The Logic of Practice*. Translated by Richard Nice. Stanford, Calif.: Stanford University Press.

Bousfield, Marie. 1989. *Births by Race in Chicago's Community Areas, 1979–87*. Chicago: Department of Planning, City of Chicago.

Brenkman, John. 1987. *Culture and Domination*. Ithaca, N.Y.: Cornell University Press.

Cicero, Joe. 1988. Commercial Revitalization Stimulates Rehab Interest. *North River News,* Spring, p. 8.

Clifford, James. 1988. *The Predicament of Culture: Twentieth-Century Ethnography, Literature, and Art*. Cambridge, Mass.: Harvard University Press.

Corral, Luis M. 1990. Neighborhoods: Albany Park Cleans Up Its Act. *Chicago Enterprise,* May, pp. 15–16, 27.

De Certeau, Michel. 1984. *The Practice of Everyday Life*. Translated by Steven Rendall. Berkeley: University of California Press.

———. 1986. *Heterologies: Discourse on the Other*. Translated by Brian Massumi. Minneapolis: University of Minnesota Press.

Dorst, John. 1989. *The Written Suburb: An American Site, an Ethnographic Dilemma*. Philadelphia: University of Pennsylvania Press.

Douglas, Mary. 1966. *Purity and Danger: An Analysis of Pollution and Taboo*. London: Routledge and Kegan Paul.

Downs, Anthony. 1964. *What Will Chicago's Residential Areas Be Like in 1975?* Chicago: Chicago Commission on Human Relations.

Engels, Friedrich. 1987 [1845]. *The Condition of the Working Class in England*. New York: Penguin.

Fabian, Johannes. 1983. *Time and the Other: How Anthropology Makes Its Object*. New York: Columbia University Press.

Flores, Raymundo, Marie Bousfield, and Eugene Chin. 1990. *Areas at Risk: Chicago's Potential Undercount in the 1990 Census*. Chicago: Department of Planning, City of Chicago.

Foucault, Michel. 1979. *Discipline and Punish: The Birth of the Prison*. Translated by Alan Sheridan. New York: Vintage.

Fraser, Nancy. 1989. *Unruly Practices: Power, Discourse, and Gender in Contemporary Social Theory*. Minneapolis: University of Minnesota Press.

Fremon, David K. 1988. *Chicago Politics Ward by Ward*. Bloomington: Indiana University Press.
Goozner, Merrill. 1990. A Startling Climb in Area's Jobs. *Chicago Tribune*, 22 April, pp. 1, 8.
Haraway, Donna. 1989. The Biopolitics of Postmodern Bodies: Determinations of Self in Immune System Discourse. *Differences* 1 (Winter): 3–43.
Harvey, David. 1985. *Consciousness and the Urban Experience: Studies in the History and Theory of Capitalist Urbanization*. Baltimore: Johns Hopkins University Press.
______. 1989. *The Condition of Postmodernity*. Oxford: Basil Blackwell.
Hinz, Greg. 1991a. Census Reveals Huge Changes. *News Star* (Chicago Lerner Newspaper), 26 February, pp. 1, 4.
______. 1991b. An Extra Ward for North Side? *News Star* (Chicago Lerner Newspaper), 5 March, pp. 1, 5.
Hodge, Robert, and Gunther Kress. 1988. *Social Semiotics*. Cambridge, U.K.: Polity.
Jameson, Fredric. 1991. *Postmodernism: Or, The Cultural Logic of Late Capitalism*. Durham: Duke University Press.
Johannesen, Richard L. 1985. The Jeremiad and Jenkin Lloyd Jones. *Communication Monographs* 52:156–72.
Kerson, Roger, ed. 1990. *The Chicago Affordable Housing Fact Book*. Chicago: Chicago Rehab Network.
Lemann, Nicholas. 1991. *The Promised Land: The Great Black Migration and How It Changed America*. New York: Knopf.
Marcus, George E., and Michael M. J. Fischer. 1986. *Anthropology as Cultural Critique: An Experimental Moment in the Human Sciences*. Chicago: University of Chicago Press.
Mayhew, Henry. 1968 [1861]. *London Labour and the London Poor*. Vol. 1. New York: Dover.
McClory, Robert. 1991. Segregation City. *Chicago Reader*, 30 August, pp. 1, 16, 18–20, 22–23, 26, 28.
Meyers, Gary S., and Don DeBat. 1990. *The Chicago House Hunt Book*. Chicago: Chicago Sun-Times.
Miller, Christopher. 1985. *Blank Darkness: Africanist Discourse in French*. Chicago: University of Chicago Press.
Mudimbe, V. Y. 1983. *The Invention of Africa: Gnosis, Philosophy, and the Order of Knowledge*. Bloomington: Indiana University Press.
Mullings, Leith, ed. 1987. *Cities of the United States: Studies in Urban Anthropology*. New York: Columbia University Press.
Murphy, John M. 1990. "A Time of Shame and Sorrow": Robert F. Kennedy and the American Jeremiad. *Quarterly Journal of Speech* 76 (November): 401–14.
Pennelle, Sandra. 1989. Prices Force Families to Live Together. *News Star* (Chicago Lerner Newspaper), 8 November, sec. 2, pp. 1–2.
Quinlan, Donal G. 1991. "Polite" Minority Finding Its Voice. *News Star* (Chicago Lerner Newspaper), 2 April, pp. 1, 7.
Rapp, Rayna. 1987. Urban Kinship in Contemporary America: Families, Classes, and Ideology. In *Cities of the United States: Studies in Urban Anthropology*, edited by Leith Mullings. New York: Columbia University Press.

Royer, Ariela. 1984. Albany Park. In *Local Community Fact Book: Chicago Metropolitan Area, 1980,* edited by Chicago Fact Book Consortium. Chicago: Chicago Review Press.

Said, Edward. 1979. *Orientalism.* New York: Vintage.

Sanjek, Roger. 1990. Urban Anthropology in the 1980's: A World View. *Annual Review of Anthropology* 19:151–86.

Scholes, Robert. 1985. *Textual Power.* New Haven, Conn.: Yale University Press.

Scott, James C. 1990. *Domination and the Arts of Resistance.* New Haven, Conn.: Yale University Press.

Shapiro, Michael J. 1988. *The Politics of Representation.* Madison: University of Wisconsin Press.

Skogan, Wesley G. 1990. *Disorder and Decline: Crime and the Spiral of Decay in American Neighborhoods.* New York: Free Press.

Sontag, Susan. 1979. *Illness as Metaphor.* New York: Vintage.

Squires, Gregory D., Larry Bennett, Kathleen McCourt, and Philip Nyden. 1987. *Chicago: Race, Class, and the Response to Urban Decline.* Philadelphia: University of Pennsylvania Press.

Stack, Carol B. 1974. *All Our Kin: Strategies for Survival in a Black Community.* New York: Harper and Row.

Stallybrass, Peter, and Allon White. 1986. *The Politics and Poetics of Transgression.* Ithaca, N.Y.: Cornell University Press.

Suttles, Gerald D. 1968. *The Social Order of the Slum.* Chicago: University of Chicago Press.

———. 1990. *The Man-made City: The Land-Use Confidence Game in Chicago.* Chicago: University of Chicago Press.

Todorov, Tzvetan. 1984. *The Conquest of America.* New York: Harper and Row.

Turner, Victor. 1977 [1969]. *The Ritual Process: Structure and Anti-Structure.* Ithaca, N.Y.: Cornell University Press.

Weaver, Richard. 1953. *The Ethics of Rhetoric.* South Bend, Ind.: Regnery Gateway.

Williams, Raymond. 1983. *Keywords: A Vocabulary of Culture and Society.* rev. ed. New York: Oxford University Press.

Wolf, Eric. 1982. *Europe and the People without History.* Berkeley: University of California Press.

4 RECENT ECONOMIC RESTRUCTURING AND EVOLVING INTERGROUP RELATIONS IN HOUSTON

Jacqueline Maria Hagan and Nestor P. Rodriguez

None of the tenants at Arborland, including myself, have taken too seriously management's threat to evict tenant families with children. It has been over a month since we received the general notice and, to my knowledge, no action had been taken against any of the families in the apartment complex. I assumed, as did many of my neighbors, that the newly established "adults only" policy was designed as a strategy to attract potential young, single, middle-class tenants to Arborland in the context of the city's current economic upswing. I imagined the policy would be presented to potential tenants but not enforced, since it would amount to losing over a third of the tenants in thc back buildings. That was until today. It's now clear that management is dead serious about enforcing its new policy.

Maria and Elizana, two of my neighbors, were quite upset—almost frantic—when they arrived at my apartment this morning. Jose, one of the two Mexican-American maintenance personnel, visited both women yesterday afternoon and told them that Jim, head security officer, was giving the manager the names of tenants who had children. Jose told the women that several families had already been evicted. He then cautioned the women to keep their children indoors when Jim was on duty. Maria was especially upset, since she had just received an eviction notice this morning in which it was stated that she and her family had to be out of the apartment in three days. She stayed home from work today fearing that she shouldn't leave her son alone. Her husband is in Chicago for the month where he has been working construction with his brother and, with no one to turn to, she has solicited my help. She asked me to call her boss and find out what she can do to postpone the eviction until her husband returns.

I called her boss, the manager of a nearby Mexican restaurant, and relayed the story to him. I was truly taken by his understanding tone and even more surprised when he said he would call the

> apartment manager and demand that Maria be given at least thirty days to move from her apartment. I then went to speak with Jose who told me that management is taking dramatic steps to "clean out" the families from Arborland. Jose told me that "the manager has offered to give us [staff] $50 for every family we turn in." I asked Jose how many of the staff were actually doing this and he said that "Jim the Prick [as he is referred by his staff] is doing most of the turning-in. Some of the other guys are too, but most of us are just warning the families and won't have any part of it." He went on to explain why many of the maintenance staff were resisting management policy.
>
> "These families have no other choice. They need to be close to their work. It's not fair to the children, who will have to change schools, and it's not fair to the parents who rely on local bus lines and their neighbors for transportation to work. I have a family and I don't believe in discriminating against families, let alone making a profit from it."
>
> With the indirect support of staff members like Jose, the direct help of Maria's boss and another neighbor in the building, we were able to convince management to give the evicted families a thirty-day notice. Unfortunately, management will probably succeed in evicting most of the families. However, neighbors, friends, and coworkers of these families are going to help the families resist. Many of these established residents are sympathetic to the precarious situation in which the newcomer families have found themselves. As evidenced in past situations in which the newcomers have been the most vulnerable and most affected by management's upgrading policies, many of Arborland's tenants have united to speak out for the newcomers and taken actions to resist management's policies, which are seen as aimed at displacing the newcomers in the complex. (Hagan field notes 5/12/88–5/14/88)

With the construction of hundreds of large apartment complexes in Houston's west side since the 1960s, analysis of the disposition of housing has emerged as a central means of understanding new emerging intergroup relations in the city. In the 1980s, tens of thousands of Latino immigrants (primarily undocumented Central Americans) located high-quality yet inexpensive housing in westside apartments, which had been previously dominated by middle-class tenants. Some apartment complexes have become homogeneous islands of immigrant settlement in the city's west side, but other apartments have been transformed into major multigroup settings as established residents and new immigrant families locate housing in the same complexes.

The westside apartment complexes' transition from housing mainly middle-class established residents to housing only new immigrant tenants or mixed populations of long-term residents and new Latino immigrants is the story of

Houston's recent two-phase restructuring of its apartment-complex industry. In the first stage of restructuring, apartment owners and managers responded to the city's economic decline and subsequent outmigration of their middle-class tenants by recomposing their tenant population with new immigrants. In the second stage, apartment owners and managers have responded to the city's economic recovery and subsequent return of middle-class tenants by reducing the presence of their low-income immigrant tenants.

Our long-term fieldwork in the west side of the city suggests that the success of restructuring often depends on the type of strategies implemented. Complexes that lowered rents considerably and shifted to an all-Latino tenant population were unable to weather the economic storm, whereas complexes that incorporated a mixed population of established residents and immigrants were more likely to survive the economic crisis. Consequently, what emerged in many westside apartment settings in the 1980s—and for the first time in the city's history—were mixed tenant populations of Mexican Americans, African Americans, Anglo, and Latino newcomers.

Arborland, a large westside complex, is the rental housing site we selected to examine the effects of apartment restructuring on intergroup relations between newcomer and established-resident tenants. The ethnographic findings from our two-year study of intergroup relations at Arborland show how restructuring changed the course of relations between Anglo, African-American, and Mexican-American established residents and Central American and Mexican immigrants in the apartment complex. Restructuring became a catalyst promoting, strengthening, and later dissolving intergroup relations. The first step of restructuring promoted cordiality, cultural awareness, and tolerance between newcomers and established residents. The second stage of restructuring initially facilitated greater cooperation among the various tenants' groups, when these groups united to resist managements' restructuring strategies. The success of management's restructuring strategies at Arborland, however, severed emerging intergroup relations in the complex, as newcomers were displaced from their apartments.

Latino Immigration, Economic Restructuring, and New Intergroup Relations in Houston

Demographic and Economic Context of Restructuring

Large-scale, long-term changes in Houston's population structure and economy significantly influence where and how new immigrants and established residents interact.

In the early 1980s the composition of Houston's immigrant population began to change. Prior to this period, Houston's Latino immigrants had come primarily from Mexico. Since the beginning of the twentieth century, Mexican migrants have been making the journey to Houston (see table 4.1) in response to

Table 4.1. Houston's Population Growth, 1900–80*

Year	Total	Latino
1900	44,633	1,000**
1908	78,800	2,000
1920	138,276	6,000
1930	292,352	15,000
1940	384,514	20,000
1950	596,163	40,000
1960	938,219	75,000
1970	1,233,505	150,000
1980	1,594,086	280,000
1990	1,630,553	450,000

*Includes incorporated city area only.
**Figures rounded to nearest thousand.
Sources: Shelton et al. 1989: 95–96; preliminary 1990 census statistics cited by Sallee (1991).

the city's growth as a global industrial center (Feagin 1988). Settling in areas adjacent to the industrial sectors in the east side of the city where they found work, Mexican immigrants helped form the well-known barrios of El Segundo Barrio, Magnolia, and Northside (Shelton et al. 1989). Until the early 1980s these three barrios housed the majority of Houston's Latino community and constituted the traditional zone of Latino settlement (see figure 4.1).

Beginning in the early 1980s, large streams of new Latino populations began arriving in Houston. Although Mexican immigration continued through the eighties, thousands of undocumented Salvadorans, Guatemalans, and Hondurans also migrated to the city (Rodriguez 1987). Their recent large-scale migration to Houston is reflected in the dramatic growth in the city's Latino community. The central city's Latino population grew from 281,331 in 1980 to an estimated 500,000 by 1989 (Shelton et al. 1989). The 1990 census figures for the entire Houston metropolitan area place the number of Latinos at 707,536 (Sallee, 1991).

Rather than settle in the traditional Latino zones in the city's east side, many of the newcomer Central Americans settled in the city's west side so that they could be close to the service industries in which they worked and, given the changing real estate market, where they could find quality rental housing at an affordable price (Rodriguez and Hagan 1989). Moving into mainly middle-class white neighborhoods, the Central American newcomers created settlement pockets that provided new opportunities for intergroup relations between these new Latinos and the area's predominantly middle-class resident professionals (see figure 4.1).

Table 4.2, which shows changes in elementary school enrollment in the west-

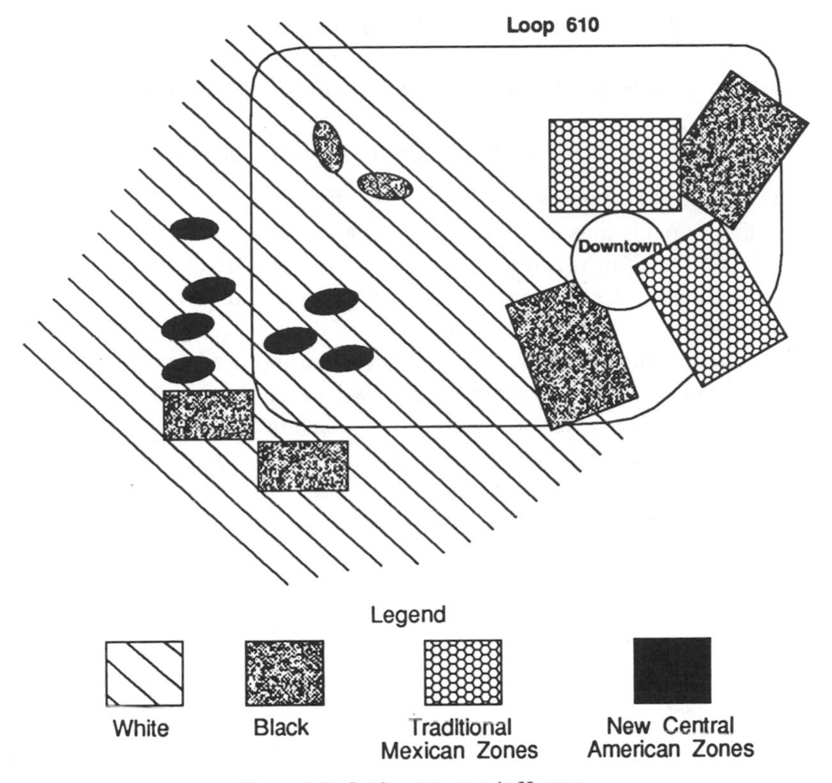

Figure 4.1. Settlement zones in Houston

Table 4.2. Percentage Enrollment Change, by Anglo, African-American, and Latino Groups, in Elementary Schools in the Western Sector of Houston, 1980–86*

School	Anglo (%)	African-American (%)	Latino (%)
Braeburn	−78	86	698
Briargrove	−8	59	743
Cunningham	−74	85	851
Pilgrim	−93	−72	325
Sutton	−57	25	245
Twain	−26	38	201

*Schools are located in the general vicinity of the Arborland fieldwork site.

ern sector of the city, illustrates dramatic population shifts in Houston during the early eighties. Interviews with school principals in Houston's west side indicate that the majority of newcomer students are Central American.

Economic Restructuring and Houston's Housing Industry

While changing demographic conditions set the stage for the development of new intergroup relations in the west side of the city, changes in Houston's economy played a catalytic role in promoting new intergroup relations. Houston had experienced almost continuous economic growth and prosperity since the 1910s (Feagin 1988). During the 1960s and 1970s, however, as the center of the world petrochemical industry, Houston grew at an unprecedented level. Expansion in the petrochemical sector spurred growth in accompanying service industries. In the personal-service sector, the construction of large apartment complexes was dramatic. Houston has 3,067 apartment complexes, comprising 400,725 units. Many of these complexes, including the city's twenty-four largest, were built in the 1965–80 period of economic growth (Smith 1989). The Latino immigrant work force that helped construct the large apartment complexes contrasted with the Anglo white-collar tenants who came to live in them.

The prosperous years came to an end in 1982, when the city entered a severe five-year economic downturn. By the end of Houston's five-year decline (1982–87), the area's economy had suffered through the repercussions of a 57 percent decline in oil prices and a 77 percent reduction in active drilling rigs in the United States (Feagin 1988). For the local economy and its work force, this translated into a 1987 unemployment rate of 10 percent and the loss of 200,000 jobs.

As several works have described, economic crisis and related restructuring start in the primary circuit of capital (Beauregard 1989; Henderson and Castells 1987; Harvey 1981). In Houston, the crisis started in the primary circuit of manufacturing capital in the oil- and petrochemical-related industries, and in a short time it affected the area's secondary circuit of real estate capital as well. The bankruptcies filed by 485 real estate firms in 1986 highlighted the crisis suffered in the city's secondary circuit of real estate capital. By 1987, vacancy rates in office buildings soared to 28 percent, and residential-space vacancy rates reached 18 percent. From 1981 to 1985, the number of vacant residential units increased from 86,961 to 220,709, representing a 154 percent increase in just four years (Smith 1989).

Massive job losses and empty factories in the city produced large numbers of rental vacancies and empty apartment complexes in the city's residential areas, especially in the westside sector of white, middle-class neighborhoods. Not surprisingly, the crisis was especially severe for large apartment complexes. Capital outlay per complex measures in the millions of dollars, so that a large apartment complex requires several hundred tenants to remain profitable (and attractive to investors). In the fall of 1987, economic vacancy rates (including physical vacancy and rental concessions such as free first-month rents) reached an all-time high of 34.3 in the apartment industry (REVAC 1990).

The start of Houston's economic downturn in the early 1980s had coincided with the large-scale immigration of Central Americans (Rodriguez 1987). Thousands of undocumented Salvadorans, Guatemalans, and Hondurans had migrated to the city. Mexican immigration was continuing unabated as well. The Central American immigration enabled some large apartment complexes to implement a restructuring strategy to survive the city's recession. Owners and managers of apartment complexes recomposed their tenant populations with the Central American newcomers. To attract the new Central American tenants, the owners and managers lowered rental prices, advertised in Spanish, changed apartment complex names to ones familiar in Spanish, offered special services for immigrant tenants, and hired Spanish-speaking staff.

Some large apartment complexes did not survive the economic downturn, even with their restructuring strategy. Lowering rents to affordable levels ($160–$260 per month) for the new immigrants eventually caused some complexes to close. Some complexes deteriorated to uninhabitable levels when maintenance services were reduced for the new immigrants. Other complexes lost new tenants due to a shrinking labor market. Moreover, newly implemented employer sanctions under the Immigration Reform and Control Act of 1986 (IRCA) drove some immigrants to other areas. The decline of the apartment industry, including its restructuring to a lower-income tenant population and a large foreclosure rate, lowered the value of apartment complexes. From 1987 to 1989 almost 6,000 apartment units were razed in the city (Rosen, 1990).

The upturn of Houston's economy in the late 1980s brought a second phase of restructuring in the large apartment-complex industry. This phase involved an upgrading of the existing apartment complexes and a reduction of the immigrant presence in anticipation of the return of middle-income tenants. The following sections describe our research setting and methods and address the effects of Arborland's two-phase restructuring process on intergroup relations at the apartment complex.

Restructuring at Arborland

Our research in Arborland shows how restructuring strategies implemented by management created and then altered the nature of two levels of intergroup relations. First, management's attitude toward newcomer tenants changed from one of accommodation to one of exclusion, if not displacement. Second, we found that the restructuring process expanded and then limited relations between new immigrants and established residents in the neighborhood arena.

Arborland (see figure 4.2) is a 645-unit apartment complex located in

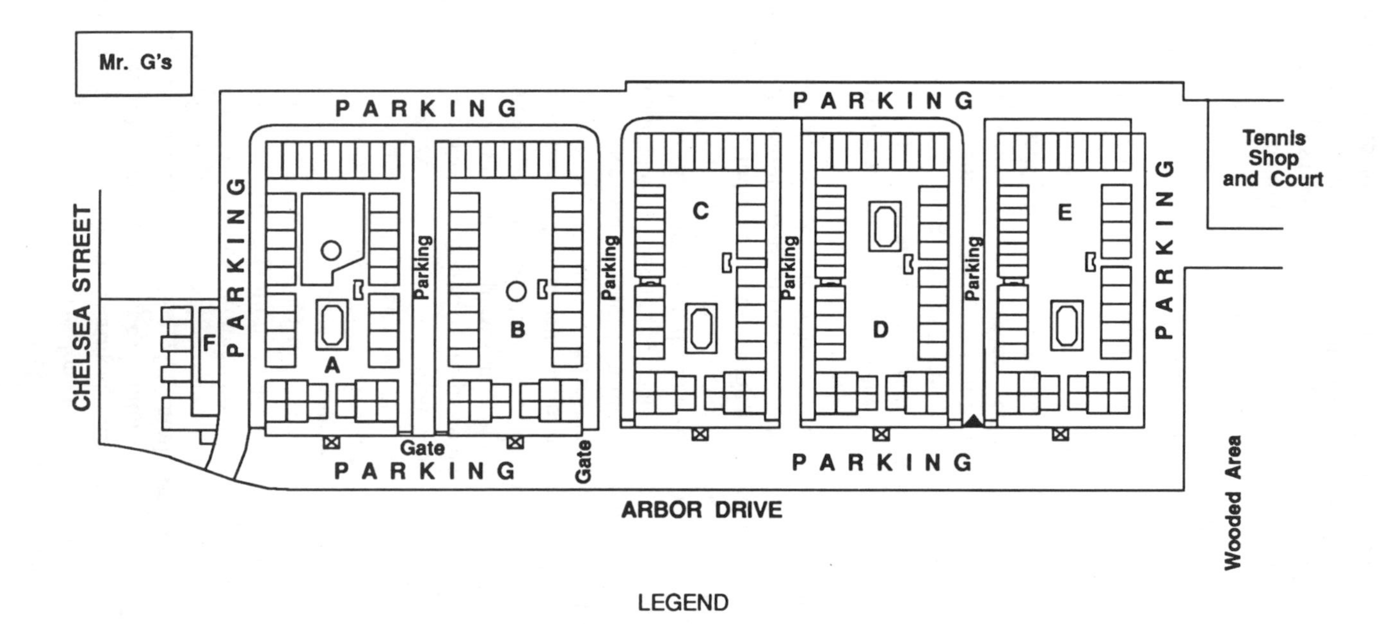

Figure 4.2. Arborland apartment complex (ground-floor plan)

Houston's west side, the most recently developed area in the city. Like many of the area's apartment complexes, Arborland was constructed in the early 1970s to house the increasing number of Anglo and African-American professionals moving to the city during Houston's boom years. Throughout the seventies and early eighties Arborland maintained the image of an adults-only complex, complete with door-to-door cleaning and laundry services, maid service, heated swimming pools, Jacuzzis, tennis courts, and its own bar, restaurant, and beauty salon. In line with the corporate targeting by many of the large complexes built during the city's boom years, Arborland offered temporary corporate housing to professionals working in the city on a short-term basis. The combination of extensive in-house services, rents of $500–$600 a month, and an adults-only rental policy attracted a relatively homogeneous tenant population of young, middle-class, mostly Anglo professionals.

When Houston's economy crashed in the early 1980s, Arborland found itself in a crisis. Almost overnight, it experienced the loss of 40 percent of its tenants. Arborland management responded to this crisis by implementing the first of a two-phase restructuring strategy—the recomposition of its tenancy. Taking advantage of the large and timely Central American immigration to the city, Arborland management vigorously advertised to attract Latino newcomers to the southwest complex.

In the summer of 1987, locating an apartment in a westside complex that housed newcomer Latinos proved to be an easy task for Hagan. Virtually all the area's complexes had mounted a litany of signs in both Spanish and English soliciting prospective tenants. Signs and billboards advertising amenities such as free English classes, on-premise Latino nightclubs, and drastically reduced rents lined the premises of Arborland and those of other complexes in the west side. In some cases, apartment managers and owners had tried to create a Latino environment by renaming their complexes with Spanish names to attract the newcomer tenants.

When Hagan entered the Arborland rental office and inquired about vacancies, she was greeted by a female bilingual rental agent well versed in pitching a hard sell. After showing several models in buildings A and B, the agent provided a map listing the several hundred vacant units, and Hagan selected a one-bedroom apartment in building E because she knew of several newcomer families residing in the same building. Following some negotiation, Hagan leased the apartment for $219 a month. No security deposit was required, and a rent-free month was thrown in.

Arborland management accommodated its newcomer tenants in numerou
ways during its initial restructuring phase. It stopped enforcing its adults-
policy, and newcomer families with children became a growing segment
idents in Arborland. When several of the newcomers established inform
nesses at Arborland (a mechanic shop, beauty salon, and dressmaker
advertised their services in Spanish on the complex's bulletin boar

ment looked the other way. A bilingual security guard, maintenance worker, and rental agent were usually on hand to assist newcomer tenants, and all apartment notices and bulletins were translated into Spanish.

As intermediaries between management and newcomers, the bilingual staff members and maintenance workers developed relatively close relationships with many of the newcomers. On several occasions, maintenance workers gave discarded rental furniture to arriving newcomer families. The Mexican-American tennis director provided free tennis classes to one young Salvadoran boy and wrote affidavits for several young newcomers applying for legalization under IRCA.

What emerged in Arborland as a consequence of management's success in restructuring was a mixed tenant population of Mexican Americans, African Americans, Anglos, and Latino newcomers. Throughout the mid and late eighties, approximately 60 percent of the tenants were Latino newcomers, the majority of whom were from Guatemala and El Salvador. The remaining 40 percent of the tenant population were African-American, Anglo, and Mexican-American residents.

The majority of new immigrants at Arborland came from rural and low-income occupational backgrounds. In Houston, they are concentrated in the low-paying maintenance and domestic sectors of the city's service economy. In contrast, the Anglo and African-American residents at Arborland came from a middle-class background, many of them being young professionals employed in white-collar jobs (Hagan and Rodriguez 1989).

In the Field

Jacqueline Hagan moved into Arborland in the summer of 1987, six months before the Changing Relations project officially began. She conducted fieldwork in Arborland in two stages. During the six months preceding the project's start date, Hagan developed a core group of informants among the tenants and the established-resident staff. With these contacts established, she began to make systematic observations in multigroup settings in Arborland and to conduct reflexive interviews among the tenants and staff.

In the period of establishing key informants in Arborland, Hagan spent most of her time getting to know the undocumented Central American and Mexican newcomer tenants. Several researchers have written about the problems of studying undocumented populations (Chavez 1988; Cornelius, Chavez, and Castro 1982). Part of the problem of gaining research access to the largely un-[illegible]ocumented tenant population had been resolved by Nestor Rodriguez, a [illegible]ted figure among the Guatemalan tenants, the largest newcomer group in [illegible]artment complex. Drawing on his initial contacts, Hagan requested intro-[illegible]s to other newcomers and began building her own network of infor-[illegible] some cases, she directly approached newcomer households, [illegible]em of the study, and let them know that her door was open if they

Established residents in Arborland public square (photograph by Tina Otto)

ever needed assistance. To gain their confidence, Hagan provided English assistance during her first four months in the complex.

Hagan built networks with newcomer tenants by attending many community events, such as baptisms, birthdays, *quinceañeras,* weddings, picnics, and soccer games. She also built networks with the Anglo tenants. She accomplished this by joining Arborland's tennis team, frequenting monthly "beer bashes" in the apartments, and becoming a regular fixture at the Jacuzzi and the complex restaurant.

Her initial strategy was to secure an informant among the Anglo rental agents in the front office. Most of the rental staff, however, were reluctant to talk about management policies toward the immigrant tenants. Hagan did not disclose her intergroup research, fearing that it might affect the information the staff provided. Thus, her interactions and observations in the front office were carried out within the boundaries of a tenant-management relationship. She did manage, however, to develop a rapport with Amy, a bilingual agent in the office, who had become disgruntled with management's changing attitude toward the newcomer population.

Members of the largely African-American and Mexican-American maintenance staff became her second group of informants. Three of the staff members (two Mexican Americans and one African American) were remarkably sensitive to the project's intergroup concerns and to the settlement experience of newcomer tenants. The working relationships Hagan developed with these three staff members proved to be a methodological breakthrough. Located between management and tenants, the maintenance staff provided an intermediary perspective from which to understand patterns of integration between management and tenants and between established-resident and newcomer tenants.

On a daily basis Hagan observed intergroup interaction involving tenants, staff, and management. These observations took place in a variety of settings (swimming pools, patios, tennis courts, grills, garages) and a variety of situations (for example, the rental of an apartment, the eviction of a newcomer family).

In her conversations with maintenance workers, rental agents, and the complex's tennis director, Hagan focused on the effects of management's changing policies concerning the immigrant tenants. For example, once signs of restructuring became evident, she cautiously steered conversations toward the effect of restructuring measures (such as placing newcomers' apartments in the back sections and enforcing restrictions against children) on the Spanish-speaking newcomer tenants.

Hagan's role as cultural broker and in-house translator for the Spanish-speaking tenants facilitated entry into the apartments and lives of many newcomer tenants. She translated correspondence and conversations, assisted immigrants moving in or out of Arborland, and approached management and staff on their behalf. This role allowed Hagan to gauge tenant attitudes toward the restructuring process in Arborland and the influence of the restructuring measures on future directions in immigrant housing and intergroup relations.

Ethnographic Findings of Intergroup Relations during Arborland's First Restructuring Phase

Our research findings indicate that the first stage of restructuring, which brought many newcomers to Arborland, created a multigroup atmosphere—

one that promoted greater cross-cultural understanding between established-resident and newcomer tenants. The spatial layout of the apartment building, featuring several common courtyards, provides the different tenant groups with opportunities for daily interaction. Each of the buildings frames a courtyard area that has a swimming pool and a barbecue area. These complex facilities proved to be important promoters of intergroup interaction among the young and their parents, especially the mothers. Newcomer and established-resident women watched over each others' clothing while doing laundry and shared recipes while cooking on the courtyard grills. Many of the established-resident tenants in the back buildings of Arborland learned to distinguish the cultural origin of various foods prepared at Arborland (such as *pupusas* from Salvador and *chuchitos* from Guatemala), and some actually created a market for the sale of ethnic foods prepared in the complex. Edna, a young Salvadoran woman, for example, took advantage of the popularity of her recipes among the established-resident tenants and began selling *pupusas* door to door throughout the complex. She claimed that the Anglo and African-American tenants were her best customers and that on occasion she had been asked to cater for one of their parties.

Newcomer children, many of whom did not know how to swim when they arrived in the United States, learned to swim from Anglo, Mexican-American, and African-American established-resident children. In some cases, it was a more established newcomer who adopted the role of intermediary for recent arrivals. Fluent in both Spanish and English and more familiar with various facets of U.S. culture (sports, fashion, school norms, and the like), these young boys and girls occupied positions of high status among the newcomer youth. Jaime, a bilingual Salvadoran teenager who had been living in the complex for eight years, was frequently given the task of orienting young newcomers at school. Although Jaime barely passed his courses (Hagan spent many an evening tutoring him), he was admired by newcomer parents and their children because of his successes in the United States. He received legal status through IRCA's legalization program in 1988. He was a member of the high-school football and tennis teams and—most important—was among the first newcomers in Arborland to finish high school, in 1991.

Initially reluctant to play this intermediary role because of the responsibility it brought, by 1988 Jaime enjoyed his elevated status but was clearly sensitive to the adjustments newcomer children must make in order to succeed in a culture foreign to them. As Jaime told Hagan:

> I was so young when I came here and I have been here so long, I had almost forgotten what it was like. Hector [his older brother] doesn't like to talk about Salvador and what it was like when we left and what we went through when we arrived. Hanging out with some of the guys here and seeing the work you do helps me remember how hard it was for us when we first arrived.

Similarly, many of the more established newcomer women, the majority of whom are from Mexico, have established a door-to-door catalog-vending business, catering mostly to more recent immigrant women, who welcome the opportunity to order household items out of a Spanish-written catalog.

These cross-cultural exchanges were initiated by established-resident tenants as well as the more recent and more established newcomer tenants. On separate occasions, Hagan was approached by two African-American residents and asked whether she would teach them Spanish. Frank, one of the young men who requested her help, worked as a manager at Circle K, a nearby convenience store, and spoke of the need to speak Spanish on the job. As Frank explained, "Our customers are mostly Spanish-speaking. With the new law, we are hiring more and more legal aliens, but most don't speak English. They are great workers, and I feel that I need to communicate with them to keep them." In 1991, Frank was taking Spanish lessons from his Guatemalan neighbor and in return gave English lessons to his neighbor.

Newcomers of different nationalities also attempted to cross the cultural barriers that separated them. Mr. G, an ethnic Chinese immigrant from Korea and the owner of a nearby convenience store, was proud to tell Hagan, "Thanks to the Mexicans, Guatemalans, and Salvadorans I can now speak better Spanish than English." According to Mr. G., learning Spanish was more important than learning English, since "most of my customers are Spanish speakers. Whites prefer to shop at the larger stores elsewhere. The Mexicans use my store because I am friendly; sometimes I give credit. It is easy for them. They can walk here and visit here." Mr. G. stocked a variety of Latino foodstuffs and installed several computer games in his store to attract new, younger clients.

Miguel, a Guatemalan mechanic, established a thriving car-repair business in the garage area of the complex. While he serviced many cars belonging to newcomer tenants, he was unable to attract business from established-resident tenants. As Miguel explained, "They [established residents] would rather use the car-care centers in the area, where they can have their cars not only repaired but cleaned and polished as well. The immigrants, on the other hand, are used to a neighbor working on their car."

Other Arborland entrepreneurs were unable to attract the newcomers to their establishments and consequently did not respond favorably to the newcomer presence. Luci, an older Anglo woman, had been operating the complex's oldest private business, a women's beauty salon, in one of the apartment units for fourteen years. The beauty shop closed its doors at the end of the first year of fieldwork at Arborland. When Luci announced that she would be closing her doors because of lack of business, she blamed the newcomers. The following comments made by Luci led to some interesting insights into the cultural distance than can exist between newcomers and residents and the competitive and conflictive nature of evolving relations under economic and demographic restructuring:

> I used to have lots of clients from the apartment building, but we have too many foreigners here, don't you think so? If I can't talk to them, I don't want them. Anyways, they have ruined my business. I hear they [newcomers] have their own hairdresser.

Observations of Luci and the operation she ran, however, paint a different picture of why she failed to draw business from tenants. Luci was an older woman who maintained a very untidy, unkempt image. Her face was thickly caked with makeup, curlers were randomly scattered throughout her hair, and she never looked very happy to see a potential customer. The interior of the shop was dark, disheveled, and cluttered with period salon fixtures and photos of hairstyles from the fifties and sixties. Her clients were predominantly older Anglo women from the area, who had been coming to her to have their hair done for years. It is difficult to imagine any of the younger women in the complex, regardless of ethnicity or newcomer resident status, seeking out Luci's antiquated style of hairdressing. Given these factors, the source of Luci's hostility toward "foreigners" becomes clearer. She no longer attracted any residents, and, rather than recognize that this might have something to do with the loss of several hundred tenants in recent years or with her business style, she blamed the most vulnerable and defenseless group within reach, the non-English-speaking tenants.

Despite the opportunities Arborland's mixed tenant population presented for greater intergroup interaction, the actual development of new relations between newcomer and established-resident tenants took place primarily among individuals, and it was usually a specific situation or development that brought them together (or sometimes kept them apart). For newcomer and established-resident women at Arborland, the common use of Arborland's facilities enabled an exchange of household ideas and chores. For Frank, the need to learn Spanish for work led him to solicit help from his Guatemalan neighbor. For many of the newcomer teenagers, making friends with an established youth in the complex became especially important for learning cultural norms at school. On the other hand, Luci's failing business became the issue that kept her apart from the newcomers. Intergroup relations developed from particular situations and were usually temporary in duration, disappearing along with the situations that caused them.

At the group level, our observations at Arborland show that resident/immigrant status and race/ethnicity continued to delineate important boundaries of social interaction among the groups. New immigrants often clustered in certain sections in the building and shied away from many activities and settings that provided opportunities for interaction (the tennis courts, the Jacuzzi, and management-sponsored beer busts). And when established residents and newcomer immigrants overlapped in these activities, there was considerable social distance among the groups. For example, Latino immigrants

New immigrants in Arborland public square (photograph by Tina Otto)

generally avoided the tennis courts at the peak hours (5:00–7:00 P.M.), when long-term residents generally packed the courts. The newcomers preferred to play early in the morning, when the courts were relatively unused and the resident tennis pro was not around.

Similarly, African-American, Mexican-American, and newcomer tenants rarely frequented the on-premises restaurant and bar, which was operated by an Anglo man. These tenant groups considered the restaurant and bar an Anglo drinking establishment. Juan, a Mexican-American informant and eight-year resident of the complex, captured the sentiments of many Latino and African-American tenants:

> I have never been to the restaurant and bar, the reason being that I don't think they would allow comingling between Anglos, blacks, and Mexicans [the term "Mexican" is often used by established-resident groups to describe anyone of Latino origin] who go there if they go there. It's not that I have anything against whites, I just

> don't like being around them when they are drinking because they start putting other groups down. Things can get out of hand.

In reality, things rarely got "out of hand" at Arborland. In the two-year period, we documented just one instance of intergroup violence, and it was largely attributed to a resident's lack of cultural familiarity with newcomer groups and newcomer response. In this particular case, a fight broke out when a group of newcomer Salvadorans opposed an Anglo security guard's tendency to group the newcomers under the category of "Mexicans" and to ascribe to them a series of negative attributes attached to Mexicans.

While conflict was not identified as a pattern of intergroup interaction at Arborland, group boundaries did exist, and occasionally we sensed a certain level of tension underlying the accommodating intergroup relations in the complex. Interviews with newcomer and established-resident tenants did uncover negative intergroup attitudes and cultural misunderstandings. For example, on Saturday mornings the pools were often trashed with beer bottles from Friday night parties organized by students; yet it was often newcomer tenants who were accused of "trashing the premises." Similarly, when a washing machine or another piece of equipment broke down, established residents often blamed the newcomers without providing evidence. On several such occasions, established-resident tenants told Hagan that different newcomer groups "broke the machines because they [newcomers] jam the machines with their foreign coins." Yet these negative feelings rarely translated into open conflict. Because group boundaries are maintained through social distancing, relations can appear harmonious and residents can legitimately remark on how well everyone gets along.

Ethnographic Findings of Intergroup Relations during Arborland's Second Restructuring Phase

Whether the tenants of Arborland would have been able eventually to tear down the social boundaries that limited interaction to levels of tolerance and cordiality remains an empirical question we were unable to answer, because Arborland management initiated a second phase of restructuring. As in the first phase of restructuring, intergroup relations were changed as a result of management's ability to withhold or release its resources to the newcomers.

As long as Latino tenants were needed to raise the occupancy of the apartment units, management had been accommodating. However, once the city's economy began to show signs of recovery in the summer of 1988, management's behavior toward the Latino renters was quickly transformed from one of accommodation to one of mere tolerance and, by 1989, exclusion.

Anticipating an economic recovery in the housing industry, Arborland management began a second phase of restructuring in the summer of 1988. This phase involved upgrading efforts to change the low-income newcomer tenancy to a more professional and corporate-related one, a tenancy anticipated as a result of Houston's economic upturn. Measures to upgrade included installing a sophisticated security system, evicting all units containing families (usually Latino) with children, changing social rules regarding management-tenant communication to "English only," creating a policy of residential segregation, and raising rents considerably.

Prior to the installation of the electronic security system, access into and out of the complex was uncontrolled, and tenants moved freely among the buildings. The new security system, installed to limit and control entry to and exit from the premises, provided three main access points to the complex: a visitors' and tenants' pedestrian entrance at building B, an entrance for automobiles between buildings A and B, and a combined automobile and pedestrian entrance for tenants (mostly newcomer) residing in buildings C, D, and E (see figure 4.2). Not only was there an inequitable distribution of entrances across the complex, but outside residents visiting tenants in buildings C, D, and E had to park their cars at building A and walk the lengthy distance of the complex to reach the rear sections. Moreover, tenants had to have a computerized card to gain access to the building. Management issued only two cards per apartment unit, making it very difficult for tenants of units shared by several persons to gain access to the complex. Established-resident tenants repeatedly complained to management about the inconvenience and security risks of the system. Management assured tenants of the upcoming construction of more access points but made no moves in that direction.

Despite the difficulties posed by the new security system, the tenants, especially the newcomers, developed strategies to overcome at least one of the problems posed by the system—insufficient gate cards. Considering the security system inconvenient and useless, many tenants went out of their way to assist the newcomers with no passes by holding the gate open for them and even lending them their gate cards.

In the early morning hours, when many of the newcomer men returned home from working night shifts, groups of them could be found waiting outside the gate. The driver of the first vehicle encountering the group ushered the waiting newcomers through the gate. When the assistance of another tenant was not available, tenants waiting outside the gate asked newcomer children to pass through the bars and over the gates. The persistence of tenant strategies and intergroup resistance continued to stump management, to the amusement of many tenants.

The difficulties experienced by newcomer tenants when management switched to a policy of writing tenants notices in English only was illustrated in a notice regarding the new security system. In the early summer of 1988, a notice was mailed to all tenants informing them of the new security system. The notice was the first to be written in English only, as far as the newcomers could remember. Shortly after the arrival of the notice, newcomer tenants began approaching Hagan and Jose, the Mexican-American maintenance worker, for a Spanish translation of the notice. When Hagan asked management to translate the notice into Spanish, she was told that this service was longer available because bilingual agents no longer worked with the company.

Although the departure of these agents was not directly linked to management policy, Amy, the befriended rental agent in the front office, told Hagan that the manager was not hiring a new bilingual agent. Amy said she thought this quite unfair, considering how much business depended on the Latino newcomers, who were "so easy to get along with, because they never complain to us." It was clear from a follow-up conversation with the manager that he was not concerned with the problems newcomers might encounter with the security system or with notices written only in English. This interpretation of the situation was echoed by Jose and Paul, two of the maintenance workers, and Amy, the reluctant rental agent. Hagan, Paul, and Jose finally received permission to use the front office to hold a seminar for the Latino newcomer tenants. Reluctant to allow the seminar explaining the new policy to be held during the weekend, management finally agreed on two weekend evenings. Hagan, Paul, and Jose prepared and mailed out a notice in Spanish informing newcomers of the seminar. Over one hundred interested Spanish-speaking tenants showed up—an overwhelming response.

A second upgrading measure introduced in the summer of 1988 involved evicting families with children. When the research began in 1987, residents were well aware of the "adults-only" policy but understood that it was not enforced. In May of 1988, management began an aggressive campaign to evict families with children, including paying fifty dollars to each security or maintenance person who reported to management the presence of a unit with children. This chapter's opening vignette highlighted the intergroup response to the policy. The policy led to a unified resistance by newcomers and established-resident tenants, the latter group responding to what they perceived as an unfair policy with severe ramifications for the newcomer tenants.

Management did yield to the demands of the intergroup alliance by extending the eviction time, but refused to acknowledge to Hagan that Arborland had ever maintained a policy of renting units to tenant families. Yet, Hagan's conversations with immigrant families and with Amy, the rental agent, indicated that newcomer families with children had never been barred from renting an apartment. One wonders whether the rapid eviction of these families was associated not only with economic restructuring in the industry but also with the pending passage of the 1988 Fair Housing Amendment, which would ban discrimination for reasons of age and make "adults-only" apartment complexes illegal. Over one dozen families known to the researcher were evicted in less than one month.

The third and perhaps most significant indication of management's switch from a policy of newcomer accommodation to one of newcomer exclusion occurred in the summer of 1988, when an implicit policy of residential segregation began to be implemented. This policy involved placing Anglo tenants in the front sections of the complex and placing newcomer tenants in the rear sections (buildings C, D, and E). To a lesser but still noticeable extent, African Americans were also placed in the back buildings. According to Gina, an African-American student and tenant (Arborland houses a number of students from a nearby college), African-American and Mexican-American students were being placed in the back buildings and Anglo students in the front buildings. When Gina was asked how this could be done, given that housing applications were submitted to the college and not the apartment complex, she explained that the housing application had a space for the designation of the student's ethnicity.

The following comment relayed by Juan Carlos, a Mexican-American staff member of Arborland, reveals the logic underlying the formation of this policy and the stereotypical image management has of its newcomer tenants:

> We are trying to change the "caliber" of the tenants. This policy [residential segregation] exists because we realize that these people [newcomer Latinos] will bring in their brother, sister, and whole family. How would you like to be showing an apartment in, let's say, A building, and you have twenty [Latino] people living in one apartment? That's why we put them in the back, because we realize that this will happen with the Latino population, especially your resident aliens.

A policy of residential segregation was reinforced through differential rents, with units in the back sections having lower rents. One might argue that the differential costs alone produced the trend toward residential segregation; however, this argument can be countered by the fact that when Hagan moved in Arborland in 1987 rents did not vary by building. A policy of different rents was implemented in the fall of 1988, several months after management implemented its policy of residential segregation. While any potential renter had the liberty to live in an apartment in the back building, the pattern that emerged was one of de facto segregation, since established residents were directed to the front buildings, while immigrants were directed to the back buildings.

From the newcomer's perspective, residential segregation was not initially problematic. Newcomers, especially the undocumented ones, preferred a clustering arrangement, because it facilitated greater interaction among kindred groups. Most of the established-resident tenants were not aware of the policy, since they rarely traveled to the back buildings. It was not until the spring of 1989 that the policy produced intergroup tension at Arborland. The passage of the 1988 Fair Housing Amendment (which actually took effect in March of 1989) forced Arborland management to allow families with children into the complex. During the spring and summer of 1989, an increasing number of families (mostly

Latino) moved into the complex. Newcomer families were rented units in the back buildings, giving rise not only to a concentration of families in the back buildings but also to a new dimension of segregation within the complex.

The rapid influx of children in the back buildings led to some negative remarks on part of neighboring African-American tenants, a group that rarely had expressed hostility. There were such comments as "Why do they have so many kids when they can't afford it?" and "The noise level has got out of hand since they let them bring their kids in." The response of African-American tenants was not surprising; it is probable that the majority of Arborland's single adult tenants, regardless of race or ethnic status, would have expressed similar sentiments if confronted with the same situation. Very few African-American and Anglo families have moved into Arborland, while many Latino newcomer families have. It is safe to assume that any arriving families, regardless of race/ethnicity or resident/newcomer status, would take the brunt of the discomfort residents felt.

In some ways, the response by neighboring tenants to the influx of newcomer families parallels the response of Luci, the beauty-shop owner, to the increasing presence of newcomers in Arborland. Luci blamed the newcomers for her failing business. Established-resident single tenants blamed the newcomers for recent legislation that caused what they saw as an invasion of their privacy. In both cases, the newcomers had no control over the issue, but because established residents felt victimized, scapegoating ran rampant.

Scapegoating can result from existing prejudices, but our findings indicate that the scapegoating by established residents in Arborland was a response to a sense of helplessness in the face of policies imposed from above. Anglos and other established residents in the apartment complex related the recent housing legislation to the presence of tenant immigrant families, not to some abstract notion of equal housing opportunity. In the same way, Luci related her business decline to the coming of Latino tenants and not to changes in hairstyles or apartment restructuring policies adopted in reaction to the city's economic downturn. These findings illustrate how imposed policies can shape interaction between established residents and new immigrants.

In the fall of 1989, rents at Arborland rose for the first time in the two-year research period. By January of 1990, when the research at Arborland ended, several newcomer households and families had left Arborland because they were unable to pay the higher rents. Some of the newcomers moved in with friends and kin living in Arborland, while others were forced to move farther west, where they reported that rents were lower but apartments were distant from work and friends.

In the spring of 1990, management began enforcing a limit on the number of occupants per unit (two for a one-bedroom apartment and four for a two-bedroom apartment). In a July 1990 visit to Arborland, Hagan learned that management was attempting to enforce this policy on a Salvadoran family who had

New Latino immigrants at Arborland (photograph by Tina Otto)

been living in a two-bedroom apartment since 1989. Although only four members of the family actually lived in the apartment unit, management contended that the unit included five members—that the granddaughter of the couple also lived in the household. In reality, the child lived with her parents at another complex but spent weekday mornings with her grandmother at Arborland while her mother was at work. The Salvadoran couple (both of whom received permanent residency in the United States through IRCA in 1990) refused to leave and requested verification from the manager of the complex where their daughter was a tenant. The Salvadoran couple, both of whom were valuable informants in the study, were very cognizant of the implications of changes at Arborland for newcomer tenants but were nonetheless shocked that management would turn on their family since they had been at Arborland so long. According to the father of the family, "They can get away with this behavior with many of the illegal immigrants, but not with us." Legal status had empowered the Salvadoran couple to protect their rights. For many of the undocumented tenants, however, fighting for housing rights was a luxury they could not afford.

The restructuring process continued at Arborland through 1990. Newcomer tenants who had managed to weather the restructuring storm in late 1990 informed Hagan that rents at Arborland had risen over one hundred dollars in the previous few months, in some cases a 40 percent increase. Tenants in other area complexes have reported rental increases of 50 percent in a single month. In fact, tenant complaints in one westside complex prompted the Department of Housing and Urban Development to investigate whether rent increases were being used to discriminate against minorities (Urban 1990).

Management continued to give Arborland its facelift during 1990. Fresh paint was put on the walls, new driveways were laid, and laundry rooms were renovated. In all these cases, however, buildings D and E, where most of the newcomers reside, were the last to receive the benefits of the improvements. For example, the old washing machines and dryers in buildings A, B, and C were replaced with new ones in the fall of 1989. In contrast, between November 1989 and February 1990, over four hundred tenants in building E had to share two washers and two dryers because the other four washers and dryers in the building had not been repaired. Many of the newcomers reluctantly accepted the inconvenience and did their laundry at building D. Established residents living in building E were less patient and persistently complained to management. When Hagan called the front office and complained for the third time, she was told that the machines were broken because "immigrants were jamming the money slots with foreign coins, and because of this we will have to replace the old machines with models resistant to tampering, which will take some time."

The first phase of Arborland's restructuring widened opportunities for intergroup interaction at Arborland. While social class differences distinguished newcomers from established residents at Arborland, all were new residents to Arborland. The common transient status shared by Arborland tenants as a result of managements' restructuring strategies had the short-term effect of promoting greater cordiality and cohesion between newcomers and established residents. Developments in the second phase, however, have created new social and economic barriers. Middle-class tenants have adjusted to higher rents, while newcomer tenants have left the complex in search of more affordable housing. Rising rents, management policies, and other restructuring measures are shutting the window of opportunity for new intergroup relations.

Implications of Apartment Restructuring for Intergroup Relations

The upgrading process that is now occurring throughout westside Houston involves three developments important for intergroup relations. One is the planned underdevelopment of apartment housing by preventing the erection of additional complexes and by continuing to destroy thousands of units. This, no doubt, will create a tight apartment housing market, especially for low-income tenants, who will have fewer alternatives. This could promote apartment housing competition between low-income established residents and newcomers.

The second development includes the infusion of out-of-state and out-of-country capital by individuals and corporations that are buying up apartment complexes and raising the rents. This could promote residential separation between established residents and newcomers in the west side to the extent that these two groups represent different income capacities. This situation can also be promoted by a third development: upgrading efforts in apartment complexes by owners who appear to be trying to leave behind their low-income newcomer clientele in favor of the more professional and corporate-related population that is supposed to increase with Houston's economic upturn.

We have observed several ways in which upgrading takes place. In Arborland, management has implemented several upgrading efforts (for example, security gates and higher rents) since the summer of 1988. In many of the surrounding complexes, which housed a greater proportion of newcomers, a different strategy is developing. Rather than being continuously upgraded as was Arborland, several apartment complexes (eleven by the spring of 1991) were being completely renovated. This involved displacing the present tenant population and closing down the complex entirely. When the renovated apartment complexes reopened, they did so under new and more glamorous names and with higher rents.

We believe that the different approaches to upgrading may be related to the composition of the tenant population. Many of the apartment complexes that have displaced their entire tenant population were homes to newcomers only. Arborland, in contrast, housed a multiethnic population. Management in the complex has been forced to make improvements to attract and retain the established-resident component of the tenant population. The heterogeneity (newcomers and residents) of the tenant population weakens the possibility of conflict between management and newcomer tenants, since Anglos act as buffers between the two through their intermediary role.

Yet the upgrading efforts have not been equitably distributed across Arborland. More renovation has been done on the front buildings of the complex, where the majority of the established residents live. In addition, by implementing differential rents, management has been able to maintain full occupancy and avoid the costs of closing down during a period of renovation.

A pattern of apartment renovation is clearly under way in westside Houston. In those complexes where newcomers are displaced, we should expect several ramifications for intergroup relations. Unable to afford the increasing rents, many newcomers are moving out to the western fringes of the city. In 1989, one complex rented units for $250; in 1990, the same complex, after renovation, rented a unit for over $400. One immigrant spoke of the overnight increase in rent that prohibited his remaining in his apartment. According to him, the suddenness of the rent increase is causing many economic and job-related problems for newcomers residing in the area, since many are forced to move away from their jobs and friends. Others are remaining in the area, but moving into poorer-quality rental housing that has not yet undergone renovation.

If this latter trend continues to develop, then what we might see in the future is another form of residential segregation. What was once household or building segregation within a complex might evolve into a residential pattern where complexes occupied solely by newcomers are situated near complexes in which only established residents live.

Conclusion

Analysis of the double restructuring process (shifting to new immigrant tenants and later to established residents) in the city's apartment industry leads to insights for theorizing about intergroup relations. First, it shows how macro-level social change specific to economic crises can influence intergroup relations. In the Houston case, restructuring in the apartment industry brought new Latino immigrants into the proximity of Anglo established residents. Our fieldwork at Arborland showed how this proximity led to the development of intergroup relations. In some cases, in search of cultural understandings of cuisine or different languages, individuals in both established-resident and new-immigrant tenant groups initiated interaction that crossed group boundaries. In other cases, in reaction to prejudices and stereotypes, some individuals, such as Luci the hairdresser, exhibited behavior that emphasized group differences. The upturn of Houston's economy, on the other hand, prompted the apartment's management to initiate restructuring measures (evicting families with children, installing a security fence, and returning to English-only tenant bulletins) that acted as catalysts for the formation of solidarity ties between some established residents and new immigrants in the complex.

Second, while previous research (see Sassen-Koob 1984; Bach 1986; Morales 1983) has highlighted the labor role of immigrants in restructuring processes, the Houston case shows the important consumer role that new immigrants can also play in these processes. It was precisely the new immigrants' consumer role as renters that prompted Houston's westside apartment owners and managers to adopt restructuring measures to bring them into the apartment complexes and then to restrict their presence in these complexes.

Third, the second phase of restructuring (getting rid of the newcomer tenants) showed how tenuous macro-change in intergroup conditions can be. In many of Houston's westside apartment complexes, residentially based intergroup interaction (and the opportunity for interaction) ended by the late 1980s, when the second restructuring phase pushed new immigrant tenants out. In Arborland, rising rents and management's drive against immigrant families with children displaced a significant number of new-immigrant tenants who had interacted with established residents or who had lived in apartment sections with a high probability of intergroup interaction.

Finally, and perhaps the most theoretically significant point, the Houston restructuring case is instructive for understanding the importance of the structural context of intergroup relations. Specifically, concepts of intergroup relations can be grounded on the cyclical structural change of U.S. capitalist society. This is an important point, we believe, because it helps to link intergroup relations to the broader socioeconomic structural underpinnings of society. The emergence of intergroup relations at Arborland resulted from restructuring strategies that were adopted in response to the city's economic structural change. This change, in turn, was linked to industrial structural changes in the global oil economy.

References

Bach, Robert L. 1986. Immigration: Issues of Ethnicity, Class, and Public Policy in the United States. In *From Foreign Workers to Settlers? Transnational Migration and the Emergence of New Minorities,* edited by Martin O. Heisler and Barbara Schmitter Heisler. Beverly Hills, Calif.: Sage.

Beauregard, Robert A., ed. 1989. *Economic Restructuring and Political Response.* Newbury Park, Calif.: Sage Publications.

Chavez, Leo. 1988. Settlers and Sojourners: The Case of Mexicans in the United States. *Human Organization* 47 (Summer): 95–108.

Cornelius, Wayne A., Leo R. Chavez, and Jorge Castro. 1982. *Mexican Immigrants in Southern California: A Summary of Current Knowledge.* La Jolla, Calif.: Center for U.S.–Mexican Studies.

Feagin, Joe R. 1988. *Free Enterprise City: Houston in Political and Economic Perspective.* New Brunswick, N.J.: Rutgers University Press.

Hagan, Jacqueline M., and Nestor P. Rodriguez. 1989. Evolving Relations Between Established Racial/Ethnic Groups and Latino Newcomers: Ethnographic Findings in an Apartment Neighborhood. Paper presented at the Annual Meeting of the American Sociological Association, San Francisco, 11–13 August.

Harvey, David. 1981. The Urban Process under Capitalism: A Framework for Analysis. In *Urbanization and Urban Planning in Capitalist Society,* edited by Michael Dear and Allen J. Scott. New York: Methuen.

Henderson, Jeffrey, and Manuel Castells. 1987. *Global Restructuring and Territorial Development.* London: Sage.

Morales, Rebecca. 1983. Transnational Labor: Undocumented Workers in the Los Angeles Automobile Industry. *International Migration Review* 17 (Winter):570–79.

Real Estate Evaluation Consultants (REVAC). 1990. Harris County Apartment Occupancy and Rental Survey. Houston.

Rodriguez, Nestor. 1987. Undocumented Central Americans in Houston: Diverse Populations. *International Migration Review* 17:4–26.

Rodriguez, Nestor, and Jacqueline Hagan. 1989. Undocumented Central American Migration to Houston in the 1980s. *Journal of La Raza Studies* 2 (Summer/Fall): 1–30.

Rosen, Pat. 1990. "City Apartment Demolitions Picking Up after a Slow Start." *Houston Business Journal,* 1 October, p. 16.

Sallee, Rad. 1991. "Minorities Now Majority in Houston." *Houston Chronicle,* 8 February, p. 25A.

Sassen-Koob, Saskia. 1984. The New Labor Demand in Global Cities. In *Cities in Transformation: Class, Capital, and the State,* edited by Michael Peter Smith. Beverly Hills Calif.: Sage.

Shelton, Beth Anne, Nestor P. Rodriguez, Joe R. Feagin, Robert D. Bullard, and Robert D. Thomas. 1989. *Houston: Growth and Decline in a Sunbelt Boomtown.* Philadelphia: Temple University Press.

Smith, Barton. 1989. *Handbook on the Houston Economy.* Houston: Center for Public Policy, University of Houston.

Urban, Jerry. 1990. "Rent Hikes Put Squeeze on Tenants." *Houston Chronicle,* 13 May, p. 1A.

5 TRANSCENDING BOUNDARIES AND CLOSING RANKS: HOW SCHOOLS SHAPE INTERRELATIONS

JUDITH G. GOODE, JO ANNE SCHNEIDER, AND SUZANNE BLANC

It is graduation time at Peterson School. The eighth-graders include children from Puerto Rico, Colombia, Guatemala, Portugal, Korea, Taiwan, Vietnam, India, and Jamaica as well as established Americans of European and African descent. The only Puerto Rican city councilman orates about their bright futures. The established white leaders of local community groups award prizes. No ethnic, racial, or national group dominates the awards. After the performance of the orchestra and chorus, which include most eighth-graders, parents cheer and applaud. At the end of the ceremony, many participants cry. The music teacher is presented with a gift. In tears, she hugs her students. The Home and School leaders, neighborhood old-timers, speak nostalgically of the wonderful experience they had producing the yearbook with the students. Parents with limited English ability speak to the teachers and to other parents, sharing in the success of their children.

For two years this class has been observed to show relatively little awareness of the boundaries between racial and nationality groups. Best friends crossed lines and maintained bonds even when they left school. For example, one day Maria, who goes back and forth to Puerto Rico for family events, was sitting next to Cathy and Eileen, two white Euro-American established residents who were her best friends. She was reading a letter from Alicia, who had recently returned to Portugal; she then passed the letter to Blanca, another close friend, who was born in Lisbon and came to the United States when she was two. Boy-girl relationships seem to be as mixed as same-sex friendships. At the eighth-grade graduation party, almost all the dancing couples were "mixed" in terms of race, ethnicity, or newcomer/oldtimer status. Interracial dating was common in this group.

Several miles away, in a neighborhood that was once similar to Peterson's but

We would like to thank the many collaborators on the Philadelphia Changing Relations project. For materials on the schools, we are especially grateful to Juana McCormack, Hong Joon Kim, Cyndy Carter, David Marin, Apparajita Mitra, and Saku Longshore. All the schools have been given pseudonyms as have all individuals.

has experienced different dynamics, we find Dixon school. It is lunchtime followed by recess in the schoolyard. During lunch, one area of the cafeteria is dominated by Spanish-speaking clusters. At another set of tables, the few African-American students sit together. In the playground, local white women serve as aides—paid supervisors of lunchroom and recess activities. They talk to each other as they break up fights and nurture crying children. A few Spanish-speaking women also work as paid aides. They similarly confine their conversations to each other, the Spanish-speaking children, and parents who have come to the schoolyard to make sure that their children are not hurt or treated unfairly by the white school staff. As recess progresses, the black security guard who helps maintain discipline talks about how the Spanish-speaking parents constantly accuse him of bias and threaten to sue him for discrimination. He is surprised that he, a fellow victim of oppression, should be a target of their animosity.

These two schools exist in the same system. They are staffed in similar ways, in neighborhoods that are both part of the historically Catholic white working-class area of the city. Yet in the ways relations between children and adults transcend or reflect the ethnic/racial boundaries of their respective neighborhoods, they are very different. This paper will explore how local conditions and mediating institutions facilitate or inhibit the transcendence of boundaries.

The Study

Our study compares four schools in three neighborhoods in eastern North Philadelphia. Two (Peterson and Dixon) are public schools, and two (St. Ignatius and Ascension) are parochial. Two of the neighborhoods (Port Richmond and Kensington) are predominantly working-class, one stable and the other declining. The third (Olney) combines working-class, aspiring middle-class, and middle-class populations. Each has experienced the recent economic/ demographic transformation differently. Subtle differences in the trajectories of the communities have created differences in class composition, patterns of residential segregation, the neighborhood role in the absorption of new immigrants, and power relations between groups. We expected these differences to be reflected in relations between established adults and new immigrants in school organizations and ultimately in children's relationships.

While public and parochial schools share the central mission of educating children to be citizens and workers, the two systems differ in their relative emphasis of different goals. Public schools emphasize individualistic achievement within a context of equal opportunity. Parochial schools emphasize the perpetuation of religious and moral values and the reproduction of the parish community. Teaching emphasizes love of God and responsibility to family and community. We expected these differences to be reflected in relations.

Ultimately, we also discovered other critical differentiating factors. Each

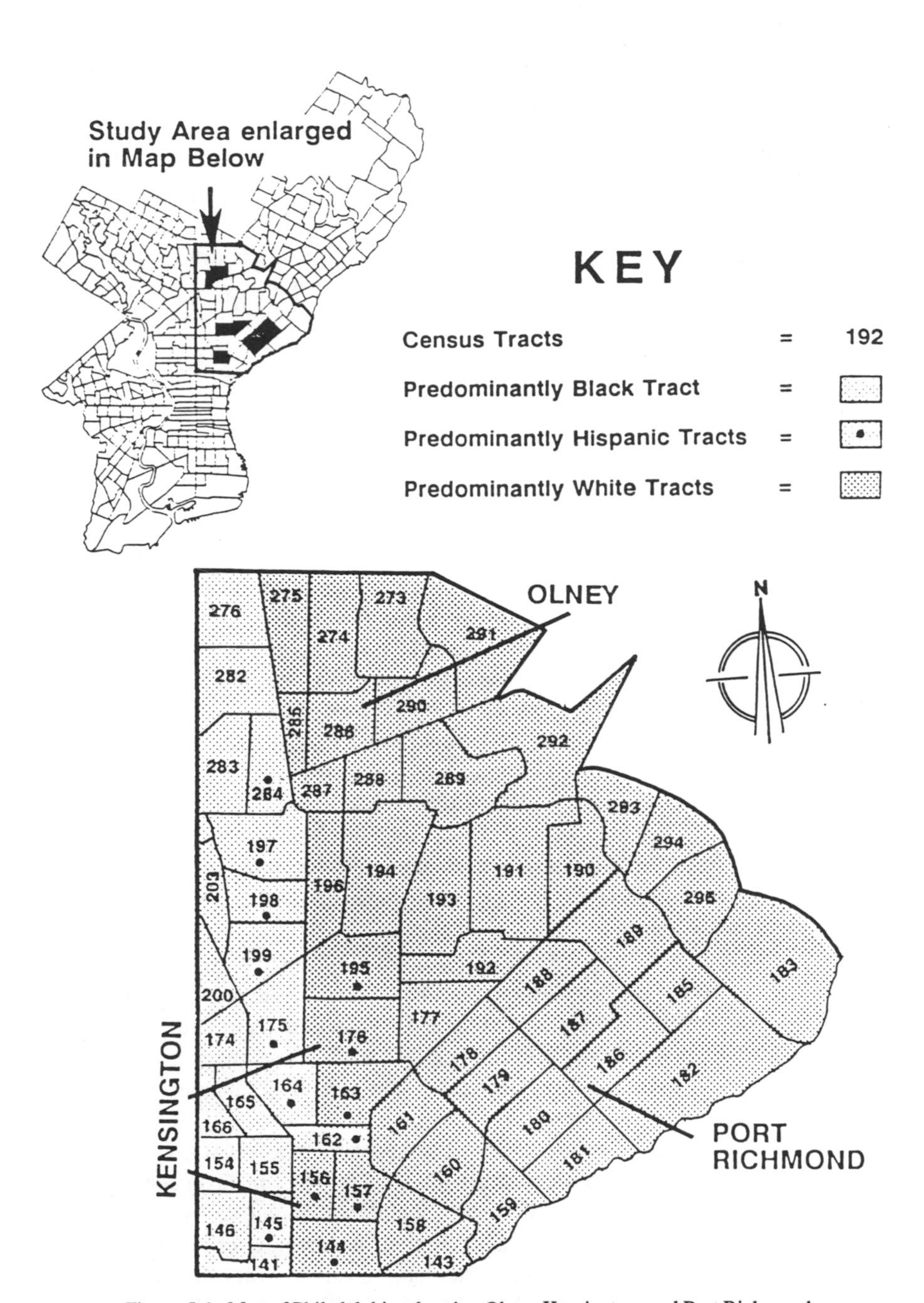

Figure 5.1. Map of Philadelphia, showing Olney, Kensington, and Port Richmond

school as an institution has a different ability to resist pressures from the outside and control its student population, resources, and staff. The degree to which populations are stable or transient depends not only on neighborhood factors but also on the results of this control. For the public school, this means clout at the district level. For parochial schools, it means the parish resource base and its ability to raise funds. It is the central argument of this paper that these differences in institutional history and structure interact with neighborhood class dynamics and school goals to engender variable patterns of ground-level relationships. The maintenance or transcendence of boundaries is a result of these complex social processes.

Why Schools?

The Philadelphia Changing Relations project focused on several arenas: community organizations, shopping strips, workplaces, and schools. These arenas were chosen because they were settings that brought newcomers and established residents together for varying purposes. Schools are often considered a critical element in the "Americanization" process of the massive turn-of-the-century waves of European immigration (Weiss 1982). Traditionally, observers have shared the assimilationist assumption that the classroom provided a relatively neutral and objective environment for immigrant children, allowing them to achieve mobility within American society (Parsons 1959). In contrast, revisionist historians and Marxist social theorists argue that American schools have merely funneled immigrant children into the capitalist class structure (for example, Bowles and Gintis 1976; Katz 1968; Tyack 1974).

More recently, there have been analyses that see school structures, curricula, and ideologies as relatively autonomous, the results of complex political and social struggles (Willis 1977; Sieber 1979; Baron et al. 1981; Wrigley 1982; Katznelson and Weir 1985).

Within such a framework we examine schools as one of the few public arenas in which established residents and newcomers engage in regular, sustained interaction. Moreover, children at age five and six start off even, without the developed social constructions of difference that adults carry. They cross group boundaries freely, unless school structures and personnel channel their contacts.

Much contemporary anthropology of schools focuses on ways in which schools teach cognitive and social skills for different roles in advanced capitalist systems. The ways in which linguistic, social, and cognitive discontinuities between home and school environments impede academic success of minority and immigrant students has been of particular interest (see, for example, Spindler and Spindler 1989; Trueba 1989; Weisner, Gallimore, and Jordan 1988).

The following analysis is consistent with the assumption that schools are sites of social and ideological production and reproduction, but does not focus on what is learned in the classroom. Rather, it extends the discussion to include an examination of the processes and forces that structure intergroup relations. These include both internal social processes and the interactions between schools and external mediating institutions: local community structures and educational bureaucracies in their citywide contexts. In this manner, ethnography contributes a different perspective to the ongoing attempt to understand the school's role in class formation, ideologies of Americanization, and the negotiation of racial and ethnic identities.

Shared Structures

While this paper focuses on the differences in social processes within schools, all schools have common structures. Each school has a core of regulars: the professional staff, a group of nonprofessional workers, parent volunteers, and the students.

Authorities

The professional staff in the public schools is organized into classroom teachers and superordinate administrators who formally mediate relations with outside constituencies. Since the school district has integrated its teaching staff more successfully than its students, the staff members are often outsiders to the neighborhood and oriented to the central administration and union in terms of their career interests. They are frequently of different racial and ethnic backgrounds. In the two schools we studied, teachers were about one-third black, one-third Jewish, and one-third Euro-American Catholic. They were also different in class identity from the residents of predominantly working-class settings. On the other hand, the parochial schoolteachers are likely to be current or former local residents.

In all the schools, the nonprofessional staff is dominated by local working-class women. This includes secretaries and nonteaching aides who supervise informal lunch and recess activities. They represent community interests and see themselves as maintaining local rules in the face of change and threats by outsiders (Goode 1990). These staff members informally control the periphery of the school and affect the access and attitudes of outsiders. In the public schools, male NTAs (nonteaching aides) and security guards are also hired to back up discipline. They are often not community residents.

Other volunteer parents in the school run the Home and School associations. These groups work with and often under the control of the principals and teachers to promote common school interests: achievement, discipline, fundraising, and ceremonial events.

Points of Tension in Public and Private Schools

The structure of the public schools creates several points of conflict and tension between adult authorities. The pressures of a large external bureaucracy are myriad. Points of tension include the relations between the principal and teachers over policy and career-related evaluations and transfers. There are often conflicts within the community of teachers. Teachers tend to be friendly with others of their own race or ethnic group, as we will see below. The lengthy and disruptive teacher strikes that had characterized the school district in the early 1980s had left a residue of hostility between strong unionists and those who saw a contradiction between the demands of the union and the interests of the children.

There are tensions between established community representatives (aides) and the "outsider" professionals in the public schools. While protective of the school, the aides see themselves as important actors who are ignored and exploited by the administration and teachers. They resent having to line up students and keep them disciplined until tardy teachers arrive. They believe that administrators do not back them up enough in discipline.

There are also conflicts between established community residents in the school's inner circle and less connected parents who are resented for not knowing the rules of the playground or for not volunteering and participating. Since many established parents can remain inactive but still have access to important networks and knowledge, the newcomer parents remain the least connected.

Parochial schools have the same basic components as public schools, but their structural relationships are different. The parish is in charge of elementary schools. While the archdiocese does provide some special services, the schools are effectively dependent on local resources. Here fundraising is essential rather than supplementary as it is in public schools. Parochial schools are not as directed by bureaucratic rules. In fact, only a handful of people manage the archdiocesan school system, in contrast to hundreds in the school district's massive central bureaucracy (Binzen 1970).

Within the parish there is an expectation of a seamless community, with the professionals (the teaching order and lay teachers) and parent volunteers united as part of the whole. The schools see themselves as families writ large, or communities with common goals. There is much less hierarchy and cleavage between professionals and parents. Over the last few decades, the proportion of lay teachers has increased. Parochial schools pay much lower salaries than those of the public schools and consequently tend to recruit local teachers with lower credentials than those of their public school counterparts. Incentives for teachers include tuition benefits for their children and the sense of community and family that pervades the school, creating a very different environment from the public school. The emphasis on moral behavioral prescriptions masks any tension or conflict below the surface.

In spite of the emphasis on community, many parish schools in changing neighborhoods are seriously affected by the underlying pressure for resources. This can affect relationships between established community residents and newcomers if the latter are seen as not making contributions to fundraising.

Daily Routines

All these schools are similar in their daily routines and offer many opportunities for spontaneous contact and play between children of different backgrounds. Most of the day is spent in classrooms, which offer the greatest opportunities for contact. Lunchrooms in three of the four schools organized seating by classroom as well, reinforcing these bonds. Recess on the playground is entirely unstructured. Here ties built in classrooms are still evident but compete with ties based on neighborhood groups and kinship.

Contact between the school and families is also structured by the daily routine. The daily round begins when children come to school early in the morning with parents or older siblings. The classroom day is punctuated by lunch periods and recesses in the schoolyard. At dismissal time in the afternoon, the morning pattern repeats itself as parents pick up children. Some parents, particularly newcomer parents, also congregate around the schoolyard at lunch and recess times. They come to talk to their children, to bring them food and snacks (mostly forbidden), and to make sure that they are being well treated.

Structural Influence on Children's Relations

How does the structure of the school channel relations? One way is through organizing classrooms in a nonrandom way. The two public schools, Peterson and Dixon, organize classrooms by ability.[1] This has the effect of keeping the same children together throughout their grade-school years. Ability tracking brings children of different background together in classrooms. It did not segregate students by race or ethnicity in the schools we observed.

Language ability is also used to organize children, and this tends to separate newcomers from established residents. ESOL (English for Speakers of Other Languages) programs in the public schools and informal language buddy system in the parochial schools tend to structure relations, isolating some groups.

Control over nonclassroom activities is limited to the way in which lunchtable assignments are given and enforced, as well as rules about moving and speaking. Gender is the most salient social characteristic affecting everyday interaction in all schools.[2]

Methodology

The school component of this ethnographic study consisted of regular participant observation in four schools largely at lunchtime, at informal play times,

1. Public schools choose whether to use ability tracking or not. Not all public schools use ability tracking.

2. We were amazed by the emphasis on cross-sex relationships in children's interaction at all ages in all schools. Second-graders talked constantly about girlfriends and boyfriends and who liked whom. Cross-gender teasing dominated informal play.

and during after-school activities. Wherever possible, we assumed the role of lunchroom or classroom aides and regularly participated in the activities of the schools. Schools were visited at least once a week throughout the study. All special public events such as concerts, plays, graduations, and parents' meetings were attended for a two-year period. Formal interviews were also held with principals, teachers, aides, and Home and School Association leaders. Informal discussions took place with many parents outside the schools, and in the last year of the research, structured household interviews were conducted with parents whom we had met through the research process. These interviews gathered information about life histories, social relationships, and social networks for members of the household. They included both newcomers and established residents.

The focus of the ethnography was to understand the way in which relationships between adults and children were influenced and channeled by day-to-day life in the classroom, on the playground, and in the lunchroom and the explicit and implicit messages of the special events and ceremonies. The role of adults in channeling interaction was also a focus.

Given the dominance of classroom structures that bring children from different backgrounds together and the opportunities for unfettered play, why are relationships in some schools still overwhelmingly structured by race and ethnicity, and why are these boundaries transcended in others? In the next section we will look at the citywide forces that shape each neighborhood. This will be followed by an ethnographic analysis of the social processes that channel relationships in each school within its neighborhood context.

The City

In order to understand the neighborhood and institutional changes which affect social relations "on the ground" in local schools, it is necessary to look at regional and citywide economic shifts and their differential impact on the three localities. Philadelphia was a major industrializing center between 1830 and 1880, when large waves of British, Irish, and German immigrants entered. At the turn of the century (1880–1920), the industrial city was a major receiving center for a wave of Southern and Eastern European immigration. In the twentieth century, black inmigration from the rural South was of significance from 1930 to 1960. Unlike earlier waves, blacks came into a declining economy. A combination of deindustrialization and the suburbanization of populations and jobs created a major transformation of urban settlement patterns, as whites moved to the suburbs and blacks settled in an increasingly segregated pattern (Hershberg 1981; Goldstein 1986).

The postwar process of deindustrialization and the contemporary restructuring of the region's economy as a service economy make the city a very different context for the post-1965 wave of immigrants who are entering the United

States. Philadelphia is no longer at the center of demographic shifts brought about by immigration. While ranking fifth nationally in city size, it is only sixteenth as an immigrant destination. Moreover, many immigrants today come from middle-class backgrounds in their home country, in contrast to the peasant origins of the earlier waves (Young 1989).

A dominant image of Philadelphia is that of a city of "ethnic villages." This image is promulgated by the media and popular wisdom. While this is popularly attributed to the retention of "culture" by the turn-of-the-century immigrants, as Yancey et al. (1985) have demonstrated, the appearance of ethnic communities is really the legacy of stable, localized industrial jobs, creating intergenerational residential stability based on class. An inexpensive housing market of low-rise row homes reinforced the pattern. Continuing local institutions such as the nationality parish system (with church communities that are divided by nationality and language), civic associations, community newspapers, and community business strips reinforce this image even today, when large-scale population turnover has occurred.

The postwar processes of deindustrialization and suburbanization have further contributed to transforming the demography of the city whose population is increasingly poorer and less white. Between 1972 and 1980, the city lost 227,000 people, or 10 percent of its population, and 35 percent of its manufacturing jobs (Byler and Bennett 1984). Preliminary analyses of the 1990 census indicate a further 9 percent loss of population (Borowski 1990). The suburbs have continued to gain both housing and jobs in newly developing sectors of the economy. Seventy-five percent of the city population today works in the restructured service sector, often in jobs that are nonunionized, part-time, or with a two-tier wage system.

In September 1990, a fiscal crisis was declared in the city. Over the previous decade, the loss of tax base as the middle class moved to the suburbs, the continued loss of business, and the visible decline in services (police, sanitation, street repair) increased the despair of those committed to their traditional neighborhoods. The school district has been in constant crisis, reflected in long and bitter strikes in the early part of the 1980s as well as serious overcrowding, particularly in the neighborhoods we studied. Philadelphia has always sent a relatively large proportion of its population to parish schools. Here too, the system has been seriously affected by the fiscal crisis of the city (Binzen 1970).

Today the city is half white and half black.[3] Racial segregation, which increased throughout the century, has divided the city spatially. In the part of the city north of the center, that area most closely related to the study neighborhoods, there is a strong pattern of blacks in the west and white Euro-American

3. Blacks moved from 34 percent of the population in 1970 to 39 percent in the 1980 census. Both these figures are believed to be undercounts. It is generally assumed that they will constitute close to 50 percent in the official 1990 census and over 50 percent in actuality.

groups in the east, with socioeconomic status rising as one moves from the southern areas to the north. The increasing black population, school desegregation, a strong civil rights movement, and the rise of black political power have focused greater public attention on race. Two models of difference coexist. One is the racial dyad, which is manifested spatially by significantly segregated residential areas. The other is the pluralistic mosaic and other positive metaphors of diversity such as the "quilt," the "salad," and the "tapestry." The city is home to an extensive human relations network that has developed throughout the century largely under the auspices of Society of Friends (Quaker), Jewish, and black leadership. These organizations are responsible for many programs to combat racism in the schools.

Neighborhoods and Schools

The economic transformation of the region has not had the same impact on all areas of the city. Our study focuses on eastern North Philadelphia, an area historically housing white Catholic working-class populations whose ancestors immigrated to the city in the late nineteenth and early twentieth centuries. These populations were once dependent on the factory jobs that clustered along the Delaware River. We have worked in three socially recognized neighborhoods that are characterized by differences in class composition, class trajectory, newcomer entry, and the nature of demographic shifts. Consequently, the creation of group boundaries, interaction, avoidance, and conflict has been different.

What happens in all the schools results from a complex process in which the nature of local transformations and demographic shifts create boundaries in the community. These affect the ground-level structures of the schools, the alliances and cleavages within them, and ultimately the nature of relationships among adults as well as children. However, as the first two cases illustrate, schools as ongoing structures are different in their ability to resist external pressures, even in the same neighborhood context.

Olney

Olney, in the north of the study area, has long attracted aspiring middle-class populations from further south because of its newer and larger housing stock. Olney thinks of itself as a village. It has a network of civic associations, public events, and a thriving local newspaper which have all flourished for fifty years. The shopping strip in Olney is a real Main Street, through which all traffic has to flow because of a pattern of one-way streets and railroad obstructions. Public events have traditionally been held here. While institutions are stable, population is not. Upwardly mobile working-class families from the south have moved up the same parish pathway for much of the twentieth century, whether they are

The shopping strip in Olney—center of community life (photograph by Karen Vered)

whites who came thirty years ago or fifteen years ago or Latinos in the last five years.

In the last decade, there has been massive turnover in Olney. Reports on real estate transactions describe this area as one of the busiest in the city. The shift accelerated when mortgage rates declined in the early 1980s. Established whites who can afford to move to the Northeast[4] or the suburbs are being replaced by new immigrants. Newcomers are predominantly middle-class, involved in small business and technical or professional fields. They include Koreans and Latinos (Puerto Ricans, Colombians, and Central Americans) as well as Portuguese, Asian Indians, and Southeast Asian refugees. Most work in circumscribed niches and do not compete with local residents in the labor market. Other newcomers to the neighborhood include aspiring middle-class blacks and whites who are looking for good schools and affordable housing and

4. The Northeast is an "internal suburb," most of whose housing stock was built after World War II. It is known to be an all-white area and has attracted many families from all three of our communities. Alienated from the city government, some residents of this area have made a move to secede from the city.

who think diversity in the neighborhood is a plus. No one group of immigrants is dominant in this most multicultural area in the city (see table 5.1).

Established residents still control the network of established institutions. Established community leaders have adopted the dominant view of the human relations institutions and see newcomers as belonging to separate, tightly knit communities that are represented by official spokespersons. Olney residents see a recent increase in local blight and decline, but tend to blame city government for their problems and not the newcomers. Instead, newcomers are expected to learn to become replacements for the established residents who have left the community.

Schools in Olney have long held reputations for achievement and success, as a steady stream of upwardly mobile working-class families came looking for a better life. This process continues today with new populations.

Peterson

Peterson is one of several public schools in Olney. The demographic composition of Peterson is 28 percent white (including Portuguese newcomers), 22 percent black (including West Indians), 30 percent Latino, and 20 percent Asian (Korean, Indian, Vietnamese, Cambodian, and Chinese). Peterson houses grades K–8.

At Peterson, a special ability to maintain a stable school community has facilitated the development and maintenance of cross-group ties. While boundaries between adults persist, they are mitigated by their children's relationships.

The school was highly thought of by its district. It was allowed to restrict entrance to kindergarten and first grade only in order to reduce overcrowding. People entering the neighborhood with older children found their children bussed elsewhere. This policy created grade cohorts which are together in the school for eight or nine years.

CHILDREN'S RELATIONS. The graduation activities described at the beginning of this chapter are one example of the way group boundaries are frequently transcended. In the day-to-day activities of the children, there were almost never occasions when boundaries between race, nationality, or language groups were visibly displayed.

In informal play, groups of all ages mixed. One day, a group of first-graders including blacks, Puerto Ricans, and established whites played a rough-and-tumble "karate" game led by their Korean classmate. Their game was stopped by a Latino aide, who chastised the Korean for teaching such a dangerous sport, but a few minutes later they were at it again.

At the same time, the sixth-grade "safeties" (teacher-selected monitors) were up to their shenanigans on the back stairs, heavy-handedly controlling access to the bathrooms. Led by a Latino, this tight-knit group included established whites, blacks, Asian Indians, and Portuguese. It was classroom-based. Fre-

Table 5.1. Community Socioeconomic Characteristics (Based on 1980 Census)

	Kensington	Olney	Port Richmond
Population	25,398	17,967	22,591
Median age	25.33	29.8	36.57
Race & ethnicity*			
White	68%	64%	98%
Black	7	24	1
Asian	n.s.	2	n.s.
Spanish speakers	25	10	n.s.
Ancestry of whites			
Multiple	28%	21%	32%
Polish	2	1	28
Irish	10	10	13
German	6	7	5
Same house since last census	68%	63%	77%
Education			
High school graduate	24%	29%	30%
Some college & college graduates	4	11	9
Whites: High school	25	36	30
Some college & college graduates	4	9	9
Blacks: High school	18	43	29
Some college & college graduates	8	14	1
Asians: High school	23	12	0
Some college & college graduates	18	47	0
Hispanic: High school	22	26	33
Some college & college graduates	5	13	6
Occupation			
Professional & managerial	7	10	9
Gray- or pink-collar (sales & admin.)	24	30	31
Blue-collar	50	45	44
Household income			
Total less than 5,000	34%	19%	14%
" " 10,000	55	38	41
" " 50,000	70	57	57
White less than 15,000	62	47	43
Black less than 15,000	64	65	95
Asian less than 15,000	48	42	0
Hispanic less than 15,000	89	52	0
In poverty	38	19	14
Not in poverty	62	81	86
Asians: In poverty	29	9	0
Not in poverty	71	91	0
Hispanic: In poverty	64	40	27
Not in poverty	36	60	73
Ratio of owners to renters	3 : 1	3.5 : 1	6 : 1
% vacant housing abandoned	77	36	64

*Since most immigrants and refugees have come between 1980 and 1990, these figures severely undercount nonwhites and newcomers.

quently, this mixed sixth-grade group of boys would relentlessly tease their female counterparts, a similarly mixed group of girls whose relationship with the boys led to a continuous round of practical jokes and sports challenges. The aides joined in with the jokes and teasing.

In Peterson's lunchroom, the only one where free seating was allowed, gender was the only principle visibly structuring tables. Even age was ignored in a lunchroom seating pattern in which girls from the higher grades "adopted" girls from the lower grades, who called them "Mommy" as they played house at the table. These pseudo-families involved mother-daughter pairs that almost all crossed race or nationality lines. However, these relationships across groups are not limited to occasional spontaneous play. As we saw in the vignette at the beginning of this chapter, interethnic friendships are strong and still intact after eight years, when the students graduate.

The story of the International Club offers another example. The International Club was a device to provide the children in ESOL (English for Speakers of Other Languages) with an extracurricular activity that "would make them feel part of the school." It was organized by the ESOL teacher. While such structures serve a ghettoizing function elsewhere, further isolating newcomers,[5] at Peterson the club soon attracted the most popular children, both newcomers and established residents, as they worked to perform a play. It was a huge success, well attended by established and newcomer parents. It became another in a regular series of public events at which the ideology of success and community becomes lived experience in this school.

Peterson emphatically and publicly proclaims its belief in opportunity and achievement through education. The building is decorated with trophies and clippings about past achievements. Neither teachers or students get carried away by the divisions into ethnic or "cultural" segments common in the neighborhood. The close ties between the children preclude this. They do not see the world as constructed of bounded entities, as the citywide human relations experts do. Peterson deemphasizes cultural differences, stressing an America where people come from many places to find equal opportunity through hard work. This was the explicit message of the International Day play. The play emphasized common goals and did not emphasize difference by performing the folk cultures of the homeland, as is so often the case in multicultural programming. The message of graduation visually demonstrates that achievement in academics, music, art, sports, and leadership occurs across all groups. This is reinforced as students from all backgrounds gain entrance to elite high schools.

5. At another Olney school, International Day was handled by an art teacher who was interested in music, dance, and other "cultural traditions." She divided established and newcomer students into nationality-based groups and organized separate dance groups that performed sequentially. She won a citywide award for her efforts and traveled with her groups to ethnic festivals all over the city. This tactic divided the students into segments and did not lead to boundary transcendence.

Thus the ideology of equal opportunity is reinforced, not contradicted, in public life.

Language and music, which reinforce group boundaries in other schools, are shared by Peterson children to cement intergroup ties. Children from different groups often teach each other words of their native language as a bonding device. One day, a group of established Euro-ethnic sixth-graders were showing off the Spanish curse words they had learned from their Latino friends. ESOL segregates students only for a short time, when they enter at age five or six until they become fluent. One never hears languages other than English spoken on the playground.

At the graduation dance, arguments over the type of music to be played were based not on ethnic group but on gender. As the boys and girls fought, an Asian boy who was in control of the music sided with the other boys and chose black rap music (Blanc 1989).

There is no oppositional culture among the children at Peterson based on a racial or linguistic dyad, as there is at other schools. While this is due in some part to the presence of so many different new populations, a nearby school with a very similar demographic pattern has experienced the development of opposition between Koreans and whites among adults and students to a much greater degree.[6]

Successful achievement and relationships between children even lead to contact and ties between adults of different backgrounds whose children are best friends. There are many examples of families who share meals and special occasions through their children's friendships.

What accounts for these unusual patterns at Peterson? In part it is the class nature of the population. Many of the newcomers have middle-class origins or incomes, or both, as do their established counterparts. Their experience has led them to share the belief that schooling leads to success. Their resources help them to assure this. There is little resistance to the school's message from students or parents. Yet an increasing proportion of students in the school live in households with incomes below the poverty line.[7]

STRUCTURE. Class is only part of the story. The key to Peterson's experience is its stability of participants in the face of rapid neighborhood turnover. The structural feature that allows children to travel through eight years of schooling together is itself only part of the explanation of stability and the sense of community.

Peterson is tracked by ability so that students tend to remain in the same

6. Frost, a few blocks away, has a population of 35 percent white, 18 percent black, 14 percent Latino, and 33 percent Asian, mostly Korean. Here the children are much more divided by ethnic group, and there is tension between the white and Korean parents.

7. In 1988, 25 percent of the students at Peterson lived in households below the poverty line (as opposed to 50 percent at Dixon). However, the percentage rose significantly the following year.

classroom cohort throughout their grade-school years. Common career goals often link peers from very different backgrounds in long-term relationships that continue into high school. Among the boys, Tomas (Puerto Rican) and Tran (Vietnamese) are best friends, as are Miguel (Portuguese) and Lee (ethnic Chinese from Vietnam). Each pair has selected a different magnet high school to attend together.

Peterson is a walking school, whose students all live nearby and walk to and from school together each day; thus school ties can be reinforced in street play. Many "best friends" in school can see each other regularly out of school. This works against attempts by parents to control their children's social networks. For example, two Portuguese girls talked of pressure by their parents to participate in Portuguese institutions: attending language school, tutoring newcomers, and participating in the day care program. However, residential proximity to their school-based best friends allowed them to maintain these relationships as well.

Teachers are also stable. Many of the parents of current children studied under the same teachers when they were in the school. There have only been two principals in the last two decades. Nobody asks to be transferred from this school where teachers feel successful. The teaching staff is biracial. At teaching staff meetings the teachers tend to sit clustered by gender and race. However, the teachers often all participate in a joint lottery pool and buy each other's home sale products. There is no racial tension, as there was at a nearby elementary school where human relations specialists were brought in to deal with conflict between teachers.

Teachers, while residential outsiders to the neighborhood, have formed local ties. For example, one runs the local summer camp at a neighborhood park. Teachers shop on the strip, attend local events, and are familiar figures. In spite of their experience and commitment, this is still a unionized public school. Teachers pay strict attention to union work rules. At one staff meeting, as soon as the buzzer rang to announce that fifty minutes was up, all participants rose, chatted with their neighbors, and walked out, even though the discussion had not finished. Yet these practices have little impact on the sense of community.

PARENTS AND AIDES. Many fissures typical in other schools do not exist. There is little division between aides and professionals. Because of the long-term cadre of teachers, aides do not see the middle-class black and Jewish teachers as outsiders. One day, they spoke warmly about a well-dressed Jewish teacher whose husband had brought their children with their nanny to observe a program she had organized. Her husband, a lawyer in a large firm, was conspicuous in the audience in his expensive suit. The aides had once been to her house for a school function and spoke admiringly of her home and clothes. They showed no class resentment or feeling of distance. The one newcomer aide, a Puerto Rican woman, was incorporated into the established clique and participated in conversations about the other newcomer parents and their rule infractions. She also provided translation and mediated some disputes with parents. The female aides have established a warm, joking relationship with the black male nonteaching aide, who sits with them to gossip during the quiet time after lunch.

The close collaboration between newcomer parents and their children's teachers incorporates newcomer parents into the school community. Since most of the newcomer parents are upwardly mobile, they are concerned with their children's progress and collaborate directly with teachers.

However, all aides and some teachers believe that things are changing for the worse. While the aides are well integrated into the school community and share in the spirit of success at concerts, plays, and graduations, as community residents they also fear decline and change. One aide, when asked about differences between her days as a student and now, said, "It was a great school then; it is terrible now." Some teachers notice change and complain about declining parental involvement. On the day after open school night, when parents were to come to meet the teachers, two teachers were bemoaning the fact that the numbers of parents who came dwindled every year.

One of the few boundaries exists between established insider parents and newcomers. There is considerable tension between the insider parents (established aides) and the outside newcomer parents at the gates. Newcomer parents who come to deliver, pick up, or meet children at lunch hour are handled by these women. Aides talk constantly about incidents of rule violation. One day, a newcomer mother who was entering the school from the playground entrance to use the bathroom was told in no uncertain terms that she must go in the front door and check in at the office. Another newcomer mother who had brought her child juice in a glass bottle and attempted to hand it to him through the fence was stopped and told that glass was not permitted and that children were not allowed to have food on the playground.

The Home and School Association parents also unintentionally create a barrier. The officers are a small group of long-term acquaintances, all of whom have grown up in Olney and have mutual friends and shared experiences. Regular activities include fundraising sales and are always run in the same fashion. These activities widen the circle of participants to include the more distant established blacks. Two black grandmothers regularly came to these events.

Officers of the Home and School Association are often the contact point for newcomer parents who respond to invitations to meetings. Unfortunately, this contact did not lead to incorporation into the school community. Established parents were uncomfortable speaking to the newcomers who spoke with accents, even though many were bilingual. They tried to assign such communication to "brokers" such as Spanish-speaking aides. The discomfort of communicating directly with newcomers was evident at the first meeting of our second year, when six Latino families came. They were the only parents in attendance besides the officers. The meeting consisted of formal presentations.

The only direct person-to-person communication with the newcomers involved collecting dues. It was clear from informal conversation that the newcomers did not understand the nature of the organization. The initial attendance and interest was never followed up, and leaders complained throughout the year about the lack of Latino participation in the fundraisers.

This boundary between the established parents who are insiders and newcomer parents who are outsiders reflects the general relationship between adult established residents and newcomers in the neighborhood. Peterson's stability as a community and its belief in its success have militated against some of the tensions and pressures typical of other schools. Many teachers spoke about their successes with pride. They commented on the school as continuing the successful absorption of new immigrants that had occurred during their grandparents' time.

St. Ignatius

The composition of the student body at St. Ignatius is almost identical to that at neighboring Peterson. Since schedules for the two schools are similar, the two

A parochial school recess illustrating the cultural diversity in Olney. Informal mixing is characteristic of the playgrounds, while relations outside of school are more separate. (Photograph by Karen Vered)

student populations would seem identical except for the uniforms that mark the parochial students. Yet social processes in the schools were very different. St. Ignatius is 31 percent white (including Portuguese), 18 percent black, 32 percent Latino, and 18 percent Asian. It also includes kindergarten through eighth grades.

STRUCTURE. St. Ignatius has been affected by the increased transiency in the neighborhood more than Peterson because it does not control new enrollments. One parent of Peterson children remembered that when she was a child, there was no room for her at St. Ignatius because it was so desirable. Today it must recruit students from other parishes as well as an increasing number of non-Catholics to sustain itself.

While the neighborhood dynamics and social composition of Peterson and St. Ignatius are identical, social processes in the latter school engender boundaries. The financial pressures on this parish school, coupled with the ideology of family and community, have generated these processes. Much of what is happening is an indirect consequence of the need to replace families who have left. Needing new members, the parish has incorporated newcomer subcommunities as separate enclaves and reifies them as such. The parish priests have provided five separate language masses and space for sodalities, dance and music groups, and clubs for each group, which further segregate activities. The parish calendar is full of festivals celebrating individual ethnic groups in an effort to make them feel at home. The school and parish are thus divided into many subcommunities. At ceremonial events, adults are clustered in these groups, which the parish helps create, each speaking a different language.

The school recruits through kinship networks within these ethnic components. It is no longer a neighborhood-based school, and children are transported to and from school by kin and friends, further reinforcing preexisting ties. Kinship and quasi-kinship relations permeate the school. Almost all the students with whom we spoke had large numbers of actual siblings and cousins in the school. Two Puerto Rican girls in one class were fictive cousins. Their mothers being "like sisters," they called them aunts and referred to each other as cousins.

As many of the established families have left the neighborhood, the heart of the fundraising enterprise that is responsible for the support of the parish has decreased, leading to increased tuition and thus increased difficulties in recruiting students. While numbers have been made up by new subcommunities, the newcomers are not familiar with the institutions of fundraising essential to American parish sustenance. In the first year of our fieldwork, the traditional Night at the Races, which had always provided an important budgetary component, had to be canceled for lack of volunteers. Such setbacks have generated resentment of newcomers on the part of the established, who see themselves as paying higher tuition and singlehandedly providing volunteer labor because of the newcomers' failure to participate.

CHILDREN'S RELATIONS. Just as at Peterson, our observations at St. Ignatius yielded many examples of cross-group play and long-term friendships among those who travel through eight years of school together. However, in this school only half as many stay for their full elementary career. Turnover is high, as children come and go each year.

There are many situations of free and unfettered play. One newcomer Korean girl who speaks no English is being "buddied" by a Korean boy in her class, who is supposed to stick by her side and help her with translations through the day until her English develops. However, she has been simultaneously "adopted" by three Latina girls who want to nurture her. In one third grade, the competition for popularity leads to quarrels and jockeying for "best friendships" with the leaders. Thus one day, an established Euro-ethnic girl complains that her popular Latina "best friend" has dropped her and become "best friends" with another (Portuguese) girl. These pairings changed daily in the class and involved all groups. One established Euro-American boy tried to create a "gang" in the class and recruited the Asian boys in his area of the room. (He was of average size and they were smaller than he, quiet and quiescent.) However, these friendships seem to have no significance outside of school, given that many children are not from the neighborhood.

At St. Ignatius, group boundaries are more visible than at Peterson. For example, in the after-school program that brought children together to play games and do homework, Latino, Portuguese, Asian Indian, and black students spent three relatively unstructured hours together every day. While they got to know each other well, they still tended to retain boundaries based on family and kinship. Comments about group differences were often heard—remarks about skin color, the oddness of names, and the peculiarity of foods. Yvette, a light-skinned Latina girl, and Ravi, a dark-skinned Indian, began to trade slurs about skin color. Yvette commented on Ravi's darkness, and he told her that her skin was yellow. She screamed, "I've got a suntan." Ravi then told her to not make fun of his color, and Pierre, a black boy, agreed. On another day, two black boys told Ravi that he looked like an Indian. He told them not to make fun of his nation.

Authorities do not view these boundaries as problems and in fact reinforce them, as they see children as appropriate extensions of families and subcommunities. It is expected that those related by kinship should protect each other and that those who come from the same background should feel more comfortable with each other. There is no countervailing force of bureaucratic rules that would encourage the organization of groups by formal decision rules like ability tracking. Since the school stresses family—literally in terms of the many extended kin networks as well as metaphorically—there is no self-consciousness about underscoring family relationships. For example, there is no concern about favoritism or special privileges for a teacher's child or an aide's child.

One group of Indian girls, including several clusters of siblings, were inseparable. This group cut across grade levels. Their parents were all close friends, and they were brought to and from school together. Known for their good behavior and fear of discipline, this little gang was often chosen to help out when the principal or a teacher needed help outside of class. They were always awarded little gifts for these favors. The public validation of this particular clique was repeated regularly. The solidity of this group, reinforced by parents and the school community, carried over into the after-school program and led to the retention of partial boundaries there.

The Portuguese children in the school were similarly close. Here, too, the school reinforced ties. Portuguese children are considered to present the school with its greatest language problems and are often assigned to each other as buddies.

The assumption on the part of insiders that newcomers feel more comfortable with their own kind has led to other informal networks created by school staff. A group of Korean boys of different ages and grade levels, including siblings, had formed a strong clique under the auspices of one teacher and often spent much of the lunch hour in her classroom. Sometimes the teacher brought them home with her. Otherwise most of these boys had specific arrangements after school to be picked up and brought to their parents' small shops. These arrangements precluded any after-school contact with other classmates.

In contrast to Peterson, in the later grades at St. Ignatius there is a tendency for black and some Latino children to switch to friendships among nonwhites. As the students and their parents talked about friendships, there were many comments by nonwhite students concerning switching to friends "more like us." This seems to be a common pattern in Philadelphia schools as children get older,[8] a tendency that makes the experience at Peterson even more unusual.

TEACHERS, PARENTS, AND AIDES. As the active, established core of the school shrinks and becomes subject to more pressure for financial and volunteer resources, insider ties become stronger in order to mask the transiency at St. Ignatius with the appearance of continuity and stability. There is no line between the lay professional staff and the parent volunteers, as there is in the public schools. In an effort to contain the rapid changes, tradition and communal solidarity are emphasized. In providing the sense of continuity that is expected of a parish school, this presentation of communal solidarity creates a greater boundary between insiders and outsiders and unintentionally excludes newcomers further.

In spite of low pay, there is great stability among the teachers, many of whom are parishioners, former parishioners, and/or parents in the school. These

8. A teacher at Frost commented on the same phenomenon, especially related to Korean separateness in upper grades there. "The kids clutch together as they get older," she said. These tendencies parallel the "hang-out" structures in the local high schools as well. In two high schools we worked in, most relationships were structured by race and ethnicity.

teachers are a devoted group. They work well together and often volunteer time during lunch hour to work on projects or to work with individual children. The lay teachers are all Catholic, white, and American-born. Their interactions with each other are extraordinarily friendly. Everything is shared: food, time, and caring thoughts. When one very young male teacher became engaged, an elaborate surprise party was planned. Everyone pitched in. Collaborations on decorating the school for occasions like Catholic Schools Week and parents' meetings occur during free time. In contrast to the public schools, there was no grumbling or cynical complaining about the school.

The closeness of the regular established parents and the lay teachers creates a boundary that is palpable. These parents exhibit the same discomfort in interacting with newcomers that was illustrated by the Home and School Association at Peterson. At a luncheon to celebrate the end of a program, the insiders' solidarity and joking behavior effectively shut out the newcomer parents. Only one member of the "insider" community approached and introduced herself to the outsiders, who otherwise stood on the periphery.

As at Peterson, established blacks participate, but at a little distance from the long-term insiders. Established blacks and other nonwhite newcomers serve as the lunch mothers. At schoolwide events, these nonwhite women stay with each other and trade teasing words with the white staff and volunteers, implying a strong we/they boundary. For example, at one cookout, the black lunch mothers cooked their hamburgers separately and joked that the others ate their meat too raw and were not to be trusted as cooks.[9]

This distance between whites and blacks is symptomatic of a deeper distrust of the school insiders on the part of black parents, who have chosen the school to avoid the lack of achievement and discipline they see in the public schools. Yet they remain wary of racism from the established white school insiders. One black mother states that black parents who have left the school have asked her why she stays in a prejudiced environment. While she does not think the school is racially biased, she clearly does not identify as an insider. Another example of this type of concern occurred when a black parent refused to let her daughter attend a white girl's birthday party until she found that another black girl would be there. This familiar dynamic of the Philadelphia racial dyad contributes to the tendency of children's networks to become increasingly divided between white and nonwhite as they get older.

The officers of the Home and School Association are largely drawn from the parent volunteers who are around the school on a daily basis. In an attempt to try to involve more Latino families, a Latino was elected president of the Home and School Association at the end of 1988. Unfortunately, as a male who worked

9. One white woman who is married to a black and whose children have predominantly black and Latino friends was formerly a member of the lunch mother core. She has since become a paid staff member. As such, she acts as part of the white parent insider group and is similarly viewed by the lunch mothers.

full-time in the distant suburbs, the president did not fill the role usually performed by a nonworking mother who can spend considerable time at school and participate in the informal communication system.[10] This further convinced the established volunteers that newcomers were not willing to participate in the essential voluntary activities of the school and reinforced the line between insiders and outsiders.

Distance between newcomer and established parents is also related to the fact that newcomers are thought not to share the moral mission of the school: to reinforce responsibility to family and community and counter the emphasis on materialism and individualism prevalent in the larger society. There is a general sentiment among insiders that newcomer mothers work too much. Their commitment to work is blamed on their too rapid acquisition of the materialism of American society—providing their children with too many things to compensate for lack of time with them. Newcomers have clothes and cars that seem ostentatious, and it is they who come to graduation with video cameras. For newcomer parents, choosing the parochial school (for expected superior academics) and encouraging mothers to have careers are part of a strategy to reestablish their middle-class status. On the other hand, established families' reasons for sending their children to the school may have more to do with religious training and fulfilling an obligation to the parish community.[11]

While emphasis on achievement is strong in this school, as in Peterson, achievement competes with instilling the moral values of caring, loving, and community. At most public events, achievements and awards are mentioned but are given less time and prominence in the agenda. For example, at graduation, awards are not listed on the program, which instead contains the religious texts, hymns, and sermons of the day. The schools attended by graduates include some of the elite magnet schools, but there is a strong preference for the local Catholic high school.

As at Peterson, newcomer parents at St. Ignatius, while outside the school community, are very involved in their children's progress, and teachers serve as primary links between them and the school. Open school nights are well attended, and newcomer parents are reported to be very helpful with homework. Since many of the parents are making big sacrifices to pay tuition and travel long distances to bring children to and from school for what they hope is a safe environment with quality education, this involvement is not surprising.

While newcomer parents at St. Ignatius relate to the school in similar ways to those of Peterson, the children's relationships are entirely different. Recruiting and retaining newcomers through the creation of subcommunities leaves new-

10. Newcomer fathers rather than mothers often played the role of school contact. This was true for all newcomer groups. This went against the traditional expectations of the school.

11. An attempt to deal with values led to a questionnaire sent home to parents, asking them to rank-order the problems that faced the school community. The problems listed for ranking were trash and graffiti, materialistic values, and crime. There were too few responses for a follow-up.

comer parents and school personnel more in control of the children's relationships, and boundaries are thus reinforced.

Kensington

Kensington, in the southern part of the study area, is a former mill area that housed working-class Euro-Americans beginning in the early 1800s. An early victim of plant closings, it has lost population and seen an increase in housing abandonment and the use of drugs. Once the setting for a dense network of civic organizations, sports leagues, and parish-based structures similar to that in Olney, Kensington since the 1970s has been dominated by empowerment organizations concerned with controlling housing stock, job training, and social services. These organizations, engendered by federal antipoverty and community development programs, employ networks of Alinski-type activists. While many of the empowerment groups are attempting to bring whites, Latinos, and blacks together to solve common problems, there is a major social movement under way to organize Latinos as a separate minority group with special problems. As part of the rhetoric of this movement, whites and blacks are seen as part of the city power structure.

Kensington is an area conscious of racial lines. Over the last twenty years, the boundary between whites and nonwhites has shifted eastward. Today, while the eastward-shifting boundary is still contested by acts of violence against minorities moving in, there is little intergroup violence in West Kensington, as the community has developed a pattern of checkerboard segregation. Latinos have moved into a narrow band between the whites farther east and blacks farther west (see figure 5.1). Small clusters of blocks are thought of as either Latino, where Spanish dominates public space, or as white, where English dominates.[12] While Kensington still retains some stable working-class families among both whites and Latinos, it has also become a locus of cheap rental housing and scattered-site public housing and is much poorer than the other two neighborhoods across all groups (see table 5.1).

The schools in Kensington have come to be seen as "inner-city" schools where a "culture of poverty" in which bad values are taught in the home must be overcome if the children are to achieve. In many schools there is hostility between the school and the parents and a resistance ideology such as that characterized by Paul Willis (1977).

12. Spanish-dominant areas are those in which Spanish is the dominant language of the street and organizations, churches, and clubs are Spanish-speaking. This does not mean that no established families are present, but that they are in the minority, tend to relate to organizations outside the area, and are recognized and protected by the Spanish-speaking locals. While adults have separate networks, sometimes English-speaking children and teens are incorporated into Spanish-dominant networks. Outsiders who are established whites avoid the area. White-dominated areas are the reverse. The area around Dixon was dominated by established whites, but many newcomer Spanish children and teens played with local whites.

A schoolyard in Kensington with factory and rowhousing. The photo illustrates the crossing of ethnic boundaries in informal play despite residential segregation and social distance between adults. (Photograph by Karen Vered)

Dixon

Dixon, the second school depicted in the opening of this paper, is situated in Kensington. Its relatively new building was built in late 1973, one of the first results of organized pressure by empowerment groups. The population of Dixon is 55 percent white, 31 percent Latino, 13 percent black, and 1 percent Asian. Dixon housed kindergarten through sixth grade in the first year of our research and kindergarten through fifth grade in the second.

STRUCTURE. As an "inner-city" school, Dixon today has little power. Its high rate of turnover of teachers and students exacerbates problems. The teachers and administration blame the parents, the parents blame the outsider professionals and the school district, and a strong boundary separates the English-speaking and Spanish-speaking adults and children.

The school handles more "transactions" (transfers of records of incoming and outgoing students) each fall than any other school we studied, and transfers continue throughout the year. In the fall of 1987, there were 500 transactions in a school of 1,100 students. Turnover occurs because renters relocate frequently and because of the circular migration of Puerto Ricans back and forth to the island. During the two years, we observed many cases of children across groups who missed school for months at a time. Family crises were much more prevalent than at other schools, and in one school year there were several child deaths and at least three families burned out by house fires.

The school district's policies seriously exacerbated the instability of the school population over the two years of fieldwork. In the first year of fieldwork, the school housed its own surrounding population as well as a large number of overflow students (almost all Latino) from the catchment area of a nearby school. In the second year, the whole grade structure of the school shifted, as the result of a districtwide restructuring. In addition, the original overflow students were removed and replaced by overflow students from still another school, so that the student population was significantly reconstituted. Established parents protested these shifts because of overcrowding, but the shifts occurred nevertheless.

Until 1989, when they were prohibited, the school was characterized by high midyear teacher transfers, forcing students to switch teachers in midstream. Since there was always a delay in scheduling new teachers, often a string of substitute teachers filled in during the lengthy post-New Year transition. Since this school was almost never given as a preference by teachers with seniority, it was often the very young and inexperienced who came. One community resident once pointed out a new teacher in schoolyard and said, "Oh, look, they've sent us another 'sweet young thing.'"

In a two-year period, 25 percent of the teachers turned over. As a result of these shifts, teachers had little sense of community. One young teacher was determined to transform her students. She decided that she must remove them from the general environment of the school; consequently, she kept them in their classroom throughout lunch period so that they would not be "infected" by the others. The one Latina teacher was in frequent conflict with her peers. Teacher absenteeism was a significant problem in the school and the focus of discussion at one Home and School Association meeting. Teachers often told researchers that they disagreed with policies and were occasionally observed resisting orders.

PARENTS AND AIDES. The teachers and the principal at Dixon tend to see the parents as the source of the troubles in the school rather than blaming the lack of support from the district. The principal had been brought in to straighten out the school after having some success in other problem schools. He was appalled at what he saw as poor values among the parents at Dixon. He disparaged their lack of interest in academic achievement and their preoccupation with safety, comfort, and other nonacademic issues. Parents were described as evasive and virtually unreachable when their children were in trouble. He blamed whites and Latinos equally. The parents he was at war with, many of them teenage parents, came from both groups, as did the children who did nothing but fight and "act out their feelings with no thought."[13] All of our meetings in the office were interrupted every few minutes by groups of students brought in for discipline. Both the principal and the series of acting vice-principals in charge of discipline received a steady stream of miscreants. The lack of a continuous vice-principal due to a contractual grievance was another structural problem that confused parents and prevented progress in gaining control.

The parents and aides clearly see the school professionals as outsider adversaries.[14] Many of the parents and aides are overtly hostile to the school administration and professional staff. Parents are conscious of the difference in class between themselves and the outsider professionals. At one Home and School Association meeting at which the use of organized games was discussed as a strategy for control, one professional mentioned tennis. There was an immediate and uniform outburst of giggles and guffaws, as one parent said, "That's too lah-de-dah for me."

Like Peterson aides, Dixon aides have complaints about being exploited and not backed up in discipline. However, here the disciplinary problems are more serious, and there are none of the achievements, successful public events, and special moments to compensate.

At Dixon, the adult social order reflects the structure of the neighborhood, which is divided into Latino-dominant and white-dominant areas. The school itself is in a white-dominant area into which more Latinos are moving every year. Street play around the school generates cliques, which include mostly established whites but incorporate some Latinos. The overflow students come from Spanish-dominant settings where the street play groups are all Spanish-speaking.[15]

Among the aides there is a strong division between English speakers and Spanish speakers. These two groups do not communicate with each other. In fact, the Latino parents derisively refer to the older white aides as *viejas* (old women). While the Latina aides deal mostly with Latino children, the older white women are inclusive in their largely nurturing interactions. One established aide was called "Grandmom" or "Abuela" by both language groups and is known for her protective care. Children show her respect and often play with her in the yard. Language is also cleaned up around her.

13. One extreme incident occurred in the first year, when a white mother concerned about threats to her daughter entered the principal's office, assaulted him, and destroyed his furniture. Criminal charges were brought.

14. In an effort to relate to the community, the principal became active in a neighborhood civic association and soon became president. However, this organization was a moribund remnant of the traditional civic organizations in this area, which had been replaced by more militant empowerment organizations in the last two decades.

15. Unlike the schools in Olney, Dixon, like the community around it, is becoming publicly bilingual. School programs begin and end with greetings in both languages (although the main program is in English), and notices sent home are available in both languages.

There is less collaboration between parents and teachers here than at the schools in Olney. There are many parents who see school as the road to success. For example, one young, well-dressed, middle-class Latino couple came to the playground frequently at lunch hour to make sure their two children were not hurt and to work on homework assignments with them. One Latino family was always in attendance at school events. Their twin daughters were soloists at all the concerts and together won two-thirds of the awards at their graduation. The Home and School Association officers focus on academic achievement and run a student-of-the-month program, posting photographs and providing pizza to those children named as successful by their teachers.

In this school and neighborhood where discipline and safety are real problems, however, the parents are primarily concerned about their children's safety both in the school and on the way home. Many parents do not trust the school to protect their children. In this highly stressed area, this is not surprising. Moreover, many downwardly mobile working-class parents reject the notion that schools provide opportunity. Some see the school as a prison that impinges on the rights of their children.

When we look at the large majority of Dixon parents, we see two groups of angry and disgruntled adults divided by the language/ethnic line. Two incidents in the first year underscored white parental opposition to the school. One was a rebellion of the parents of special education children when the principal refused to permit the group to leave school for a Special Olympics event. Seeing this event as another example of avoiding academic activity, the principal refused to approve a bus. That night, at the spring concert, established parents were abuzz with anger and rebellion. During the course of the evening, the physical education teacher, who was reported to be equally "angry with HIM," and the parents conspired to develop an alternative plan for transportation.

The other incident concerned a rule to prohibit shorts during a week of very high temperatures. An angry group of parents gathered in the schoolyard to protest, but no resolution was forthcoming, and they left. Again very negative statements about the school and the principal were made. The white working-class parents often appeared in the schoolyard in housedresses and slippers or skimpy clothes. The principal firmly believed that more formal dressing made people take school more seriously.

Separately but equally vociferously, the Spanish-speaking parents often gathered to complain about the way the school was treating their children. The Latino parents who congregate around the schoolyard at recess and lunchtime are actively concerned about bias against their children in this white-dominated area. They are aware of the active Puerto Rican rights movement in the city and often use its rhetoric. All established residents, white and black, parents or staff, are seen as part of the power structure from which they are excluded.

They insist that Latino children are being differentially picked on by staff and teachers. Since their observations are confined to the yard, they blame the white aides and the black security guard. One woman whose child was suspended complained that the Puerto Rican children tended to be suspended more and spoke derisively about what *el viejo* (the old man, referring to the principal) and *el moreno* (the black, referring to the security guard) had done. One day a Latino couple came to the security guard to complain that a white bully was always beating up their child and that the guard did not stop it. The guard told them that their child usually started the fights. With that, they cursed him and marched to the office to seek "satisfaction."

CHILDREN'S RELATIONS. How do these internal divisions affect the relationships among children? Why did the principal report that race and ethnicity did not structure relations? While ethnicity and race tend to organize adult interaction and some children's interaction at Dixon, they only partially structure the main dynamics of the school: physical contests, displays of toughness, and discipline.

While one can see clearly demarcated white and Latino spaces in the school, as in the neighborhood, there are many mixed groups and activities. This results from the influence of toughness and street life in organizing relations as well as the influence of classroom organization. A major organizing principle at Dixon has to do with "toughness" and fear. Children sort themselves into groups depending on their willingness to take part in challenges, risk taking, chases, and fighting. There are tough girls as well as boys. A large group of children are afraid of the physical challenges in the playground and stick near the aides who protect them. They also try to stay in the cafeteria after lunch and beg to be helpers in cleanup activities, to avoid going outside. Others bring toys and try to play in the corners, out of view of those engaged in chasing and fighting. The children who avoid the contests and challenges tend not to be divided by racial or ethnic boundaries. It is common to see cross-group comforting of crying children who have been hurt or threatened. Similarly, toughness ties together Latinos and whites in some of the "gangs."

The spaces of the lunchroom and the playground are organized to some degree by race and language, as was described in the opening of this chapter. In the Latino section of the lunchroom, several tables are occupied by the "infamous" Latina girls' gangs—street structures from the Latino-dominated area from which overflow students come. Next to them are the tables at which the newcomers in the all-day bilingual program sit. The other tables in this area are also Latino-dominated, and Spanish is heavily used, even though Spanish ability varies considerably between newcomers and the up-to-third-generation established Puerto Ricans.[16]

16. It is very difficult to categorize Puerto Rican children as newcomer or established. Life histories of parents usually include periods on both the mainland and the island. We rarely found "newcomers" who had not been on the mainland before. A child's language ability depends on what is spoken at home. In several cases of Anglo fathers and Puerto Rican mothers, Spanish was spoken at home because of the presence of monolingual grandparents. There were some families with attenuated links to the island and some children who had never even visited there. They tended to have retained "Spanglish," a mixed-vocabulary language, but no fluency in Spanish.

This is the only school in our study where a language other than English is prevalent in the lunchroom and playground. Yet only 10 percent of the students are considered beginners in English. Most are partially or totally bilingual. Spanish is deliberately used in informal activities, to create boundaries around some groups like the Latina gang, for playing island street games, for cursing, and for planning aggressive events. It is quite common to hear conversations that begin in one language and switch back and forth, depending on audience and topic.

Virtually all the black students sit together at several tables, violating the ostensible rules of seating by class. The rest of the lunchroom is more mixed, reflecting toughness, classroom, and street-group lines. One table is the locus of a mixed "gang," older boys, including Latinos and whites, who all wear black leather jackets and punk hairstyles to display their solidarity.

Fighting on the playground is often a ritual performance for an audience. There is a lot of scuffling, chasing, and menacing behavior. One day, a group of black boys ran after an established white boy for a half-hour, appearing to be in earnest. After they finally caught him, everyone smiled, and they tousled his hair. This was the end of the incident. Most of the ritual fights are performed by one segment for other groups as audience. Many times, established Euro-American boys fight among themselves while Latino children form the audience. One day the white and black girls in the lunchroom stood around watching as the older Latina girls issued threats to each other in both English and Spanish about a grudge fight to be held later. They then reported these rumors to us in awe.

Serious fighting reflects street life. "Getting people" after school because of past actions or "looks" often leads to continuous cycles of conflict that last several days. Drug transactions define patterns of turf ownership in the area around the school. Some of the fighting that occurs during school hours is related to "getting back" at people for incidents that occurred on the street, as children mimic patterns of turf protection. The principal sees this pattern as a psychological weakness, a senseless "acting out" of uncontrolled feelings rather than socially generated techniques to mimic or maintain an informal street power structure. At Peterson and St. Ignatius there is little evidence of such "street culture" except for the interest children show in high school gangs that they learn about through their older siblings.

Punishment is a major focus of life at Dixon. Here the issue is mass control. "Good" children are a minority, while those who get into trouble are the majority. Many public rituals like sending children "against the wall" as punishment are viewed as badges of honor. We were told by some students that they were the way one obtained entrance "into the gangs."

As at all the schools we studied, at Dixon there are examples of close and lasting ties across groups. Besides the mixed "gangs" there is the "blackboard bunch," a threesome of sixth-graders in charge of the blackboard in the main office who are given assignments and responsibilities by the administration. The group included one established white boy, one established Latina girl, and one newcomer Latina girl. They were described as having been "inseparable" since third grade.

On the other hand, ESOL and after-school activities divide children. Several clubs are almost exclusively one group or the other. ESOL segregates children at Dixon more than at the other schools. In one fifth-grade class, there are twenty Latino students and seven Euro-American students. Fourteen of the Latinos are in ESOL and are removed from class for varying periods of the day, depending on their proficiency in different subjects. This significantly affects the boundaries in the class: the established students do not get much chance to know the ESOL students, and the Latinos are divided into two playground groups, depending on language proficiency and time spent together.

Dixon's institutional structure is characterized by division. The schisms between professionals and parents reflect class conflict and external pressures. Those between the Euro-American and Latino adults reflect community structure. Both types of division are reinforced by the school's inability to control student and teacher populations. An additional result of the inconsistent feeder policies is the distance that puts a barrier in the way of friendships and parents' participation. The insertion of children from a Spanish-dominant area helps to generate a boundary. Street culture and the structure of the ESOL program tend to undercut the formation of classroom-based friendships. However, the division of children into those who take risks and those who seek protection has generated the most significant ties across groups.

Port Richmond

Port Richmond is located directly to the east of Kensington. While both communities began as working-class neighborhoods built around adjacent factory employment, residents of the two localities fared differently in the changing economic structure of the city. A greater percentage of Port Richmond residents either maintained blue-collar factory employment or shifted into gray-collar or lower white-collar jobs. Most residents sustain a working-class standard of living (see table 5.1). Many residents have stayed in the neighborhood over succeeding generations, so that it is not uncommon for two or three generations of a single family to live within several blocks of each other. The intergenerational flavor sets the tone for the neighborhood. As one teacher put it: "If you get into trouble at school at 10:30 and Babci (Grandmother) lives on Orthodox Street, she'll know about it by 11:00." Others have moved back to the neighborhood because of the convenience of the community and the good housing value. In addition, a number of former Kensington residents have moved here as their neighborhood declined.

In 1980, Port Richmond was 98 percent white. This is a community bent on reproducing itself. Residents fear that the Latinos and blacks from adjacent Kensington will bring down housing values and the quality of life. Associating poverty with skin color, many residents develop an insularity and hostility toward both nonwhites and city government, which they see as encouraging integration. Their efforts to hold onto a working-class life-style in the face of economic and infrastructure decline extends automatically to their children: local parochial schools are favored because of their discipline and the absence of nonwhites at the grade-school level.

The community retains the flavor of an urban ethnic village. As one drives into the area from Kensington, the streetscape is dominated by four late-nineteenth-century parish churches within six blocks of each other: one German, one Polish, one Italian, and the "regular" parish church, which is identified as Irish. There are also several large Protestant churches. The church is the basis of local social life. Each church has its own school, so that during the school year streets and parks are overwhelmed by children in the competing colors and plaids of their uniforms. The community maintains an aura of stability, order, and safety. Neighbors keep close track of each other, so that a sense of closeness and uniformity prevails.

Polish institutions clustered in Port Richmond: Union of Polish Women in America, Polonia Federal Savings, and many shops. (Photograph by Karen Vered)

The ethnic atmosphere of Port Richmond is supplemented by the presence of successive waves of Polish émigrés. It is the most institutionally complete Polish neighborhood in the city and is also one of two neighborhoods where Polish newcomers have traditionally settled. In 1980, approximately 30 percent of the population claimed Polish heritage. Émigrés include people who came to the United States after World War II, around 1968, and recently (post-Solidarity). While all classes are represented in the newcomer population, they include many more university-educated "intelligentsia" than are present in the native-born population. The differing values and rapid economic success of some of the intelligentsia generate jealousies between newcomers and established, as they do in Olney.

Ascension

Ascension is a microcosm of Port Richmond. It is all white in population. As the Polish-nationality school, it draws a large percentage of community residents from all émigré waves.[17] The principal estimates that approximately 10 percent of the school population consists of Polish émigré students. In reality, the numbers are probably higher and the gradations of newcomers much more complex than perceived by the school hierarchy. Native-born Polish-American children mix with the American-born bilingual and bicultural children of the post-World War II and 1968 wave immigrants, as well as newcomer children who have been in the United States from a few months to several years. Outside of school, the adult groups are structured by immigrant waves. They socialize among themselves, and these ties influence children's relations.

STRUCTURE. In contrast to St. Ignatius, the majority of Ascension's students come from the parish. The school is seen as the primary means of reproducing the parish structure and the community. As such, it is highly subsidized by the parish and the stable established population. As a large self-supporting entity, Ascension remains immune to outside pressures. In return for parish support, students are expected to become active members of the parish community. At graduation mass, the monsignor tells the students that they are leaving the close, secure community of the school but admonishes them always to maintain their ties to the parish. Many of the active parents attended the school as children, the principal went to school there, and over half of the teachers are former students, wives of former students, or residents.

Only two categories are recognized within the school: foreigner and com-

17. In this case, both newcomers and established residents are of Polish descent and of the same race, unlike the situation at the other schools, where newcomer/established distinctions coincide with nationality and racial differences. However, there are class differences between established Poles and newcomer émigrés. Polish-Americans from the 1880–1920 wave are working-class, as are the post-World War II displaced persons and the post-1968 émigrés who still live in Port Richmond. In contrast, many current newcomers are from the intelligentsia. (The rest are skilled and technical workers.)

munity member. New immigrant children are expected to be different from the native-born children when they enter school. For both parents and children, the symbol for foreignness is ascribed language ability. According to the accepted wisdom of the school, newcomers do not speak English. They are considered a burden to the school in that they require special translation and educational services and seldom participate in parish or school events. They are seen as "taking" from the community and not giving back. This constellation of expectations was illustrated the first day that we visited the school. We followed a well-dressed émigré woman into the school building. Since she asked us directions in English, we knew that she was bilingual. When the principal saw the newcomer, she immediately exclaimed, "Oh, no. Not another one," and ran to get the only bilingual teacher to translate. The teacher, principal, and school secretary then proceeded to talk over the woman's head as if she were not there. Everyone assumed that she did not understand and exhibited the same discomfort in attempting direct communication without a special broker that we saw in other schools.

Even as a Polish-nationality parish school, Ascension stresses American identity over ethnicity. The school gradually gave up teaching Polish by the mid-1950s. This transition symbolizes both changes in generation, as more American-born students entered the school, and Polish-American reaction to attempts by upper-class post-World War II Polish émigrés to take over the institutions of the ethnic community (Schneider 1988; Blejwas 1981). Poland is not featured in the curriculum, and no special ethnic events are included in the school year. Speaking Polish on school grounds is effectively discouraged through unspoken rules. A bilingual child and her sister chattered with each other in Polish outside the school yard but switched to English on entering the grounds. Two bilingual children who were best friends told each other secrets in English, not Polish. A newcomer child spoke Polish to her mother as she followed her into the schoolyard after lunch but switched to English as she joined a game of ring-around-the-rosy with her classmates. Children who break the rules face hostility from teachers, aides, and fellow students.

Nevertheless, a certain ambivalence toward Poland and the Polish language remains in the parish. As the largest Polish parish in Philadelphia, Ascension has several Polish masses and is the location for a number of cultural events.

CHILDREN'S RELATIONS. Assumptions about language structure children's relationships. Foreignness is something that newcomer children are expected to get over in their first year in the school. During that time, they are exempted from language-dominant subjects like reading and social studies. Several bilingual parents voluntarily provide ESOL classes for one hour several times a week. Each newcomer child is assigned a bilingual buddy, who was meant to be his or her translator and guide. The buddy relationship is often a strain on children placed in this role. Two girls charged with translating for a new boy complained that he told teachers they had not informed him about assignments; thus he got out of homework, and they got into trouble.

Even though newcomer children may maintain friendships with established children outside of school, within school they speak only Polish and play only with their buddies. For example, one newcomer eighth-grader quickly learned English and found American friends outside of school. Within three months of moving to Philadelphia, she talked of traveling with her English-speaking friends to the malls in the Northeast on public transportation. But in school her only contact was a bilingual seventh-grader. She refused to speak English unless pressed, even in ESOL class, because "nobody thinks I speak English here."

After a year in the school, new children are expected to speak English and become American like all the others. The confusion caused by this rigid transition is evident in children's behavior. One boy kept trying to avoid work in his second year, claiming that he was having trouble with English. The teacher would have none of this and started failing him halfway through the semester. More often than not, however, children have become established fixtures within the school after their first year there. Newcomer children adopt American ways and move easily through the social structure of the school. Both teachers and students know who is native-born and who came from Poland, but this is never discussed. When one boy needed extra time off to process citizenship papers, the school authorities frowned on this, expressing anger that the child would expect "special treatment."

Children reflect the ambivalence of the parish about identification with the Polish language and Poland. Both bilingual and monolingual children clustered around a Polish poster advertising a cultural event, expressing curiosity about the language. American children unsuccessfully attempted to use the few words of Polish learned from their grandparents to communicate with a newcomer. As one researcher attempted to discuss the émigré experience with a group of seventh-graders during gym one day, both the students and the fieldworker suddenly realized that all the members of that particular team happened to be either newcomers or American-born children of émigrés. When the team took the gym floor, one boy exclaimed "Polish power"—acknowledging the mutual background publicly for the first time in two years.

Parents and Aides. The aides at Ascension resemble the aides at all the other schools. They are working-class women with American outlooks who have children in the school. A number of them went to the school themselves. Even the two aides who came with the 1968 émigré wave are bilingual and stress American identity and views while at school. However, in their own homes, both expressed ambivalence over the need to maintain a bicultural identity and the way their Polish background was frowned upon at school. One woman who is very active in both the parish and the school stated that she had to try twice as hard to be included because "they think that you are stupid if you speak with an accent."

The primary criterion distinguishing foreigner from community-member parents is participation, not date of arrival. The principal labeled one post-1968 émigré family "newcomer" because they did not help out at parish events. Others who had arrived at the same time but participated more were considered "American." One of the two émigré women who are active members of the Home and School Association and work as aides was not even recognized as a newcomer. The other teaches ESOL, so is designated as coming from Poland, but the principal states that she participates and is part of the community.

The difference between newcomer and established parents has class overtones. The current wave of émigrés are mostly intelligentsia who expect more from the school than the American-born parents and are not afraid to say so. The principal and some teachers complain that these parents want more from the school than the Polish Americans. (In fact, established parents are likely to ask teachers to be lenient with their children, like many parents at Dixon, while Polish parents demand a higher level of academic offerings, like their class counterparts in Olney.) Other teachers react positively to the eagerness of the Polish children and the interest in progress shown by their parents. The Polish parents are also the ones who are most likely to show up at school events with a video camera, thus bringing out working class jealousies over rapid economic achievement by newcomer parents.

Newcomer parents, like those at St. Ignatius, are characterized as wanting much from the school but contributing little. Polish-American parents complain that newcomers never come to fundraising events, although this absence has not affected their ability to raise funds as it has at St. Ignatius. Some of the nonparticipation is excused: "They have so little money," or "They don't speak English." The "poor immigrant" image is invoked again at the Home and School meetings, when the few Polish parents who do attend are said to come because of the monthly tuition raffle.

As at Peterson and St. Ignatius, established parents at Ascension are frustrated over the lack of participation by newcomers but do little to encourage participation. Most of the Home and School Association meetings are focused on fundraising activities, while newcomer parents are more concerned with the academic activities of the school. The newcomers who do come must deal with the cliques of a well-established community. All the newcomer parents sit with one of the bilingual aides, who translates for them. When parents gather to wait for their children to finish their dance classes, newcomer parents sit in clusters and speak Polish while Polish-American parents speak English in their groups. As at Dixon, the content of their segregated conversations is almost identical.

The fissure between the groups of parents and children is further reinforced by the mobility of the newcomers. Many of the new émigrés from an intelligentsia background move away from Port Richmond once they achieve stable middle-class employment. For the Polish-American parents who cannot afford such moves, this mobility represents newcomers' taking unfair advantage. When they move out, they are not serving the parish or school by recreating the community. Since the school sees itself as providing special services and attention to newcomers, leaving the community represents another way of taking and not giving back. Foreigners are people who do not participate in the ongoing dialogue of the community—its attempts to maintain stability and cohesiveness through sharing in the activities of the neighborhood and the school.

Conclusion

Popular wisdom in Philadelphia asserts that schools teach tolerance, but the message is undermined at home by parents' biases. Our study demonstrates that in fact schools do not invariably teach tolerance but actually help create, reinforce, or transcend boundaries. Moreover, children's relationships are often different from those of adults. How does this happen? These four schools illustrate that the processes involved are not simple. Neighborhood dynamics do impinge on the relationships within the school. Yet a comparison between Peterson and St. Ignatius, in the same neighborhood, shows that the nature of the neighborhood does not simply determine the nature of the school.

In Olney, with its aspiring middle-class population, decline is seen as approaching but not as insurmountable. Here newcomers as well as many established residents have an optimistic view of their future. They are in less competition for scarce jobs and less dependent on public resources. In Olney, the schools continue to produce successful students as upwardly mobile parents, established and newcomers alike, collaborate with professionals to push academic achievement as the path to being good Americans. Peterson and St. Ignatius have much in common in their history, demography, and community setting. Both schools have positive reputations as they shift from white Euro-American populations to a multiracial and multinational composition. While there is little collaboration among the adults, teachers find the parents to be generally attentive to their children's academic needs, fulfilling the expected role of good parents.

In spite of these similarities, the schools are very different in their ability to transcend the ethnic segmentation of the community. Peterson's stability helps it succeed as a school that provides equal opportunity to "Americanize" newcomers. It provides community for teachers and students. The students who travel together through eight years of grade school develop bonds that cross boundaries. Their residential propinquity helps reinforce school-based ties. The continuity of staff mitigates the commonly found alienation between established parents and outside professionals. As the children cross racial and ethnic boundaries, they bring their parents, the professionals, and the nonprofessional staff and volunteers with them. Boundaries are transcended in everyday life and at the regularly occurring public events celebrating success. This works against contradictions between the ideology of public schooling and school experience. Peterson avoids the reproduction of preexisting group boundaries that occurred at Dixon and the parochial schools. This occurs partially because of, rather than in spite of, an absence of emphasis on multiculturalism in the school discourse.

St. Ignatius is less shielded from community change. Its response to turnover—expanded recruitment of outsiders—reinforces group boundaries and prevents the school from achieving its goal of community cohesion and reproduction. Parish practices reinforce tightly knit kin and friendship networks in the school, creating boundaries between established insiders (the tightly knit network of professional and nonprofessional staff and parent volunteers) and the newcomers (the subcommunity networks of kin and friends who control their children's contacts and restrict their own). Established community beliefs in ethnic segments are reinforced. Yet the class nature of the neighborhood helps the school maintain its academic mission.

Similarly, the structural differences generated by participation in the public or parochial system are mitigated by differences in neighborhood process, as a comparison between St. Ignatius and Ascension reveals. In Port Richmond, the tightening of the community boundary in the wake of postindustrial changes and fears of being taken over by dangerous outsiders has strengthened the school's efforts to shape relationships. Ascension achieves the goal of being an almost seamless web of professionals, staff, and parents more than St. Ignatius is able to do. The hegemony of Ascension's established worldview is easier to maintain. Only the newcomers bring different goals and inject a note of discord and internal division. Adults are segregated, while children are incorporated through informal practices that transform them from newcomers into regular students. For the parish as a whole, the American part of a hyphenated identity is what is important in the face of threats from the outside.

Neighborhood factors also engender differences in the public schools. In Kensington, precipitous economic decline has generated greater neighborhood stress, division, and tension. Because of this decline, the public school's professed goal of promoting individual achievement is impossible. Dixon has very little control over its student population or resources (such as experienced teachers and a stable assistant principal); the dizzying instability of personnel and school-district-generated feeder policies affects the school's internal control as well. There are no conditions to militate against the effects of turnover and absenteeism, the insertion of a segment of newcomers from a Spanish-dominant area outside the neighborhood, the influence of street drug culture on the social organization of the school, and the hard and fast boundaries between Spanish- and English-speaking adults that are characteristic of the neighborhood. Professionals and parents are at odds, and neither established nor Latino parents attempt to enlist each other in their common battles. All components differ in their explanation of problems, and no group satisfactorily achieves its goal. Nonetheless, children do cross borders and form friendships, often around the dynamic of risk-taking or avoiding trouble. However, these relationships are fragile, as the forces of flux supersede constancy in everyday life.

Thus external structures, neighborhood and system type, while significant in affecting the propensity for conflict and tension within and between the components of the school's ground-level structure, work themselves out in complex interaction. Schools as institutions shape their social orders and their ideology differently depending on their ability to control the effects of macro-structural change. Peterson and Ascension have been most able to reproduce themselves and achieve their institutional goals in the face of external change: one as an academically achieving "melting pot" and the other as a tightly knit Polish-American parish school. The other two schools have been more affected by external pressures.

In all the schools, relationships between children tend to cross boundaries to a much greater extent than, and often independent of, adult relationships. At Peterson, stability encourages cross-group student ties, which bring adults together. At Dixon, conflict between professionals and separate parent segments do not impede children's links forged by street dynamics. Only at the parochial schools are adult ideologies clearly reflected in children's relationships. The role of language in creating boundaries flows from the social order rather than the other way around.

For adults the story is different. One pattern consistently found in all four schools is the distance and discomfort in relationships and communication between adults of foreign origin and working-class established adults. The working class is likely to be actively competing with newcomers for housing, jobs, and city resources. They are likely to find themselves head to head with minorities in their attempt to maintain their life-styles or move up. Their answer to this stress is to focus on the commonalities of their American life-style. In all schools they seek to retain control and continuity in local institutions, the one area of life where they have had some power, as they observe local and citywide decline around them. They are simultaneously threatened and resentful, especially if newcomers are seen to be better off or more materialistic. Their welcome is subject to the caveat that newcomers must want to "fit in," to learn the rules, become members of the community, and participate in traditional community responsibilities. They are disappointed when newcomers do not share this view. While established residents talk about wanting participation from newcomers, they want it on their terms.

At Ascension and St. Ignatius, this resentment is strengthened by the perception that newcomer families are too financially successful and not doing their share in support of the parish. At all schools they are seen as aloof, not joining in protests or fundraising activities. Yet in the public schools, where fundraising is not as critical, more blame is placed on the school district for the problems of the school, and newcomers avoid becoming scapegoats.

The differences and similarities among these four schools illustrate the interaction between micro- and macro-factors. While common patterns occur across schools, each case is unique. The particular combination of larger political and economic factors with the institutional history and present-day personalities and procedures of each site produces differences. Focusing exclusively on either macro-level factors or micro-level events limits both the research understandings and the practical applications of field study. Maintaining a double focus yields richer analysis and more appropriate interventions in attempting to facilitate interaction among groups in American schools.

References

Baron, Steve, Dan Finn, Neil Grant, Michael Green, and Richard Johnson. 1981. *Unpopular Education.* London: Hutchinson.

Binzen, Peter. 1970. *Whitetown U.S.A.* New York: Random House.

Blanc, Suzanne. 1989. Formal Barriers and Informal Networks: Negotiating the Home/School Border in a Multi-cultural Community. Paper delivered at the American Anthropological Association Meetings, Washington, D.C., 15–19 November.

Blejwas, Stanislaus. 1981. Old and New Polonius: Tensions within an Ethnic Community. *Polish American Studies* 38:55–83.

Borowski, Neill A. Census: Philadelphia Lost 9%. *Philadelphia Inquirer,* 30 August 1990, p. A-1.

Bowles, Samuel, and Herbert Gintis. 1976. *Schooling in Capitalist America.* New York: Basic Books.

Byler, Janet, and Douglas Bennett. 1984. *Employment Trends in Southeastern Pennsylvania 1972–82.* Working Paper 11. Philadelphia: Institute for Public Policy Studies, Temple University.

Goode, Judith. 1990. A Wary Welcome to the Neighborhood: Community Responses to Immigrants. *Urban Anthropology* 19:125–53.

Goldstein, Ira. 1986. The Wrong Side of the Tracts: A Study of Residential Segregation in Philadelphia, 1930–1980. Ph.D. diss., Temple University, Philadelphia.

Hershberg, Theodore, 1981. *Philadelphia: Work, Space, Family, and Group Experience in the 19th Century.* New York: Oxford University Press.

Hogan, David. 1968. Education and Class Formation: The Peculiarities of the Americans. In *Cultural and Economic Reproduction in Education,* edited by Michael Apple. Boston: Routledge and Kegan Paul.

Katz, Michael B. 1968. *The Irony of Early School Reform: Educational Innovation in Mid-19th Century Massachusetts.* Cambridge, Mass.: Harvard University Press.

Katznelson, Ira, and Margaret Weir. 1985. *Schooling for All: Class, Race, and the Decline of the Democratic Ideal.* New York: Basic Books.

Parsons, Talcott. 1959. The School Class as a Social System. *Harvard Educational Review* 29:297–318.

Schneider, Jo Anne. 1988. In the Big Village. Ph.D. diss., Temple University, Philadelphia.

Sieber, Timothy. 1979. Schooling, Socialization, and Group Boundaries: Study of Informal Social Relations in the Public Domain. *Urban Anthropology* 7:273–82.

Spindler, George, and Louise Spindler. 1989. Instrumental Competence, Self-Efficacy, Linguistic Minorities, and Cultural Therapy: A Preliminary Attempt at Integration. *Anthropology of Education Quarterly* 20:36–50.

Trueba, Henry. 1989. *Raising Silent Voices.* Cambridge, Mass.: Newbury House.

Tyack, David. 1974. *The One Best System.* Cambridge, Mass.: Harvard University Press.

Weisner, Thomas, Ronald Gallimore, and Cathie Jordan. 1988. Unpackaging Cultural Effects on Classroom Learning: Native Peer Assistance and Child-Generated Activity. *Anthropology and Education* 19:327–53.

Weiss, Bernard J. 1982. Introduction to *American Education and the American Immigrant, 1840–1940,* edited by Bernard J. Weiss. Urbana: University of Illinois Press.

Willis, Paul. 1977. *Learning to Labour.* Farnborough, U.K.: Saxon House.

Wrigley, Julia. 1982. *Class Politics and Public Schools: Chicago, 1900–1950.* New Brunswick, N.J.: Rutgers University Press.

Yancey, William, and Eugene Ericsen. 1979. Antecedents of Community: The Economic and Institutional Structure of Urban Neighborhoods. *American Sociological Review* 44:253–62.

Yancey, William, Eugene Erickson, and George Leon. 1985. The Structure of Pluralism: We're All Italian Around Here, Mrs. O'Brien. *Ethnic Studies* 8:94–116.

Young, Robert. 1989. Who Has Come to the Philadelphia Area, Where Did They Settle, and How Are They Doing? Paper delivered at the "Who Are These Strangers Among Us?" conference, Balch Institute for Ethnic Studies and Nationalities Service Center, Philadelphia, 28 October.

- loss of the plurality of the community

- politized structuring of the comm.

I. Background

II. Voicing the subject

→ for any. purposes

-

6 THE POLITICS OF DIVERSITY IN MONTEREY PARK, CALIFORNIA

JOHN HORTON

Monterey Park is by freeway only minutes east of downtown Los Angeles with its skid row and gleaming monuments to Pacific Rim capital, beyond Chinatown, Little Tokyo, and Latino East L.A., in the commercial and residential sprawl of the San Gabriel Valley at the gateway to the desert spillovers of the megalopolis. Transformed by a new wave of immigration into "America's first suburban Chinatown," in 1990, Monterey Park had an official population of 56 percent Asian, 31 percent Latino, 12 percent Anglo, and 1 percent African-American and other (U.S. Bureau of the Census, 1990; see figure 6.1).[1]

Late spring, 1988. Our research site is the city council. Seated behind microphones on a long, raised, blond-wood podium are the five council members: two Anglo men and two Anglo women, all variously identified with the politics of slow growth and "Official English"—responses of established residents to rapid demographic and economic change; next to them, a lone Chinese-American woman, an advocate of harmony and "managed" economic growth.

During heated debates, citizens fill the two hundred padded red seats of the auditorium, protest at the podium, and watch the official vote on the electronic scoreboard. During quieter meetings, the crowd dwindles to some fifty to

The principal members of our research team included Linda Shaw (who supervised ethnographic training), Jose Calderon, Mary Pardo, Leland Saito, and Yen-Fen Tseng. They contributed to my analysis, and their field notes appear in the text. All notes not attributed to them are mine. The Monterey Park project also received valuable assistance from Lucie Cheng, Paul Ong, Ping-Chun Hsiung, Jerry Kimery, Liang-Wen Kuo, Michelle DiMiscio, and Qunsheng Yang. Our research was funded by the Institute of American Cultures, the Asian American Studies Center, the Academic Senate of the University of California at Los Angeles, and the Changing Relations project of the Ford Foundation. Patrick McCloskey and Wendy Dishman provided editorial assistance for this article, and David Radick helped with the graphs and tables.

1. Recognizing that population labels are ongoing politically contested constructions, unless otherwise indicated, we employ terms current in Los Angeles: Asian or Asian American, Anglos (applied mainly to Americans of European origin), whites (equivalent to "Anglos," but often more inclusive of other groups), Latinos or Hispanics (people of Mexican, Central American, Puerto Rican, or Latin American origin), and African Americans. The usage varies with social context, but the trend favors terms referring to national or regional origin.

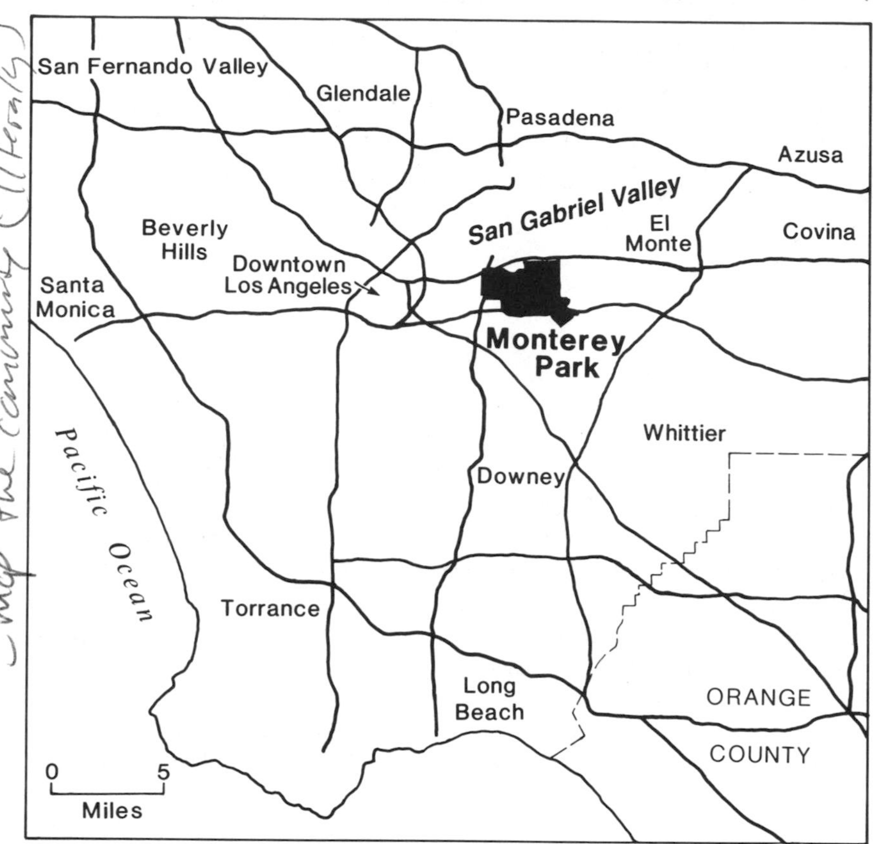

Figure 6.1. Monterey Park intersected by Los Angeles freeways

seventy-five people, but always includes a core of older, mostly Anglo residents who never miss a meeting. The council chamber is their turf. One "regular" commented publicly as she moved slowly toward the podium, "I feel at home here." Indeed, except for a scattering of Latinos and even fewer Asians, the council looks like a white island surrounded by the sea of Chinese signs and faces that fill the city's major business streets. Recent immigrants don't feel at home in the council. They attend occasionally, sometimes in the protection of large numbers needed in the defense of specific causes.

Late spring, 1990. Three of the Anglo council members, including the most vocal supporter of "Official English" and restrictions on immigration, have been retired by a recent election. The new council consists of two Anglo women, one an advocate of slow growth and the other a critic of the "antibusiness bias of the slow-growth movement"; a Latino who is president of the local chamber of commerce; the Chinese-American woman; and a newly elected

Chinese immigrant male. They have come together to celebrate the inauguration of the new mayor, Judy Chu, the American-born Chinese (ABC):

> At least for tonight, Chinese citizens did not have that bad feeling of being unwanted in City Hall. The elderly white council-watcher who a year ago had announced that she felt at home in the chambers was now struggling to find a seat. She made her statement by sitting up front in a section normally reserved for city staff. Everywhere mingling with established residents were well-dressed Chinese, many recording the event on film. Large baskets of flowers with red-ribboned messages of good luck from Chinese individuals and associations lined the front walls and were in grave danger of being toppled by the entertainers: a gyrating Chinese dragon, a fan-waving Japanese American woman dressed in a traditional kimono, an energetic troupe of Mexican American folk dancers. Public officials were present to sanction the event—a local Rabbi; the State's Attorney General, John Van de Kamp; March Fong Eu, the Secretary of State; and Dr. Omero Suarez, President of Monterey Park's East Los Angeles College, Latino territory with a fast-growing Asian student population. With these gestures, diversity and multiculturalism were being institutionalized in the Monterey Park City Council, the former bastion of established resident reaction to the new Asian immigration. (Horton field notes 1990)

The event dramatized a major change—the defeat, at least temporarily, of nativist politics and a step toward a new politics of diversity. Our report is about that change.

Change is reflected in the very physical appearance of the city. Monterey Park still looks unfinished, caught in some time warp between a picture-card-perfect Middle America of parks, public buildings, and neat single-family dwellings and the more recent encroachment of condominiums, traffic, and a thriving Chinese commercial enclave. The sights and sounds of the sixties and the nineties clash. On North Atlantic, a major commercial street, one encounters in succession the Ai Hao supermarket (the name, meaning "Love Chinese," might shock old-timers and is not translated into English); more Chinese signs with enough English to identify Little Taipei Restaurant, Red Rose Hair Design, Flying Horse Video, Cathay Bank, Remax Realty, and Bright Optical Watch, patronized by a large, regional, mostly Mandarin-speaking population; empty lots and run-down houses; the abandoned shells of Fred Frey Pontiac and Pic 'N' Save. Hughes Market and Marie Callendar's Restaurant remain as clues to an earlier Monterey Park. North Atlantic Boulevard is the last area of the city open to major development. Its future depends on the outcome of the ongoing battle between developers and the local forces of slow and managed growth.

Chinese dragon dancers, inauguration of Mayor Judy Chu, Monterey Park, spring 1990 (Photograph by Judy Chu)

This is Monterey Park, variously called "Little Taipei" (a term used by both established residents and newcomers), "the Olympic City with a Heart" (Monterey Park was on the torchbearer's route during the Los Angeles Olympics), and "All-American City" (a national award given in 1986 in recognition of programs promoting harmonious relations—just before a period of disharmony). The city evokes strong and contradictory senses of place. Some long-established Anglo, Latino, and Asian-American residents locate their Monterey Park in the golden age of a familiar past. Immigrants look to the future. Asian tourist buses make an obligatory stop at Monterey Park to show the making of an Asian-American city in a country that until recently had no place for Asian immigrants.

As ethnographers, we joined reporters, other researchers, and the merely curious to observe how newcomers and established residents shaped the process of transformation. As an ethnically and linguistically diverse team of sociology professors and graduate students, we began our fieldwork in the fall of 1988, during the current period of political as well as demographic and economic transition. Although the population had tipped decisively in favor of "minorities," the Anglo "majority" still controlled City Hall. They were vacillating between flight, containment, and cooperation, while Asians and Latinos were finding ways of turning their numbers into power. The media generally seized on the moments of conflict between newcomers and established residents.[2] We began to unravel strands of a more complex story of change and accommodation.

2. Some examples of the abundant media coverage of controversy in Monterey Park include Arax 1987; CBS 1989; Lemann 1988; Tanzer 1985; and Wood 1990.

Signs of change, Monterey Park 1991 (photograph by John Horton)

Our story is about the many-dimensioned restructuring of Monterey Park and the larger San Gabriel Valley. What we found at the macro-levels of demographic and economic change fits Edward Soja's definition of restructuring as "a 'brake,' if not a break, in secular trends, and a shift towards a significantly different order and configuration of social, economic, and political life. . . . As such, restructuring falls between piecemeal reform and revolutionary transformation, between business-as-usual and something completely different" (Soja

1989:159).[3] In the context of Los Angeles and Monterey Park, we came to understand the fashionable term "restructuring" to mean a major transformation within the dominant order of property and power relations.

A part of the story of restructuring that particularly concerned us was the extent and process of political change. How was evident economic and demographic restructuring affecting political relations between newcomers and established residents? Were the older patterns of Anglo and developer domination continuing under the aegis of nativist restrictions on immigrants and without the representation of newer Asian populations in city politics? Was the community polarized between newcomers and established residents? Or were alliances being formed across these barriers on the basis of shared ethnic and class interests? Were local institutions themselves being restructured in the uncharted direction of something we tentatively call multiculturalism—the recognition and appreciation of diversity—and ethnic pluralism, the empowerment of ethnically diverse populations?

To answer these questions, we interviewed over one hundred local activists, read daily reports in Chinese and English newspapers, and conducted two exit polls during local elections. Primarily, we used ethnography—observing and participating in local political networks—in an effort to understand the experiences and perceptions of newcomers and established residents as well as the interactions between them. Also, as researchers playing roles ranging from resident activists to involved outsiders, we were very much aware that our knowledge was the result of our own social, ethnic, and political statuses; how we were perceived; and our practices in the field.[4]

We begin with a brief analysis of the macro-layers of social life as revealed through economic and demographic data. Newcomers and established residents developed their political relationships within the context of material conditions set by the economic and demographic restructuring of the larger San Gabriel Valley and Los Angeles. Next, we examine how these changes were talked about and played out in the local political process. In this way, we can link the macro-level of social life, major social and demographic conditions, to the micro-level, how individual actors make history.

The Demographic and Economic Restructuring of Monterey Park

With 7.7 square miles and population of just over 62,000, Monterey Park is one small city among eighty-four cities incorporated within the larger County

3. For a discussion of the contradictory effects of economic restructuring in the United States and Los Angeles, see Harrison and Bluestone 1988; Davis 1987, 1990; and Ong et al. 1989.

4. Our perspective is one of critical ethnography in the sense that we were players as well as observers in the political and cultural terrain of Monterey Park. For the many issues raised by doing critical ethnography in the context of diversity see Van Maanen 1988; Marcus and Fischer 1986; and Rosaldo 1989.

of Los Angeles, which encompasses 4,090 square miles and a population of 8.8 million people. In spite of its small size, Monterey Park is a microcosm of the demographic transition affecting greater Los Angeles. In 1970, Los Angeles was predominantly an Anglo city, a frontier for Americans migrating westward to the golden land of opportunity. By 1990, the influx of immigrants from Mexico, Central America, and Asia had turned the Anglo majority into a numerical minority (see table 6.1). Today, Los Angeles is second only to New York as the city of destination for immigrants, the majority of whom are people of color. It is the primary destination for Asian immigrants (Portes and Rumbault 1990:34). Latinos, predominantly Mexicans and a growing number of Central Americans, constitute the largest population among immigrants and refugees in Los Angeles County. They are followed by Asians, who are the fastest growing minority in California and the United States (see figure 6.2).

After Filipinos, Chinese-speaking immigrants from Taiwan, Hong Kong, mainland China, and Southeast Asia form the largest Asian immigrant and refugee population in Los Angeles. The more affluent prefer the suburbs to the traditional and congested Chinatown. Increasingly, since the 1970s, Chinese businesses and residents have been settling into the already ethnically mixed Monterey Park and the surrounding western San Gabriel Valley. Today, that region of seven small cities with a total population of nearly 350,000 is approximately one-third Anglo, one-third Latino, and one-third Asian.

Table 6.1. Racial Distribution of Los Angeles County (in thousands)

	1970	1980	1990
Non-Hispanic whites	4,990	3,985	3,619
	(71.0%)	(52.7%)	(40.8%)
African American	763	943	993
	(10.9%)	(12.5%)	(11.2%)
Latinos	1,027	2,016	3,230
	(14.6%)	(26.7%)	(36.4%)
Asians/Others	250	534	1,054
	(3.5%)	(7.1%)	(11.6%)

Source: Paul Ong, School of Architecture and Urban Planning, Los Angeles.

Note: The term "Latinos" refers to persons of Hispanic origins who are not African American or Asian American. Statistics for 1970 are estimated from published data. According to data for the West region of the United States, 97.7 percent of the Hispanic-origin population were classified either as "white" or as "other." This factor was used to adjust the Hispanic-origins count for Los Angeles. The number of non-Hispanic whites was estimated by subtracting the estimated number of Hispanic-origin whites from the total number of whites. Statistics for 1980 are taken from the STF-3 tape file for Los Angeles, and the 1990 statistics are taken from the PL94-171 file provided by Greg Lipton, City of Los Angeles.

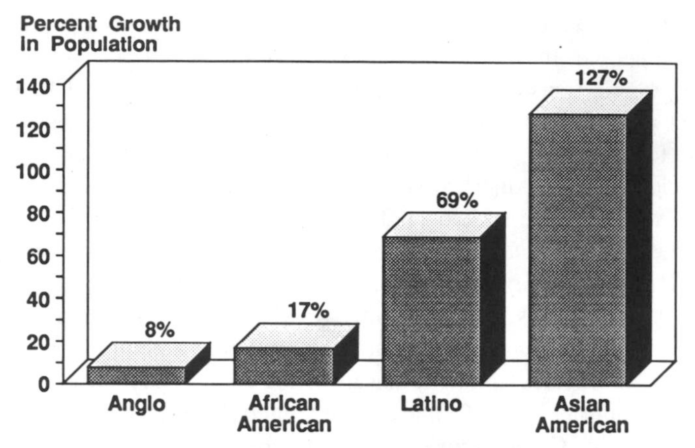

Figure 6.2. Ethnic change in California, 1980–90

Monterey Park stands out as the only city in the region and the continental United States with a majority Asian population. The internationalization of the city began slowly at first. In the late 1950s and early 1960s, upwardly mobile second- and third-generation Americans of Mexican descent, Japanese Americans, and Chinese Americans were buying homes and beginning to break the color barrier in Monterey Park. By 1980, primarily as a result of the increased immigration of Chinese, the city was almost evenly divided between Anglo and minority populations. The 1990 census, which, according to city officials, seriously undercounts Asian immigrants, signals a new demographic order, a break rather than a mere continuation of earlier trends (see figure 6.3).

Encouraged by developers and realtors selling Monterey Park in Taiwan, Hong King, and China as "the Chinese Beverly Hills," between 1980 and 1990 the number of Asian residents in the city increased by 91 percent, while Anglos declined by 47 percent and Latinos by 10 percent. The majority of Asians are Chinese immigrants, followed by a smaller number of second-generation Chinese, a dwindling population of Japanese Americans (who formerly were the dominant Asian group), and smaller numbers of Vietnamese refugees and Korean immigrants (see table 6.2).

A New Class of Immigrants

Many of the Asian newcomers arrived in Monterey Park with superior education and financial resources. In this middle-class suburb with an income level above the average of Los Angeles County as a whole, established residents take

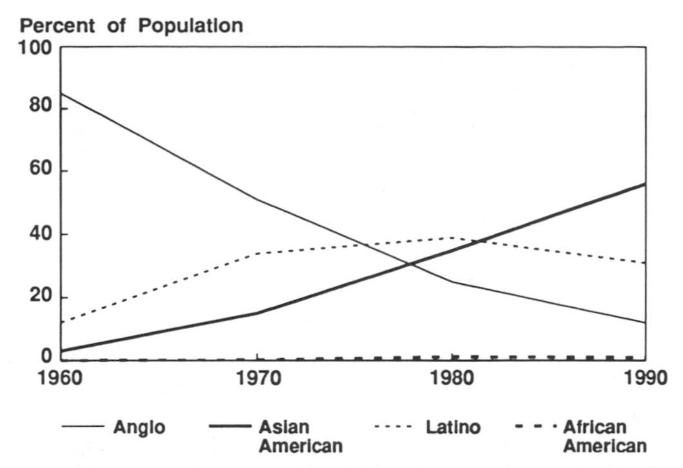

Figure 6.3. Population change in Monterey Park, 1960–90 (source: Community Development Department, Monterey Park)

particular note of affluent immigrants who do not conform to the traditional immigrant stereotypes. One elderly white resident expressed a frequently heard complaint: "Before, immigrants were poor. They lived in their own neighborhoods and moved into ours after they learned English, got a good job, and became accustomed to our ways. Today, the Chinese come right in with their money and their ways. We are the aliens."

Although the Asian population in the United States is in fact polarized, con-

Table 6.2. The Changing Asian Population of Monterey Park

	1970 (%)	1980 (%)	1990 (%)
Chinese	29	41	63
Japanese	61	40	17
Vietnamese	*	5	8
Korean	2	6	4
Filipino	6	4	3
Pacific Islander/Other	2	4	5
Total	100	100	100

*no data

Source: Population and Housing Profile, Monterey Park Planning Department, p. 1; 1980 U.S. Census, Table 248; 1990 U.S. Census Summary Tape, File 1, May 13, 1991.

taining both rich and poor, the woman's remark does reflect a reality of Monterey Park. According to the 1980 census and 1986 test census, Asian families in Monterey Park had higher incomes and higher levels of self-employment and employment in professional/managerial occupations than Anglo and Latino residents. The discrepancy is greatest between Asians and Latinos. The high status of Monterey Park Chinese was dramatically confirmed by our exit poll conducted during the April 1990 Monterey Park City Council elections. Sixty-six percent of the Chinese voters (74 percent of whom were foreign-born) had a college degree, compared to 43 percent of the Japanese Americans, 36 percent of the Anglos, and 23 percent of the Latinos. They also had higher incomes and were younger than American-born established residents. (See table 6.3.)

Relations between newcomers and established residents are conditioned by the large size, non-European origin, and class of the new immigrants—structural factors that could favor either confrontation or accommodation. Another important factor is the transformation of the economic order from locally based and Anglo to international, Chinese-dominated, and shaped by the dynamics of the regional growth machine.[5]

Chinese Economic Dominance

By the 1980s, Chinese businesses had established their economic dominance in the city and revitalized what had been a sluggish service economy in a small town that had never quite made it big. Our survey of Monterey Park businesses in August 1989 showed that fourteen out of twenty-one banks were primarily owned by and run for Chinese. The same applied to six out of eight principal supermarkets. Four major Chinese newspapers are based in Monterey Park. Asians from all over Los Angeles and the world came to shop in the stores and eat at the many restaurants of Monterey Park.

This new economic order does not stop at the borders of Monterey Park, which is today merely the first and most concentrated center of an expanding regional Chinese enclave located in the San Gabriel Valley. According to our analysis of Chinese telephone books, in the 1980s the valley was replacing the City of Los Angeles and the older Chinatown as the largest regional center of Chinese business (Kuo research notes 1989). In 1983, 48 percent of all listed Chinese businesses in Greater Los Angeles (including Orange County, another destination of Asian, especially Vietnamese, immigration) were located in the city of Los Angeles, and 35 percent in the western San Gabriel Valley. By 1989, the valley had taken the lead as a business center with 47 percent, as compared to 20 percent for the city of Los Angeles.

But probably more significant for the reactions of established residents than

5. For a discussion of the political economy of land and growth struggles, see Molotch and Logan 1987 and Plotkin 1987. For sources specific to growth and slow-growth struggles in Monterey Park, see Lemann 1988 and Horton 1989.

Table 6.3. Voters' Profile by Ethnicity, City Council Election, Monterey Park, April 10, 1990

	Anglo	Chinese	Latino	Japanese
		In Percentages		
All voters	36	25	26	13
Candidates				
Kiang	40	90	30	69
Purvis	53	26	48	34
Reichenberger	44	15	21	36
Hatch	37	10	19	25
Balderrama	45	36	67	44
Barron	42	19	47	37
Foreign-born	6	74	20	1
College or more	36	66	23	43
Age 45+	69	33	48	57
Income $50,000+	35	54	31	50
Party affiliation				
Republican	35	47	15	37
Democrat	59	22	80	59
None	3	22	3	1
Length of residence in M.P. (30 years+)	56	18	42	37
Measure S (restrictions on residential development)				
Yes	67	51	65	70
No	19	22	19	15
Didn't vote	7	13	9	8
No response	7	14	7	7
Bilingual education				
Yes	41	68	57	40
No	46	20	29	45
Undecided	12	7	11	11
Respondents (absolute number)	349	239	255	131

Source: John Horton and Yen-Fen Tseng, Department of Sociology, University of California at Los Angeles, 1990.

the existence of a powerful Chinese enclave is the fact that its rise coincides with a wider regional problem—the uncontrolled urbanization of suburbs that had prided themselves on the "Leave It to Beaver" dream of safe, tranquil, and affordable communities. Like other cities in Los Angeles County, Monterey Park is experiencing gridlock, the proliferation of minimalls and condominiums, and high-density commercial and residential overdevelopment. In the 1980s, the Asian newcomers' demands for commercial and residential land were fanning inflation and changing land use. Affordable housing evaporated for renters. Owners among established residents willingly sold out to newcomers or remained to face a changed community. By the early 1980s, the city had become a victim of regional developers. What made Monterey Park unusual was that many of the developers were immigrants and had Asian faces.

The Political Restructuring of Monterey Park

Restructuring is not part of the local vocabulary, but long-time residents with a sense of history perfectly understand the concept of a break from a real or imagined past. They date this break to the late 1970s or early 1980s, when they began to ask, in the words of a prodigal son of a local Japanese-American family, "God damn it, Dad, where the hell did all these Chinese come from? Shit, this isn't even our town anymore" (Leland Saito field notes, 1990). The Chinese are an easy scapegoat for the many problems of unplanned regional development. So many new buildings and new faces. One couple remarked that they kept their bearings in the storm of change by naming new structures according to the old ones they had replaced: for example, the Chinese bank that replaced a doughnut shop was now "The Chinese-Donut Bank," an image reinforced by its round door, and there was also "The House-of-Pies–Chinese Restaurant." Less often we found established residents who welcomed change as the revitalization and upgrading of their community. An elderly and frail Anglo man living alone with his dog in a small, decaying house had this to say: "This is a good place to live. The Orientals buy up old houses and fix them up. My neighbors are Cambodians, and they are the best neighbors I have ever had." Such opinions are rarely recorded by the conflict-hungry media.

Newcomers have their own sense of change. For them, the present, the thriving commercial enclave, is a source of pride, a symbol of success and of the contributions of immigrants to the United States. The Chinese would add that this economic success came about legitimately on the free market, without welfare assistance and at no cost to taxpayers. A Chinese developer put his view this way:

> We Chinese immigrated here and became more and more dominant through the free market system. We did not "take over" this area by force, and we don't intend to overwhelm the rest of the residents. Those who sold out their houses at a dear price were doing so willingly. They could have refused to sell their property and remain the majority in this area. I was really disgusted to read in the newspaper that some old residents claimed that they sold out because they were upset about the community quality being brought down by Chinese. . . . I think that Monterey Park is fortunate to have established a unique environment not only in Los Angeles or Southern California, but literally in this nation. The city has become identified as a land of new opportunity, a legend

of a revitalized town. It has been a successful story. We have made Monterey Park an important cultural and economic center. (Yen-Fen Tseng field notes 1989)

Change means many things for different residents. From our sociological perspective, we could conclude only that restructuring is about both structure and agency, the concrete results of human actions. In the words of Mike Davis, that astute observer of L.A. politics, restructuring is about "the strategies of the powerful, the struggles of the less-powerful" (1989:10). In Monterey Park, we learned that restructuring has been the outcome of a complex battle between developers and residents over land use, and between established residents and immigrants over representation, diversity, and the very meaning of American culture and citizenship.

Our first research task was to pinpoint the local site of the political restructuring of Monterey Park. In this changing community, we found that the arena was not a single place, an old-boy network, or a specific organization, but a fluid set of networks and sites—the city council, neighborhood organizations, civic and political clubs, and public events and festivals. The city council was our first introduction to local politics and a focal point of offstage pressure and negotiation. In council, we began to identify major political issues and players, and their trails led us toward the groups, events, and networks that made up the political arena of the city and the fluid site of our ethnography. We begin here with the city council.

The City Council and "Hard-Ball Politics"

Monterey Park is a city with its own charter, fire department, police department, library, and a host of services affecting new immigrants and established residents. Like many cities in California, its form of government is the council-manager system. The city manager runs the show. He is hired by a city council elected in nonpartisan races. (Until late 1990, California law prohibited political parties from participating formally in local politics.) The low-paid, part-time council members, elected in local races, usually did not have the time, knowledge, resources, or interest to control important day-to-day decisions. In general, they were rubber stamps for the "growth machine," concerned with developing and selling the city's major commodity, land.

Today in California, the council-manager system is under siege by strong mayors (for example, in Los Angeles and San Francisco), local activists, and interfering councils. Monterey Park exemplifies this trend toward a politicized city government. The mayor has remained a rotating one-year position but is assuming increased symbolic and political significance in the community and media. The council has become a battleground over development. The city manager, beholden to the council with its changing and quirky politics, fears for his job. The council is torn between the need to raise revenues in face of dwindling taxes and state and federal support, and the demands of local activists to curb growth.

During the period of our study, from 1988 to 1990, the situation was so politicized that the city staff was loath to talk to the researchers, lest it be drawn more deeply into the political maelstrom. One staff member summed up the atmosphere as "hard-ball politics." Even the smallest technical issues on a design plan can become points of battles.

Political Players

The major players in city politics represent four overlapping reactions to the demographic and economic structuring of the city. First, *advocates of business and economic growth,* ranging from high-powered developers to local businesspersons favorable to managed growth, unite in opposition to slow-growth interests, which they label variously as "no growth," "anti-Chinese," and narrowly "NIMBY" (not in my backyard). This group includes immigrants and established residents with similar class interests. With the important rise of slow-growth movements, growth advocates are more on the defensive than in the past and can no longer count on the city council's unconditional acceptance of the virtues of growth and development.

A second group, *nativists and slow-growth advocates,* emerged from the grass roots to protest what they saw as collusion between local government and the unwanted results of immigration and development. Their leaders and activists are overwhelmingly Anglo, although their programs have drawn strong support from established-resident Latinos and Japanese Americans. Nativists target immigrants and foreign capital as the nation's number-one problem and have strongly supported "Official English." Nativists and slow-growth advocates unite in their desire to restrict development and preserve their conception of a livable suburb. However, in a city where developers may be Asian, nativism and slow growth as well as race and class often overlap. One of the most important political developments in Monterey Park has been the gradual separation of anti-Chinese and antigrowth politics and the isolation of the more right-wing nativist tendency.

The *internationalists,* a third group, skillfully combine the developers' emphasis on multiculturalism with the more populist goal of community control over the course of development. Working toward cross-ethnic alliances on specific issues, internationalists include white liberals as well as minorities and newcomers. Finally, a fourth group, *advocates of the rights and representation of immigrants and minorities,* speak for Asian newcomers, Latinos, and Asian Americans. Their emphasis on organizing "minorities" is particularly repugnant to nativists, who see them as undermining American (Anglo-dominated?) institutions. Differing in their conceptions of strategies for empowerment, some minority advocates move in a nationalist direction, while others unite with the internationalists in strong support of multiethnic coalitions.

Stages in the Political Process

Since the mid-1980s, city politics in Monterey Park have moved from a pattern of diversity and accommodation over development, to containment of developers and immigrants, to "managed growth" within a framework of diversity. The following outline of political history since the mid-1980s gives a sense of the interplay of actors and tendencies in Monterey Park.

1985–87: The Politics of Nativism and Slow Growth

In 1985, the National Municipal League and *USA Today* named Monterey Park an "All-American City" for its innovation in engaging the participation of newcomers and established residents in the solution of pressing civic problems. In fact, members of newcomer and ethnic "minority groups" were then the majority on the five-member city council, with two Latinos and a long-time resident, Lily Chen, who became the first Chinese-born mayor in the United States.

But the appearance of harmony was deceiving. A year later, in 1986, all three were swept out of office by the forces of slow growth, led by RAMP, the Residents Association of Monterey Park. The council was criticized for being soft on development, thereby granting too many variances to developers. The new Anglo, slow-growth majority on the council successfully passed moratoriums on commercial and residential construction. In 1987, the voters of Monterey Park approved a master plan restricting commercial development.

The slow-growth movement draws a political line between populists and profiteers. The xenophobic strain within the movement has broadened the attack to include immigrants. Taking advantage of divisions between the Chinese enclave and established residents, between English and Chinese speakers, they have promoted restrictions on the Chinese language. The most divisive issue in Monterey Park surfaced in 1986, when three white English-only advocates on the City Council passed an ordinance declaring English the official language of the city. The ordinance also declared that Monterey Park was not a sanctuary and urged local police to cooperate with federal officers in apprehending illegal immigrants. However, the ordinance was rescinded when one of the council members changed his vote in response to the persuasion of a multiethnic group of local protesters, Citizens For Harmony in Monterey Park. This victory was short-lived. Later in 1986, the citizens of Monterey Park voted 53 percent to 47 percent for Proposition 63, the statewide "Official English" initiative. Interestingly, perhaps because Monterey Park was engaged in a local struggle over the language issue, its support for the state proposition was much smaller than in neighboring cities in the San Gabriel Valley, with an average 73 percent "yes" vote.

The fight for English against Chinese was clearly a containment strategy that pitted old residents against new immigrants, particularly Asians. English-only declarations written into law give legal justification for depriving new immigrants of the tools for empowerment and mobility, while blaming them for all the complex problems brought by rapid changes in the United States and world economies (Horton and Calderon 1991).

1988–90: From Containment to Negotiation

The 1988 election introduced a new tendency into Monterey Park politics. On the one hand, the election of a slow-growth leader and the defeat of two pro-growth incumbents attested to the continuing strength of the slow-growth movement. On the other hand, the winner with the biggest vote was a Chinese American, Judy Chu, who combined the implicit promise of Asian representation with the explicit promise of support for managed growth within a framework of diversity.

Chu provided a bridge between Asians, Anglos, and Latinos on the issue of controlled growth and diversity. However, the alliances were not made easily. In 1989, much of the discourse in the council was dominated by the proposals and comments of Councilman Barry Hatch, who took advantage of his tenure as mayor to promote his anti-immigrant and Official English policies. However, by the spring of 1990 city council elections, it became clear that the Chu formula was beginning to prevail over the politics of language restriction. A Chinese immigrant, Samuel Kiang, got the largest vote. Also elected were Fred Balderrama, a Latino businessman, and an Anglo businesswoman, Marie Purvis. All gave at least lip service to diversity and managed growth, although the strength of the slow-growth forces was seriously diminished. Incumbents Barry Hatch, the leader of the Official English movement, and his onetime supporter Patricia Reichenberger were defeated.

The Defeat of Nativism

One of the most significant political outcomes in Monterey Park was the defeat of overt nativism and a move away from confrontation over the perceived consequences of immigration to pragmatism, greater Chinese and Latino representation, interethnic alliances, and endorsement of multiculturalism at public events. Our data collected during an exit poll at the April 1990 elections and our ethnographic descriptions of what took place between 1988 and 1990, when Barry Hatch tried to implement his strategies of containment, provide a revealing glimpse of this moment of political change. We focus on Hatch as a symbol of the xenophobic tendency in Monterey Park politics. While serving on the city council from 1986 to 1990, he set a strident tone of xenophobia that was widely publicized by the media and reinforced the questionable image of a city hostilely divided between newcomers and established residents.

Electoral Evidence

Although Asians constitute the majority of the population, they are underrepresented as citizens and voters. Our exit poll probably comes close to representing the actual breakdown of voters by ethnicity: 25 percent Chinese, 26 percent Latinos, 13 percent Japanese, and 36 percent Anglos. The Chinese were clearly the newcomers—74 percent were foreign-born compared to 20 percent for the Latinos, 6 percent for the Anglos, and 1 percent for the Japanese Americans (see table 6.3).

Analysis of the exit poll shows one obvious reason for the defeat of Hatch. While his politics divided newcomer from established resident, the actual political picture is a more complex pattern of ethnic and special-interest voting that crosses over ethnic and newcomer/established resident lines.

Barry Hatch, who in 1987 easily outrode a special recall election condemning him for his racist support of "Official English," in 1990 was the last choice of all ethnic groups. In an election in which voters had three choices among six candidates, Samuel Kiang, a Chinese immigrant, got significant support in all communities: he was the first choice of Asians, the fifth of Anglos, the fourth of Latinos.

Chinese and Japanese Americans, clearly wanting more representation, favored the single Asian candidate, while Anglos, having more choices, tended to spread out their votes. Anglos, the strongest supporters of Hatch and nativist politics, were clearly divided in their support of Hatch (37 percent) and Kiang (40 percent). If we compare Anglos who voted for Hatch and those who voted for Kiang, we see that they are divided on the two factors—bilingualism and cross-ethnic voting—relevant to an operational definition of nativism versus internationalism. For example, 60 percent of the Hatch supporters were opposed to bilingualism, compared to 30 percent who supported Kiang. Hatch voters also generally preferred Anglo candidates. Only 15 percent of the Anglos for Hatch made Kiang their second or third choice, while only 14 percent of those Anglos who supported Kiang cast another vote for Hatch. While nativist tendencies can be found among all established residents—Anglos, Asian Americans, and Latinos—the overall pattern does not support the image of a town divided between newcomers and established residents (see table 6.4).

Poll data indicate the outcomes of a complex process of decision, negotiation, and changes in Monterey Park. Ethnographic data describe the actual process—how individuals and groups were evaluating and coming to terms with the politics of xenophobia and making up their minds before election day. Here we document that process by showing how Hatch's strategies of containment were resisted, rejected, or transformed by politically active Latinos, Asian Americans, and Anglos. There is also ethnographic evidence that his onetime supporters in the slow-growth movement were abandoning Hatch as a political liability.

Table 6.4. Anglo Profile of Hatch Voters versus Kiang Voters

	Hatch voters (%)	Kiang voters (%)
Candidate Choices		
Purvis	35%	56%
Barron	35	35
Balderrama	27	56
Kiang	15	—
Reichenberger	59	24
Hatch	—	14
Education		
College or more	35	47
Income $50,000+	33	49
Bilingual education		
Yes	29	54
No	60	30
Undecided	11	14
Measure S (restrictions on residential construction)		
Yes	74	66
No	17	23
Age 45+	75	61
Respondents (absolute number)	121	133

Source: John Horton and Yen-Fen Tseng, Department of Sociology, University of California, Los Angeles, 1990.

Ethnographic Evidence

Until his defeat in the elections of April 1990, Councilman Barry Hatch continually inserted an anti-immigrant tone into the political debate. A conservative Republican and local leader of the Official English movement, he portrayed himself as the embattled defender of the unifying principles of "Americanism"— the family, God, the neighborhood (slow growth), and English (Anglo domination). For him, the unity and strength of America is being threatened by power blocs of minorities, immigrants, criminals, and their defenders in the liberal establishment of government, education, and the media. The following excerpt from a controversial letter written on Monterey Park stationery to U.S. presidential candidates, dated July 28, 1988, and signed "Barry L. Hatch, Mayor Pro Tem," captures the essence of his position on immigration:

> As a candidate for office in the government of this great nation, you are ignoring the most serious threat the United States has ever faced. The runaway invasion of this sovereign nation by illegal al-

> iens, drug runners, terrorists and criminals is rapidly placing in jeopardy the safety and quality of life of our citizens. . . . We want, and the nation demands, leaders with principles, patriotism and realism. Control our borders—preserve our nation. If you cannot support America, we cannot support you.

One local strategy of Hatch and the more xenophobic fringe of Monterey Park activists has been to impose their vision of America at public places and events—City Hall, the library, the parks, and civic events and festivals like the Fourth of July and Play Days, which commemorates the founding of the city. Their vision is of national unity purged of ethnic and foreign references and defined by traditional symbols of patriotism and Anglo domination. By 1989, this strategy was losing, severely compromised, or even transformed into expressions of empowerment on the part of minorities and newcomers.

Hatch's demand that the city require two-thirds English on all business signs ended in a compromise ordinance requiring only slightly more English signage. His move to fire the city's independent and progressive library board was overturned by a federal court order. In spite of his complaints about the increasing number of Chinese books in the city library, the library continues to receive Chinese books and to cater to Chinese patrons. Hatch did not even succeed in erecting a patriotic George Washington statue. Meanwhile, other symbols of traditional Americanism were changing. Celebrations of the Fourth of July and the city's founding day, Play Days, were becoming more multicultural than before. Hatch's idea of city-sponsored block parties to celebrate the "good old days" turned into celebrations by and for the Latino and Chinese majorities.

Resisting the Preacher

The dynamics of resistance to Hatch emerge in the field notes of Mary Pardo. She regularly attended council meetings to follow the political activities of women and also participated in their struggles to establish a day care center and oppose a neighborhood parole office. The following quotes from her field notes in the summer of 1989 highlight the role of women—Latina, Anglo, and Chinese—in resisting the patriarch of Americanism. The setting is the final city council meeting to decide on the George Washington monument. Three women make their statements against the issue before the council majority votes "no":

The first is a middle-aged Chinese immigrant woman and longtime resident. A Republican, she has become a strong supporter of Judy Chu and her politics of multiculturalism. Lately, she has been attending meetings of a local Asian Pacific American Democratic Club, which has been active in building bridges between American-born Chinese (ABCs) and immigrants and between Chinese, Latinos, and Anglos. She wants to defend her patriotism and oppose the monument: "I have lived in Monterey Park for twenty years. I am also a member of the Parks and Recreation Commission. As an immigrant, I truly respect the land of freedom. I am all for erecting the George Washington monument. But the monument should be erected through private donations."

Next speaks an elderly Anglo woman, a member of the politically progressive Monterey Park Democratic Club. Her tactic is to avoid confronting the controversial issue of Americanism and oppose on the basis of costs—a pragmatic approach popular across the political spectrum: "I have circulated a petition many times. But this time, I got signatures very easily from a cross section of the community. This leads me to believe that 90 percent of the city is opposed to using city monies for the monument. I also asked people how they would prefer the money be spent. Here are some of the responses: help the handicapped, for child care, for the police, for the library, the parks, the hungry. There are many needs in our community."

Next, a middle-aged Latina resident speaks. She has fought for Latino representation on the city council. Now she dares to confront Hatch's conception of patriotism: "I oppose the statue and mean no disrespect for George Washington. Being an American is not having a statue in front of City Hall or wrapping yourself in a flag, but having two brothers and uncles buried in a cemetery [war victims]. And it is also standing up to city council and speaking out."

Hatch's reaction is a classical display of how to lose battles by condescension, drawing a line between his true Americanism and the self-interest of everyone else. He starts in with his usual vigor, not shouting but agitated and driven:

> I am interested in people's agendas when they get up here and speak. You know that there is a twenty-foot statue of Confucius at Cal State Los Angeles [the local state university]? Where are our American philosophers? I asked the students up there what they knew about it; they said they didn't know why it was there.
>
> What are people's agendas? I served in the military too, you know. What is the motive of coming up here and talking about what love of country means? I think these are very disturbing attitudes.
>
> What do you mean patriotism isn't wrapping yourself in a flag? Hispanics from all over can say "Viva la Raza," but they're not going back home. I want to bring a formal recognition, a statue here, and I am embarrassed by the attitudes [scolding, adamant tone]. I am appalled by these views. Why didn't some of you come up and oppose the thousands of dollars being spent on a video technician? We have volunteers, but no, they had to spend twenty thousand dollars on a full-time technician. [An Asian video camera operator in the back of the auditorium gives an audible "humph" and a laugh.] All of you are so self-centered. . . . How much are we spending on new immigrants? How about

> spending a few dollars on men who made this great country possible?

Hatch's remarks were particularly directed to the comments of the Latina and Chinese women. Returning to her seat and fuming, the Latina speaker confided to Mary: "See, this is what he does. I'm going to walk out of here. I'm not going to sit here and listen to this" (Mary Pardo field notes 1989).

Later, in an interview, the Chinese speaker reflected on how Hatch made her feel, and why Chinese residents of Monterey Park do not want to participate in local politics.

> A lot of Chinese people do not like to get involved, specially in our city hall, because someone can embarrass you. That makes you feel uncomfortable. Like, me, I don't feel it. I just go there and fight back. If you insult me I let you know it, and I won't let you push me around. It really takes some courage. At least if you don't have a language handicap, you can speak back.

She has learned from her own experience as an immigrant. As a member of a minority group, she once had to "go with the wind"—that is, adapt to the pattern of Anglo dominance. Now it was Hatch's turn to adapt.

> You know things are changing, and you cannot go against the wind. You have to make a change for the best. I went to city council not because I am against the monument but because Hatch raised it to a racial issue. After I spoke against it, he gave a lecture. He said that at Cal State L.A. there is a statue of Confucius. He said that he asked some young students how it felt to have Confucius looking down on them. He is the one that looks down on people. He brings out this Confucius statue right after I spoke. That made me have a bad feeling. (Pardo interview 1989)

In the end, the city council voted against Hatch and the George Washington statue but, as a patriotic compromise, decided to hold a bicentennial celebration for new citizens. However, the event, like the proposal for a Washington monument, was a flop. Only one Chinese immigrant was there to receive a flag from the welcoming natives.

Later, at a community meeting I attended, two residents exchanged their perceptions of this nonevent. An Anglo woman very active in community affairs saw the failure as another example of "our reaching out" and getting no response:

> I was very disappointed when they had the bicentennial program at Barnes Park. I wasn't on the committee, but I'm sure they worked very hard. They sent out invitations. The park looked beautiful with the flags. And there was about twenty people there.

> I don't know what happened, but something fell through. That's a celebration where nobody took part. Three women council people attended. They had all these flags ready to give out, and presentations, and certificates, and there was just this one little Chinese lady, and that's all. And the American Legion baked cakes and made punch. I'll tell you, we all had plenty of cake that day. For twenty people, you know. So it was too bad.

A Chinese immigrant in his late thirties, a citizen and a professional, politely offered an explanation:

> I saw announcements in the local Chinese newspaper. They do cover well the city activities. I can offer just right off my hat the reason why there is a small turnout, only one person. The people's perception of the city is wrong. . . . What happened in the city council is that there are a lot of negatives against the Chinese people. So people just feel that whatever the city does is against us. Actually there is a lot of good programs that the city has put out. But people just, you know, have the perception that they're against us.

Sensing this kind of opposition and sensitive to the charges of racism, even Hatch's onetime supporters began to abandon him shortly before he came up for reelection in 1990. A leader of the slow-growth movement explained the reasons in an interview:

> Supporting Hatch may have been a tactical mistake. We don't need that sort of person there representing us now. . . . he caused enough trouble during his period in office so that we were busy working on things other than development. The recall [a special referendum mounted by developers to recall Hatch and Reichenberger on the grounds of racism] in particular was a tremendous amount of effort that we made to save his butt. (Horton field notes 1990)

When we began our study in 1988, Hatch had commanded considerable respect, particularly among elderly Anglo residents. They would often praise him for "not being afraid to stand up and say what he thinks." We understood this to mean, "He is not one of those two-faced politicians; he is not afraid to say what many really think." Several years later, the same Hatch sympathizers were qualifying their praise: Hatch was too "divisive," "against everything," and without "positive solutions to anything." We understood this to mean that they had had enough warfare and wanted to get on with solving the community's many problems.

This mood of ambivalence toward Hatch emerged at "Homecoming" in the fall of 1989, before Hatch's defeat. The event was a banquet given by established residents for their friends who had fled the city (called laughingly by one participant "the betrayers"). Several hundred people, overwhelmingly Anglos, wined, dined, recalled the "good old days," and joked about a bewildering present. These were the people whom one might have expected to harbor sympathy for Hatch. Strategically sitting at different places, Leland Saito, Mary Pardo, and I observed reactions to a "roast" delivered by an elderly Anglo business man who had been a member of the city's preimmigration power structure:

> Monterey Park is speeding up the assimilation process. You might say that this is a "melting wok." [Fair amount of audience laughter.] I enjoy the city, my neighbors. There are many new residents and a dwindling supply of old residents. Smiles are an integral part of the Oriental faces. I enjoy seeing them, except at stop signs. [Lots of laughter. A middle-aged Latina sitting next to Mary whispers, "Because they go right by them."] Barry Hatch has gotten us lots of attention. He says that he is interested in promoting the use of the English language. Well, I've seen him at city council meetings, and presumably he's speaking in English, but I don't know what the hell he's talking about; and I'm probably better off than those who do. [Expressions of surprise and a fair amount of laughter, but one of the most senior Anglo woman, born in Monterey Park, says disapprovingly to John, "That's naughty."] (Horton field notes 1989)

Thus, from the voices and interactions in the field we began to understand reasons for the isolation and defeat of one nativist leader in Monterey Park. His rigid, nonnegotiating stance continually drew a line between "real Americans" and "the others"—the immigrants and established minorities. This strategy of polarization paralyzed politics in a community where no single ethnic group had the numerical strength, or ultimately, the political strength, to define who and what Americans are. Hatch alienated Chinese immigrants, established minorities, and politically progressive forces, who saw him as racist. As for Hatch's friends, established residents who might dearly love to turn back the clock to earlier days, they too began to understand that he was a political liability in a multiethnic community where a direct confrontation on issues of race and immigration meant war. These established residents still disliked "Little Taipei," but the Chinese were here to stay, and their support was required in solving such pressing issues as the course of economic development. The irony was that Hatch, having campaigned for the little guy against big government, fell prey to the very antigovernment sentiments that had elected him in the first place.

Transforming Definitions of America

Resistance to Hatch and, more generally, to city government does not tell the whole story of political transformations. In other sites, newcomers and established residents, citizens and noncitizens, without fanfare were taking the initiative, moving beyond the past to construct new definitions of America and Americans. Opposition to Hatch's white colonial view of America is voiced by immigrants and minorities. But this should not obscure the fact that patriotism is strong among both newcomers and established residents in Monterey Park. Both groups participate in patriotic events, including those intended to teach a certain brand of Americanism, and they transform the meaning of America in the process.

One example of a turn toward multiculturalism occurred during Play Days in the spring of 1989. The weeklong event is an annual celebration of the founding of Monterey Park and culminates in a parade and fair in Barnes Park. That year the theme "A Stroll down Memory Lane" was billed as "a universal slogan," intended to "bring together citizens to recall good times in the past." Hatch proposed that one of the elements of Play Days be city-sponsored, old-fashioned "block parties." Old-timers say that years ago on every Fourth of July streets were blocked off and neighbors brought out their tables, chairs, and food and celebrated into the night until it was time to set off firecrackers. It was in that real or imagined tradition that Councilman Hatch promoted block parties as a patriotic, small-town buildup to celebrating the founding of the city and the Fourth of July.

One of our field researchers who lives in Monterey Park, Jose Calderon, attended the block party in Hatch's own neighborhood. His notes describe a happening that did not exactly go Hatch's way. Hatch never showed up. In fact, few Anglos were present. The people who did attend transformed the event into a sneak preview of Cinco de Mayo for Chinese immigrants. The block party took place at the small Sierra Vista Park, directly across the street from a large Chinese retirement complex. Although the complex is built and run in the American style, the tiled roof gives it a very Chinese appearance in the eyes of non-Chinese locals.

> As the Mark Keppel High School band began to play [the high school is now predominantly Asian], I looked around briefly at who had come to the party. To the right of the little recreation center, there were about four rows of folding chairs filled with some twenty-five elderly Chinese. About fifteen steps away, directly in front of the serving tables, there was another group of elderly Chinese sitting in the shade of a tree and near a picnic table. Attached to the tree was a banner with a round symbol and Chinese characters on it. I immediately thought, what does that banner represent? Wait until Barry Hatch sees this! To the left of the rec center some young people, mostly Latinos, were playing baseball as their parents watched. The only Anglo present in the entire area was the guy from the city's Recreation Department.
>
> When the band finished, David Barron, a Latino and the city

clerk, went to a microphone set up on a table and thanked everyone for coming. He introduced the Monterey Park queen and princesses, who are selected every year to represent the city at public events. Interestingly, they wished everyone a "Happy Cinco de Mayo." I thought to myself, they are turning this into a Cinco de Mayo event. Someone is confused. I looked around for Barry Hatch, but he was nowhere in sight, although he lives nearby on Orange Avenue. I wondered how he would react to a block party attended overwhelmingly by elderly Chinese.

Next Barron asked me to come up front and talk about the Cinco de Mayo event scheduled for the next day. I kept thinking, this block party is truly turning into a Cinco de Mayo event. At the microphone, I presented the agenda for the next day's activities, and, seeing the character of the audience, I especially gave a plug to the Chinese Lion dance. I mentioned that tomorrow would be the first day that the Cinco de Mayo committee had made an effort to involve the Chinese culture by inviting the Chinese Lion dancers to perform. This was part of an effort to pull our communities together. Even as I spoke, I did not know that the majority of people who were there did not understand a word I was saying.

After I was done speaking, I began to pass out leaflets on the Cinco de Mayo event to everyone who was there. When I gave leaflets to the Chinese, they accepted them humbly as though I were doing a wonderful act. Some bowed, shook my hand, smiled, reached out toward me, patted me on the shoulder. But, hard as I tried, it seemed as if they didn't really understand what the leaflet was all about. One older Chinese man accidentally took the leaflet upside down and shook his head in approval (while acting as if he were reading it). I dared not point out to him that he was looking at it upside down.

When I was done passing out leaflets, Barron announced that everyone could eat in a few minutes and began to pull out box after box of hot dogs. It was interesting that the food the city offered was hot dogs, because last year there had been a big battle over what type of American food should dominate at the Fourth of July. Of course, Barry Hatch's choice was "hot dogs."

As the hot dogs began to cook, an elderly Chinese man walked toward me, grabbed me by the arm, and pointed me in the direction of the picnic table where a number of Chinese were sitting near their banner. I went over there and saw that they had brought boxes of Chinese food. They pulled me to the table and gave me an entire plateful. They circled round, and I kept saying "Thank you. Thank you." They kept shaking their heads, over and over, as though in appreciation.

I went back to serving hot dogs. The baseball players came and devoured them, while the Chinese mostly ate their own food.

> Barry Hatch never showed up to his lesson in Americanism. Overall, it was a good event—but certainly not what Hatch had dreamed of. Rather than "A Stroll down Memory Lane," the theme of the block party was "A Stroll down the Lane of Tomorrow." (Jose Calderon field notes 1989)

Calderon's notes illustrate how the demographic fact that the town is first of all Asian and second Latino influences the form and content of all intergroup activities. Although it may be perfunctory, cultural diversity is becoming an obligatory theme in all public events. On the one hand, faced with the threat of immigration and change, established residents like Hatch have revived patriotic events like the Fourth of July. On the other hand, given the ethnic composition of the city, the form of the celebration and the "appropriate American" food and music have become matters of political debate.

Fourth of July 1989 was another example of the transformation of the meaning of "American." That day there were hot dogs prepared by a third-generation Japanese American, but also egg rolls donated by the predominantly Asian Kiwanis Club. Given the dearth of volunteers among established-resident adults, the food was sold mostly by Asian volunteers from a local high school. They were acutely aware of the symbolic character of the food. As one of our researchers approached the food table, a Chinese girl shouted, "Get your hot dogs here, they're so American." A male competitor retorted: "No, hot dogs are an American cliché. Expand your cultural experiences. Eat an egg roll." Meanwhile, on stage, an old-timer white band was playing old-timer American tunes. Next, a Chinese girl prodigy in a white dress seated herself sedately at a grand piano and regaled the audience with a Chopin nocturne. Following her performance, the crowd, now mostly Latinos and a few Asians, danced to hot salsa.

> Now, the heat of the day was giving way to shade, and family groups spread themselves strategically on the grass in expectation of the fireworks. A young immigrant was lying down on a blanket, chatting to his wife in Chinese and playing with his tiny child. The man's bare feet extended into the sidewalk toward the circle of Latino teenagers hanging out around their parked car. Into their own rap, they showed no visible signs of established-resident-resentment. All seemed comfortable in their separate spaces. Two young Asian women drove by, their Chinese and laughter audible from the open windows. They were at home. At least on this Fourth of July, there was a feeling of security among the Latino and Asian families lounging, walking, and picnicking in the park. Since the defeat of Barry Hatch, this diversity has crept into the city council, only a year ago the very sanctuary of established-resident opposition to change. The trend is clear, but the future remains open and unpredictable. (Horton field notes 1989)

Multiethnic Indians—Play Days parade celebrating the founding of Monterey Park, 1989 (photograph by Mary Pardo)

Conclusions

The defeat of right-wing strategies of containment in Monterey Park and the rejection of strictly Anglo symbols of America are signs that the dramatic demographic and economic restructuring may be accompanied by a transformation of mediating political and cultural institutions in the direction of multiculturalism and ethnic pluralism.

From our perspective, the changes are profound and cannot be dismissed as merely a superficial diversity that disguises older forms of domination. There are new political players. Asians may not have much political power in the continental United States, but they, along with Latinos, certainly exert influence in Monterey Park and the western San Gabriel Valley. In this corner of the country, the days of uncontested Anglo power are over, and new political norms are emerging. It is not yet clear whether this signals the replacement of one ethnic group by another in the same structure of class domination or the internationalization of the local class struggle. Some evidence of the latter possibility can be seen in the development of interethnic alliances between Asian Americans,

Latinos, and Anglos on all sides of growing regional struggles over economic development, representation, and language.

Internationalization may also be occurring in cultural institutions charged with defining America and Americanism. In Monterey Park, to the chagrin of some old-timers, public festivals are less a lesson in assimilation to one standard American culture than the practice of diversity. Moreover, this multiculturalism is more than the obligatory display of fixed ethnic traditions that make up the cultures of the city. As Immanuel Wallerstein has observed, if we wish to understand the cultural forms of politico-economic struggles, "we cannot afford to take 'traditions' at their face value, in particular we cannot afford to assume that 'traditions' are in fact traditional" (Wallerstein 1983:76). He meant that cultural and ethnic formations are the changing outcomes of the way groups have been incorporated into the capitalist world system. Ethnographers more attuned to the microcosm of urban life remind us that ethnic identity is also the mundane work of local actors who come together at the porous borders between immigrants and established residents to fashion new definitions of themselves and America (Rosaldo 1989:196ff).

Why are these changes coming about at this time in this particular place? The reasons for the apparent shift from the politics of containment to "diversity" in Monterey Park need to be sought in the macro- and micro-layers of community life, which are interrelated through the practices and understandings of local residents.

Structural Conditions of Political and Cultural Change

In retrospect, Monterey Park's massive demographic and economic restructuring seemed favorable to some form of political and cultural restructuring. The demographic and economic changes closed one era and fostered confusion and alienation, but also opened up the possibility of community revitalization and unity between newcomers and established residents in the battle to control the course of community development. One factor behind the move from containment to accommodation has been the irreversible ethnic tipping of a basically middle-class, multiethnic community by newcomers with regional and international connections and the economic and educational "capital" to enter the ranks of the middle and upper middle classes. Their arrival changed the course of community life but did not threaten the livelihood of established residents or lock newcomers and established residents into a competition for scarce resources. Moreover, the very heterogeneity of both immigrant and established-resident populations precluded any easy division between them. As people from Taiwan, Southeast Asia, mainland China, and Hong Kong, the newcomers have many different national and class identities. Likewise, established residents as Anglos, Latinos, and Asian Americans varied widely in terms of their own origins and experience of incorporation into American society.

Agents of Change

The trend away from scapegoating immigrants, the failure of right-wing nativism, and the preference for negotiation within a framework of pragmatism and diversity were not dictated by material conditions. They were negotiated through political struggle and interaction on the foundation of these conditions. Under many major and often unpublicized minor circumstances, established residents accommodated to change, and newcomers were incorporated into and, in turn, transformed local struggles for control over the definition of a developing America.

As our ethnographic vignettes reveal, one important expression of political change was the rejection of overt racism on the part of established residents and the willingness on the part of some influential immigrants and minorities to intervene in the local political and cultural processes. One reason for cooperation was simply the desire to come to terms with the reality of demographic tipping. As the reality of a permanent, relatively high-status Chinese community sank into the political theories of established residents, they began to conclude that if you can't beat them, then it is time to move or accommodate to change. Some local activists have gone even further to see Monterey Park as a national model of multiculturalism. After seeing a rough-cut of *America Becoming,* the film comparing the six cities of the national Changing Relations project, one established resident of Monterey Park commented, "Well, at least we came out better than Chicago."

Another significant accomplishment behind the move toward diversity in Monterey Park was the separation of economic from ethnic issues. In the initial stages of the class struggle between the growth machine and the slow-growth movement, these issues were often conflated by slow-growth advocates, who scapegoated immigrants for the many problems of development. The separation of growth control from immigrant control was facilitated by the leadership of councilwoman Chu and her supporters, who directly attacked the xenophobic strain in the slow-growth movement by combining the defensive goal of growth control with a progressive demand for harmony and multiculturalism. One source of hostility between newcomers and established residents was thus mitigated by Chu and her supporters, who set a new tone of cooperation and redefined a major political tendency associated with local populism. Residents were beginning to work together across ethnic and immigrant barriers to find solutions to the persistent problem of growth. We also observe that moments of unity were achieved in the fight against crime, earthquakes, toxic waste, a leaky dam, and the state's bowing to agricultural interests with the local aerial spraying of malathion to eradicate the medfly (Mediterranean fruit fly).

The major application of these findings has to do with the meaning and possibility of diversity in the political and cultural life of an internationalizing America. The lesson of Monterey Park is that nativism and scapegoating of immigrants are not inevitable outcomes of the new influx of people and capital. On a more theoretical level, our findings point to the fluidity of American and ethnic identities constructed on the basis of situationally defined political and class interests. A final issue is methodological—the importance of ethnography in helping us grasp the practical connections between the macro- and micro-levels of community life. In Monterey Park, profound demographic and economic restructuring opened basic institutions to political change. But grass-roots actors made it happen. One of the political movers—a white woman, a resident of thirty-two years, and an activist who had been involved in running successful campaigns of several Asian-American candidates for the city council—put the issue this way:

> No one promised me that Monterey Park would remain the same. When I moved here, I created change. When other people moved in, they created change.
>
> There's nothing we can do in terms of stopping the change, so you do what you can to create a sense of community. That's the most important thing. (Quoted in Chu 1990:J1)

References

Arax, Mark. 1987. Monterey Park: Nation's First Suburban Chinatown. *Los Angeles Times,* 6 April, p. 11.

Calderon Jose. 1990. Latinos and Ethnic Conflict in Suburbia: The Case of Monterey Park, California. *Latino Studies Journal* 1(2):23–32.

Chu, Henry. 1990. Film on Monterey Park Conflict Previewed. *Los Angeles Times,* 25 October, San Gabriel Section, J1.

Columbia Broadcasting System. 1989. *Screams of Hatred and Tears of Despair.* A "60 Minutes" segment.

Davis, Mike. 1987. Chinatown, Part Two? The Internationalization of Downtown Los Angeles. *New Left Review* 164:65–86.

———. 1989. Homeowners and Homeboys: Urban Restructuring in LA. *Enclitic* 2(3):9–16.

———. 1990. Quartz City: Excavating the Future of Los Angeles. London: Verso.

Harrison, Bennett, and Barry Bluestone. 1988. *The Great U-Turn: Corporate Restructuring and the Polarizing of America.* New York: Basic Books.

Hatch, Barry. 1988. Letter to U.S. presidential candidates. City of Monterey Park, 28 July.

Horton, John. 1989. The Politics of Ethnic Change: Grass-Roots Responses to Economic and Demographic Restructuring in Monterey Park, California. *Urban Geography* 10(6):578–92.

Horton, John, and Jose Calderon. 1992. Language Struggles in a Changing California Community, in *Language Loyalties: A Sourcebook on the Official English Controversy,* edited by James Crawford. Chicago: University of Chicago Press.

Lemann, Nicholas. 1988. Growing Pains. *The Atlantic* 261:56–61.

Marcus, George E., and Michael M. J. Fischer. 1986. *Anthropology as Cultural Critique: An Experimental Moment in the Human Sciences*. Chicago: University of Chicago.

Molotch, Harvey, and Jonathan Logan. 1987. *Urban Fortunes: The Political Economy of Place*. Berkeley: University of California Press.

Ong, Paul M., Eulalio Castellanos, Luz Echavarria, Ann Forsyth, Yvette Galindo, Mary Richardson, Sarah Rigdon Bensinger, Paul Schimek, and Holly Van Houten. 1989. *The Widening Divide: Income Inequality and Poverty in Los Angeles*. Los Angeles: School of Architecture and Urban Planning, University of California.

Pardo, Mary. 1990. Identity and Resistance: Latina Activists in Two Los Angeles Communities. Ph.D. diss., University of California at Los Angeles.

Plotkin, Sidney. 1987. *Keep Out: The Struggles for Land Use Control*. Berkeley: University of California Press.

Portes, Alejandro, and Ruben G. Rumbaut. 1990. *Immigrant America: A Portrait*. Berkeley: University of California Press.

Rosaldo, Renato. 1989. *Culture and Truth: The Remaking of Social Analysis*. Boston: Beacon.

Soja, Edward W. 1989. *Postmodern Geographics: The Reassertion of Space in Critical Theory*. London: Verso.

Tanzer, Andrew. 1985. Little Taipei. *Forbes* 135: 6 May, pp. 68–71.

U.S. Department of Commerce, Bureau of the Census. 1987. *1986 Test Census, Central Los Angeles County California*. Washington, D.C.: Government Printing Office.

Van Maanen, John. 1988. *Tales of the Field: On Writing Ethnography*. Chicago: University of Chicago Press.

Wallerstein, Immanuel. 1983. *Historical Capitalism*. London: Verso.

Wood, Daniel B. 1990. Monterey Park Seeks Harmony. *The Christian Science Monitor*, 18 October, p. 6.

CONTRIBUTORS

SUZANNE BLANC has an M.A. in linguistics from the University of Pennsylvania. She is currently pursuing a Ph.D. in anthropology at Temple University. Her dissertation will examine U.S.-born and immigrant girls' negotiation of adolescent identity. She has previously written about community-based education for women and about reproductive rights.

MICHAEL J. BROADWAY is an assistant professor of geography at the State University College, Geneseo, New York. He is the author of a number of articles dealing with the restructuring of the beef-packing industry and its consequences for rural communities in the Great Plains. He is currently involved in a project that focuses on the role of the meat-processing industry in the transformation of rural America.

DWIGHT CONQUERGOOD is associate professor of performance studies and communication studies and research faculty at Northwestern University's Center for Urban Affairs and Policy Research. His teaching and research interests are in cultural studies and ethnography. He has conducted fieldwork in refugee camps in Thailand and the Gaza Strip, as well as with street gangs in Chicago. In addition to publishing several articles in journals and edited volumes, he has coproduced two award-winning documentaries based on his fieldwork: *Between Two Worlds: The Hmong Shaman in America* (1985) and *The Heart Broken in Half* (1990).

KEN C. ERICKSON is a practicing anthropologist working for the Kansas State Board of Education. His applied and research interests are reflected in his publications, which concern the workplace in complex society, anthropology and education, bilingual education, qualitative research methods, and Vietnamese-American social organization.

JUDITH GOODE, a professor of anthropology at Temple University, has done urban ethnography in Colombia and, for over a decade, in Philadelphia. Her two foci have been the role of food in maintaining communities and work occupations. She is past president of the Society for Urban Anthropology. Her publications include *The Anthropology of the City* (with E. Eames) as well as other books and articles.

GUILLERMO J. GRENIER is the director of the Florida Center for Labor Research and Studies and chair of the sociology/anthropology department of Florida International University at Miami. He is the author of *Inhuman Relations: Quality Circles and Anti-unionism in American Industry* (Temple University Press, 1988) and of numerous articles on labor and ethnic issues. He is working on several book-length studies, including *Miami Now: Immigration, Ethnicity, and Social Change in America's City* and *This Land Is Our Land: Newcomers and Established Residents in Miami.*

JACQUELINE MARIA HAGAN is an assistant professor of sociology at the University of Houston. Her ethnographic research focuses on the influence of immigration policy on the settlement of Latino newcomers, especially women immigrants, in the United States.

JOHN HORTON is an associate professor sociology at the University of California at Los Angeles. His writings have focused on contemporary social and political movements and on class, gender, and ethnic inequalities. Continuing his current interest in the internationalization of Los Angeles, he is working on a monograph, *Pacific Rim City: Immigration and the Political Restructuring of Monterey Park, California.*

LOUISE LAMPHERE, professor of anthropology at the University of New Mexico, was codirector of the Changing Relations project funded by the Ford Foundation through SUNY Binghamton. Her interest in immigration and interethnic relations began with her research on Central Falls, Rhode Island, published in *From Working Daughters to Working Mothers: Immigrant Women in a New England Industrial Community* (Cornell University Press, 1987). She is completing a book entitled *American Working Mothers: Mediating the Contradictions of Work and Family,* coauthored with Patricia Zavella and Felipe Gonzales, which compares the work and family experience of Anglo and Hispano working-class women.

NESTOR P. RODRIGUEZ is an associate professor of sociology at the University of Houston. He specializes in immigration and community development research. For the past eight years he has conducted extensive fieldwork among undocumented Latino immigrants in the Houston area.

JO ANNE SCHNEIDER was project director for the Philadelphia site of the Changing Relations project. She received a Ph.D. in anthropology from Temple University in 1988. Her research interests focus on intergroup relations, public policy, and class and ethnicity in the United States. She is completing work on a nonacademic discussion tool on intergroup relations, *Talking about Race and Nationality,* and a book on the Changing Relations project with Judith Goode. Other related publications appear in the *Journal of Ethnic Studies, Social Science and Medicine,* and *Pennsylvania Magazine of History and Biography.*

ALEX STEPICK is an associate professor of sociology and anthropology at Florida International University. He won the Margaret Mead Award in 1988 for his work with Haitian refugees. His book with Arthur Murphy, *Social Inequality in Oaxaca,* was published by Temple University Press. He is writing several book-length studies with Guillermo Grenier, including *Miami Now: Immigration, Ethnicity, and Social Change in America's City* and *This Land Is Our Land: Newcomers and Established Residents in Miami.*

DONALD D. STULL is professor of anthropology and research fellow in the Institute for Public Policy and Business Research, University of Kansas. His research, publications, and films have centered on applied anthropology, collaborative research, contemporary American Indian affairs and policy, and the consequences of economic development and rapid growth for communities on the High Plains.

INDEX

The text includes tables (T), figures (F), and plates (P), occasionally on the same page. Locators to these elements will indicate which kind (e.g., 45T indicates a table on page 45).